AF597997

The Netscape Programmer's Guide

SIGS Reference Library

Donald G. Firesmith
Editor-in-Chief

1. Object Methodology Overview, CD-ROM, *Doug Rosenberg*
2. Directory of Object Technology, *edited by Dale J. Gaumer*
3. Dictionary of Object Technology: The Definitive Desk Reference, *Donald G. Firesmith & Edward M. Eykholt*
4. Next Generation Computing: Distributed Objects for Business, *edited by Peter Fingar, Dennis Read & Jim Stikeleather*
5. C++ Gems, *edited by Stanley B. Lippman*
6. OMT Insights: Perspectives on Modeling from the *Journal of Object-Oriented Programming, James Rumbaugh*
7. Best of Booch: Designing Strategies for Object Technology, *Grady Booch (edited by Ed Eykholt)*
8. Wisdom of the Gurus: A Vision for Object Technology, *selected and edited by Charles F. Bowman*
9. Open Modeling Language (OML) Reference Manual, *Donald Firesmith, Brian Henderson-Sellers, & Ian Graham*
10. Java™ Gems: Jewels from *Java Report, collected and introduced by Dwight Deugo*
11. The Netscape Programmer's Guide: Using OLE to Build Componentware Apps, *Richard B. Lam*

Additional Volumes in Preparation

The Netscape Programmer's Guide

Using OLE to Build Componentware Apps

Richard B. Lam, Ph.D.
Research Staff Member/Manager
Learning Technologies

IBM T.J. Watson Research Center

COPUBLISHED BY THE PRESS SYNDICATE OF THE UNIVERSITY OF CAMBRIDGE AND SIGS BOOKS
The Pitt Building, Trumpington Street, Cambridge CB2 1RP, United Kingdom

CAMBRIDGE UNIVERSITY PRESS
The Edinburgh Building, Cambridge CB2 2RU, UK http: //www.cup.cam.ac.uk
40 West 20th Street, New York, NY 10011-4211, USA http: //www.cup.org
10 Stamford Road, Oakleigh, Melbourne 3166, Australia

SIGS Books & Multimedia http: //www.sigs.com
71 West 23rd Street, Third floor
New York, NY 10010

© 1998 by SIGS Books & Multimedia.

All rights reserved.

This book is in copyright. Subject to statutory exception
and to the provisions of relevant collective licensing agreements,
no reproduction of any part may take place without
the written permission of Cambridge University Press.

Trademarks
Netscape, Netscape Communications, Netscape Navigator, Netscape Navigator Gold, and JavaScript are trademarks of Netscape Communications Corporation. Microsoft, Visual Basic, Visual C++, Windows, and Win32 are registered trademarks of Microsoft Corporation. Borland is a registered trademark of Borland International Corporation. STL<Tool kit> is a trademark of ObjectSpace, Inc. Java is a trademark of Sun Microsystems, Inc.

Limitation of Liability/Disclaimer of Warranty
The author and publisher make no representation or warranties on the accuracy or completeness of the contents of this book or CD-ROM, and specifically disclaim any implied warranties of merchantability or fitness for any particular purpose and shall in no event be liable for any loss of profit or any other damage, including but not limited to special, incidental, consequential, or other damages.

Any product mentioned in this book may be a trademark of its company.

First published in 1998

Printed in the United States of America

Design and composition by Kevin Callahan.
Cover design by Brian Griesbaum

Typeset in Amasis

A catalog record for this book is available from the British Library

Library of Congress Cataloging-in-Publication Data is available

ISBN 0-521-64820-3 paperback

About the Author

Dick Lam is a research staff member at the IBM T.J. Watson Research Center. He currently manages the Learning Technologies group, which investigates Internet and groupware technologies used in the K-12 and higher education markets. Dick has a BS in chemistry and a BS in mathematics from James Madison University, and a PhD from the University of North Carolina at Chapel Hill. He has published numerous papers on a variety of scientific, mathematical, and programming topics, and is co-author of the textbook *A Jump Start Course in C++ Programming,* published by Wiley–Interscience.

Foreword

I think that Richard Lam should be given some kind of medal.

The book you hold comprises the type of mortar that holds our ever-morphing information technology (IT) infrastructure together. . . and the mortar is the hard stuff. Hard to make right, hard to make even, hard to make reliable.

The bricks are easy, relatively speaking. Here I have Netscape. Over here I have Windows 95. Up here is Lotus Notes. Stacked over there are tools such as Visual Basic, Borland and Visual C++, JavaScript, HTML, and others. And scattered out there are a thousand thousand points of light. These bricks are all supposed to fit together somehow; it should All Just Work. But if you just stack these bricks on one another, the first bump or jostle brings them down . . . usually on your head or foot.

As for the mortar that binds them, ah, there's the rub. Now you're into the arcanities of DDEs, OLE 2.0, Netscape plug-ins, and the like, where you have to discover the right incantations, the proper forms and ceremonies to get things to work rightly, work evenly, work reliably. It's hard. It's tedious. It's arbitrary or even counterintuitive. It's fraught with peril and full of pitfalls. And it sucks up hours like a camel fresh off the desert sucks water.

Dr. Lam has spent those tedious, perilous, precious hours so that you don't have to. To switch metaphors in midstream, his book . . . like the secret navigational logs of seventeenth century ships pilots . . . gets you from start to finish, safe harbor to safe harbor, while avoiding most reefs and shoals.

Now, admittedly, this book is not the stuff of dreams. Extracts are unlikely to appear in Newsweek or WIRED, and it will grace few coffee tables or nightstands. But neither is it one of the easy books (such as one or two written by yours truly), where the author gets to sit back and opine, with plenty of room to duck and dodge.

This is the type of book that will sit propped open by monitors and mice, stained with Jolt and greasy fingerprints and Cheez-It crumbs. This book says, "Do thus, then do thus, and this will happen," with empirical proofs (or refutations) easy to come by. His work and efforts are there for all to see and prove. That is a major risk to take, but it makes the book all the more valuable to those who need it.

Richard has piloted those treacherous seas, come safely home, and thrown open his logs for all who wish to follow. The price of this tome is a fraction of an hour's time with a consultant, yet few consultants could give you this much information on these subjects.

Richard Lam deserves a medal; but he'll be content with his royalties. So stop reading this foreword and buy the book, already.

Bruce F. Webster (bwebster@bfwa.com)
Chief Technical Officer, Object Systems Group

Preface

Netscape Communication Corporation's widely acclaimed Netscape Navigator software has achieved market leadership. Whether it maintains this early lead is anybody's guess, but Netscape has done and continues to do an excellent job of providing an extensible and programmable browser. Their commitment to an open architecture and rapid deployment of application programming interfaces (APIs) offers many opportunities to exploit the flexibility of client-side operations on the World Wide Web (WWW).

This book explores some of the client-side programmability features available today using well-defined Netscape APIs. In the first few chapters, some time is spent to introduce OLE Automation. Examples are developed for communicating with Netscape through both OLE and DDE. The addition of new protocol handlers and viewers is described, and an example protocol handler is written to extend the Netscape browser for accessing Lotus Notes databases while maintaining security. Netscape's plug-in API is also presented, and a general plug-in is developed that can contain any Visual Basic form.

The book is aimed at software professionals programming for the Windows 95 environment. The text and example programs should appeal to any programmer interested in extending the Netscape Navigator browser for distributed software development. Along the way, we will learn about OLE components, interlanguage calls between C++ and Visual Basic, and CGI web form processing coupled with JavaScript and plug-ins. We construct several general tools that can be used for non-web-related projects as well.

You should be familiar with the Windows and Win32 APIs, and with programming 32 bit applications and dynamic link libraries in the Windows 95 environment. A knowledge of C++ and its advanced features is assumed, as well as knowledge of programming in the Visual Basic environment.

The example code presented here was developed using Microsoft Visual Basic 4.0 and Borland C++ 4.5. This mix of languages and tools was chosen for several reasons. First, Visual Basic provides, in my opinion, the best graphical user interface development environment for Windows 95. However, it is not object-oriented in the strict sense, but object-based because of the lack of inheritance. On the other hand, C++ combines object-orientation with the performance of C, and Borland's C++ implementation has proved superior for my needs in terms of advanced language features and usability. We will see several code examples in this book where advanced C++ features such as templates, exception handling, and run-time type identification (RTTI) are used.

The recent introduction of the Standard Template Library (STL) and support for ANSI string classes provide C++ with standard collection class and string support that was sorely lacking. I have chosen ObjectSpace's STL<Toolkit> implementation of the STL for the code developed in this book. The code should port with few changes to other compiler environments and other implementations of STL as better compiler support for templates becomes available.

Using a mix of languages has not been very practical for a project up to now. However, Visual Basic's support for

Microsoft's Common Object Model (COM) (that forms the basis for the OLE 2 standard) is quite good. We will demonstrate how to construct OLE objects in Visual Basic that communicate directly with Netscape. Of course, OLE objects can be developed in C and C++ too. We will also develop C++ tools to facilitate OLE component development, and show why C++ is necessary for programming some of the Netscape extensions.

You will see how components written in different languages can be combined, and how to tie them together with the OLE functions in Netscape. Using different languages for specific tasks is equivalent to using the proper tool for the job. While reading this book, you should start to see the power that OLE provides in developing component-based software using a multiple language and application strategy.

Acknowledgments

I wish to thank IBM Research for providing a stimulating work environment, and to thank Peter Fairweather for giving me some time to work on this project despite the usual software delivery deadlines.

I also thank my colleagues Jim Cooper, Lei Kuang, Cyndi Vincent, Eric Marshall, Sherman Alpert, and John Vergo for their encouragement and technical expertise. Thanks also to Steve Gates for his review of the text and code examples, and for his helpful discussions. Finally, I wish to thank my wife, Kathy, for her unwavering devotion and support.

Dick Lam
Yorktown Heights, NY

Contents

Chapter 1

Overview of Netscape Client APIs

World Wide Web (WWW) browsers are indispensable tools for navigating the Internet. Web pages have replaced the once ubiquitous bulletin board systems as the place to go for information on virtually any topic. The number of web sites continues its incredible expansion rate, and browser technology is evolving just as rapidly while vendors strive to keep up with the demands for new ways to visualize web-based information. Thus, many extensions to the Hypertext Markup Language (HTML) have found their way into common use, and many others are being considered.

Browsers themselves have increased their functionality, replacing the need for separate client programs for gopher and ftp access, for example. Netscape[1] is arguably the leader in browser technology. The Netscape Navigator browser now supports the standard protocols for Uniform Resource Locators (URLs), including http, gopher, ftp, file, mailto, news, and telnet. A built-in newsgroup reader and Internet mail client are also included with Netscape's browser, along with an address book maintained in HTML format.

The breadth of browser functionality has increased in part because of the intuitive nature of browser use. Access to web sites anywhere in the world is only a mouse click or a few keystrokes away. Before the advent of the web, connections to remote sites were made through special purpose communications programs, using complicated sets of login instructions, scripts, or macros. Some people feel that browsers are the ultimate user interface, offering great flexibility in maneuvering around the Internet and in delivering information—all this without presenting a bewildering array of menu options, macro instructions, and toolbar buttons to the user.

As browsers subsume many desktop tasks previously handled by stand-alone programs, there has been an explosion of technologies designed to extend browsers to handle different kinds of data and requests. Of course, the Java[2] language developed by Sun Microsystems is the browser technology receiving the most press these days. Java is an object-oriented language designed to deliver custom web-based programs to a browser through a downloaded bytecode stream. The browser's Java interpreter then runs the program on the client machine. Java offers embedded, cross-platform executable content coupled with the security features necessary for protecting client machines from malicious programs.

While offering great power and promise, there is a dearth of tools for programming and implementing Java programs as of this writing. By the time you read this, the situation will have changed. However, there are a number of other technologies for extending Netscape that have been around but not utilized to their fullest extent. In many ways, these techniques complement Java or handle problems not appropriate for Java solutions.

This book discusses several ways to enhance Netscape, effectively turning the browser into a custom engine for implementing sophisticated distributed applications. Java, HotJava, and scripting languages such as JavaScript[3] will not be discussed in detail here. Rather, we concentrate on object-oriented components that you can write to control the browser, load URLs, get files through ftp, register new protocols and viewers, and handle new web data types and requests. Along the way, several tools will be developed to take advantage of Microsoft's OLE 2 component software architecture. Custom OLE software components are used in conjunction with other component-aware applications (i.e., Netscape) to build new distributed applications.

In the remainder of this chapter, we briefly look at each topic to be covered in later chapters. The tools used to build components, the structure of the code examples, and the contents of the enclosed CD-ROM are also described.

OLE

Most of the component technology we illustrate in this book is built on Microsoft's OLE 2 technology[4]. OLE 2 is much more than is implied by the acronym OLE (Object Linking and Embedding) that delivered a means of embedding or linking applications together in Windows 3.x. OLE (no longer an acronym) is an extensible architecture for building component software based on the Microsoft Common Object Model (COM). Hereafter, OLE will be used to refer to OLE 2 in this book.

COM provides methods to implement components that are language independent and that may exist either as part of the same process or in an entirely different process running on either a local or remote machine. OLE provides a standard set of interfaces for components—this includes interfaces to implement the old embedding and linking functionality. But OLE defines interfaces for a whole range of other services, including structured storage, persistence, OLE Automation, compound documents, and drag & drop.

For our purposes, we will be concerned only with OLE Automation objects and controllers. In Chapter 2, we dive in to create some OLE objects in both Visual Basic and C++. We look at all of the steps necessary to write OLE objects, create type libraries, and register them with the Windows 95 operating system. This sets the stage for our use of OLE components in accessing and controlling Netscape in later chapters.

In Chapter 3, we develop a code generation tool to automate the writing of C++ OLE objects as either dynamic link libraries or executables. Then OLE Automation controllers written in both Visual Basic and C++ are described. A C++ base class is defined that lets you derive new classes that can call class properties and methods written in Visual Basic. This sets the stage for developing componentware that uses the best attributes of both languages—Visual Basic for GUI development, and C++ for system-level, collection class, and database access functions.

DDE

Netscape provides a Dynamic Data Exchange (DDE) interface to control the browser. The DDE functions allow you to open new instances of browser windows, load URLs, activate specific windows, and register DDE servers to handle specific URL requests. In Chapter 4, we build a Visual Basic OLE object to handle the Netscape browser's DDE interface. A general dialog box object is also written to provide a progress bar for loading URLs, and for calling the DDE interface object.

Protocol Handlers and Viewers

The Netscape browser includes two automation objects that can be accessed through OLE controllers. Chapter 5 discusses Netscape.Network.1, an OLE object that exposes the browser functionality for network access. This object allows programs to access URLs transparently using the same underlying protocols as the browser—security protocols, SOCKS support for interaction through firewalls, caching, etc. We build a controller object that accesses URLs through Netscape's automation interface to transfer files.

Chapter 6 illustrates how to define a new protocol (analogous to http or ftp) using both DDE and OLE interfaces. The Netscape.Registry.1 object is used by a general Visual Basic program for registering the new protocols with Netscape. Then we write our own protocol handler for executing local programs on the client. HTML documents containing links that invoke the new protocol through our newly defined URL are demonstrated.

The use of custom protocols is further explained in Chapter 7, where we develop a handler which allows Netscape to obtain information directly from a Lotus Notes database. Some basic LotusScript OLE objects are used to construct OLE servers for handling Notes database access. In the process, we show how custom Notes client applications can be integrated seamlessly into the browser, respecting the built-in security protocols of Lotus Notes.

In Chapter 8, the Netscape.Registry.1 object is used again to show how other applications can register themselves as a viewer for a particular MIME (Multimedia Internet Mail Extension) data type. We define a custom MIME type for scientific data, and develop an OLE Automation object which is used by the browser to enable graphical views of the data. MIME viewers are implemented using both DDE and OLE interfaces, and registration programs are developed to inform Netscape of the new MIME viewers.

Plug-ins

Netscape has recently defined a new plug-in API, which has caught on with a number of vendors. Plug-ins are dynamic code modules that are native to a particular browser platform. Plug-in windows appear completely integrated with the browser. Under Windows 95, plug-ins are written as a DLL, with the ability to

- draw into and process events from a window embedded in the Netscape browser's client window,
- obtain network data via URLs,
- generate data for other plug-ins or Netscape to handle,
- override and implement protocol handlers.

Plug-ins exist to directly play animation scripts, display embedded presentations, download OCX custom controls, etc. In Chapter 9, we develop a general plug-in that can be used to embed your own Visual Basic forms directly into the Netscape browser. Example plug-ins for playing a video using the MCI control and for editing a Rich Text Format (RTF) document using the RichText control are developed.

In Chapter 10, we conclude with a plug-in that plots X,Y data as a line graph. The data is generated from an equation typed by the user directly into an HTML form. JavaScript is then used to evaluate the equation and write the data to another browser window containing the graph plug-in.

Security Issues

Browser security is an issue that raises a lot of interest. Many people ignore the issue entirely, or trust to new languages such as Java to handle any problems. As you will see when you start looking at the example browser programs provided in this book, several programs open up security holes. For example, links on a web page that launch local programs (you will learn how to do this) can obviously do severe damage to a user's machine. Likewise, plug-ins are simply DLLs, and can call any system functions the plug-in author desires. Thus, you must be able to trust the source of any applications you download from the web.

Naturally, there must be tradeoffs between security and functionality. Java is certainly not immune to these problems. More and more Java programmers are discovering the limitations of secure applets (little or no access to files, restricted access to servers, etc.). In the program examples shown in this book, I have favored functionality over security. After all, browser extension technologies to handle new kinds of web programming are not limited to the public Internet. Intranets are a rapidly growing market segment, and internal company webs have far fewer security worries. Nevertheless, as you read through the code examples and get ideas for extending Netscape in your own web-based applications, keep in mind the security concerns of your users.

Code Examples

All of the code in this book is included on the accompanying CD-ROM. The code is organized on the disk by chapter. Each subdirectory under a particular chapter includes the complete source, project files, and the corresponding executable or dynamic link library for the example.

The code examples have been tested with various versions (both release and beta) of the Netscape Navigator or Netscape Navigator Gold products. You may use the code freely to develop your own programs with no copyright restrictions. However, the code is designed to be tutorial in nature, and thus is not intended for anything but pedagogical purposes.

Tools

The C++ examples were built using Borland C++ 4.5, and each project includes a Borland .ide file. The STL<Toolkit> from ObjectSpace[5] is assumed for all of the STL template classes. The ObjectSpace implementation of ANSI strings is also used extensively. I have avoided using any of ObjectSpace's extensions to either the STL or string templates to keep the code portable to other STL and ANSI C++ implementations.

The Visual Basic projects (*.vbp) were built with Visual Basic Professional or Enterprise edition 4.0. No third-party VBX or OCX controls are used.

Naming Conventions

The naming conventions for filenames are:

File type	Naming convention
C++ header	X.h
C++ source	X.C
Visual Basic class	clsX.cls
Visual Basic form module	frmX.frm
Visual Basic code module	modX.bas

Class names, class methods, functions, and variables referred to in the text (e.g., *main()*, *x*, *A::setX()*, etc.) are shown in italics.

C++ Class Diagrams

Class diagrams in this book are used to clarify relationships among components of a project or framework. Figure 1.1 shows how different class types are denoted. Note the use of an arrow to denote classes derived from a base class. The arrow points from the derived class to its base class. Abstract base classes (classes that contain one or more pure virtual functions, or that specify interfaces only) are shown with a drop shadow, and a shaded box indicates a template class.

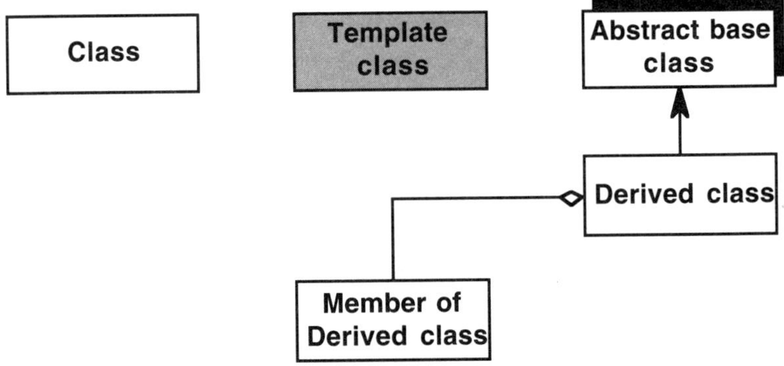

Figure 1.1. Illustration of class relationship diagrams used in this book.

References

1. Netscape Communications Corporation, http://www.netscape.com
2. A. van Hoff, "Java and Internet Programming," Dr. Dobb's Journal, August 1995.
3. T. Tessier, "Using JavaScript to Create Interactive Web Pages," Dr. Dobb's Journal, March 1996.
4. K. Brockschmidt, "Inside OLE," 2nd edition, Microsoft Press, Redmond, WA, 1995.
5. ObjectSpace, Inc., http://www.objectspace.com

Chapter 2

Introduction to OLE Automation

Much of this book has to do with the construction of OLE components. There are two principal reasons for this. One is that Netscape itself is an OLE Automation client—that is, Netscape defines several OLE interfaces that other applications can access. These interfaces pave the way for using Netscape's underlying network functions directly. Thus, there is no need to write your own code to transfer a file from a network server, for example. You can just use Netscape's built-in functionality to ftp a file, ignoring all of the complexities of TCP/IP socket communications, SOCKS protocols for reading and writing data through firewalls, multithreaded connections, caching, etc.

Secondly, Netscape also acts as an automation controller. There are published interfaces to the browser that you can use to construct your own OLE client objects. If you build client objects with these OLE interfaces and register them with the Netscape browser, Netscape will directly call your interface functions in response to certain requests. Your objects are seamlessly integrated into the browser, with the capability to interact with the user, act as a viewer for various data formats, read and write to files or databases, or control other OLE objects.

Before we work with OLE and Netscape though, we need to agree on some common terms.

Terminology

An **OLE object** is a software component that may be written in any language, as long as that language supports the Common Object Model (COM) specification. We will use both Visual Basic and C++ to develop OLE objects. An OLE object defines one or more **interfaces** that are used to work with the object.

These interfaces are expressed as **classes**, defined either by a Visual Basic 4.0 class module or a standard C++ class. Each class contains some standard methods each object must support, along with other **properties** and **methods** you define.

A property is a (usually) private member variable of a class that may be accessed through public property functions (*Property Get* and *Property Let* in Visual Basic). These functions can restrict property values to certain ranges, make a property read-only, and allow other objects to obtain and use the value.

Methods are public subroutines or functions defined as part of the class. They can call other public and non-public members of the same or other instances of an object. Methods can also access any other object's functionality through that object's corresponding public interfaces.

In-Process and Local Servers

An application that obtains a pointer to one or more interfaces of an OLE object, calls methods, and gets or sets properties defined in the object is called an **automation controller** or **OLE client**. Depending on how an OLE object is implemented, a controller accesses an object's properties and methods through an **in-process** or **out-of-process** call.

If an OLE object is implemented as a dynamic link library (DLL), it is loaded by a controller process and its interfaces are then entirely self-contained in the address space of that process. The object is referred to as an **in-process server**. Alternatively, an OLE object can be compiled into an executable (.exe file). When a controller loads the object, the executable program is started and the object thus runs in its own process. It is referred to as an **out-of-process server**, or more simply as a **local server**.

Obviously, an in-process server may have some performance advantages over a local server, as the in-process server is running in the same process as its client. Thus, there is no interprocess communication mechanism needed for every call that goes between the client and server. However, there are reasons to prefer local servers in some circumstances.

In terms of robustness, a local server can crash and not simultaneously crash the client application. By contrast, an error occurring in an in-process server becomes an application-level error. Also, using a local server can effectively gain you a thread of execution, whereby asynchronous tasks in an application can be handed off to the local server. This is not possible with an in-process server, which runs in the same thread as its client. Finally, in-process servers do not support DDE, so when we write an OLE server in Chapter 4 to access Netscape's DDE functionality, a local server will be used.

See Brockschmidt[1] or the Visual Basic "Creating OLE Servers" book[2] for additional information on the relative advantages of in-process and local servers.

Creating a VB OLE Server

Let's create an OLE server using Visual Basic. Start by creating a new project with a single form named *frmMain* (this project is available on the CD-ROM as project simple1.vbp). Insert a new code module named modMain.bas. Add the following subroutine to the main module:

```
Sub main()
    ' startup code for an OLE server
End Sub
```

Next, add a ProgressBar control to the form and name it *pbProgress*. Add a label control named *lblMessage* above the progress bar and set its caption to "Loading." You can also add some numeric labels underneath the progress bar so the ending form appears as:

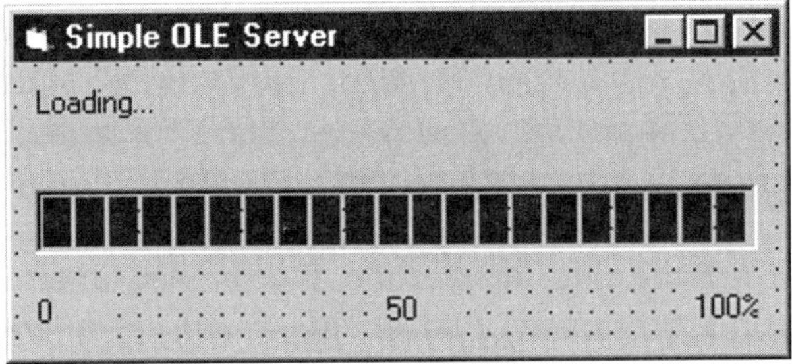

Figure 2.1.

Now insert a class module called clsShowProgress.cls to the project. Set the class module properties to *Public=True* and *Instancing=1* (Creatable SingleUse). This denotes that each client will get exclusive use of a copy of the server.

What we're building is a simple dialog box with no user inputs—it just tracks the progress of some operation. In a later chapter, we'll come back to this project and embellish it for use with lengthy operations started by Netscape. For now, we will define some methods to set the caption property of the label, establish the range for the progress bar, and write a method to update the current state of the progress bar.

We first need an instance of our form, which we obtain by declaring the following private variable in the declarations section of *clsShowProgress*:

```
' instance of the form
Private myform As New frmMain
```

There are three property functions to set the range of the bar and set the message shown in the label above the bar.

```
Property Let BarMinimum(minvalue As Integer)
   myform.pbProgress.min = minvalue   ' sets minimum
                                      ' of range
End Property

Property Let BarMaximum(maxvalue As Integer)
   myform.pbProgress.Max = maxvalue   ' sets maximum
                                      ' of range
End Property

Property Let Message(msg As String)
   myform.lblMessage.Caption = msg    ' sets text to
                                      ' display
   myform.Show
End Property
```

The last general class method is a public function that increments the current value of the bar.

```
Public Sub IncrementProgress()
    ' increments the current value
    myform.pbProgress.value =
    myform.pbProgress.value + 1
End Sub
```

Clients will use this server by first creating an instance of the Simple1.clsShowProgress object. This should create an instance of the form, so we will put code into the *Initialize* method of the class to load the form.

```
Private Sub Class_Initialize()
    Load myform
End Sub
```

We also need to unload the form when the object is deleted, so we do this in the *Terminate* method of the class.

```
Private Sub Class_Terminate()
    Unload myform
End Sub
```

Note that the *Message* method includes a statement to actually show the form after the caption property has been set.

Now we specify the Visual Basic project options, setting the name of the project to Simple1, and marking it as an OLE server. Finally, we set the Startup Form to be *Sub Main* and compile the project as an OLE executable.

Registering a VB Server

If you run the Windows 95 REGEDIT.EXE program, and expand the HKEY_CLASSES_ROOT tree, you can scroll through the entries and find an entry for Simple1.clsShow-Progress. This indicates that Visual Basic has already registered your object in the system registry, and other applications will be able to access it.

If the entry is not there, you can register it by simply running "Simple1 /r" from the command line. You can remove the object from the registry by running it with the "/u" switch. Later, we will see how to register in-process servers.

Testing the VB Server

Create a new project called test1.vbp to exercise our new OLE server. Our test application does not need a form, just a main routine residing in a modTest.bas module.

```
Sub Main()
    Dim start As Long
    Dim i As Integer
    Dim progress As Object
```

```
    ' create an object with late binding
    Set progress = CreateObject("Simple1.
                                     clsShowProgress")

    If progress Is Nothing Then
        MsgBox "Could not create object", vbOKOnly
    End If

    ' set the range
    progress.BarMinimum = 0
    progress.BarMaximum = 10

    ' set the label
    progress.Message = "Testing the OLE server"

    ' loop to increment the progress
    For i = 1 To 10
        progress.IncrementProgress

        ' one second delay
        start = Timer
        Do While (start + 1) > Timer
            DoEvents
        Loop
    Next i
End Sub
```

After creating the object, the range of the OLE server's progress bar and the label caption are set through properties, and the *IncrementProgress* method is called in a loop to demonstrate the update of the ProgressBar control.

You will notice the declaration of *progress* in the test code as an *Object*. The actual reference to the OLE server object was made by calling the *CreateObject* function. This is an example of late binding of the test client with the server object. We could also have Visual Basic detect the type of object at compile time (early binding), thus cutting the amount of overhead needed to invoke properties and methods on the object.

To use early binding, add a reference to the Simple1.clsShow-Progress object in the Tools, References dialog box. Then change the code above from:

```
Dim progress As Object
Set progress = CreateObject("Simple1.
                                clsShowProgress")
```

to:

```
Dim progress as New Simple1.clsShowProgress
```

Late binding is slower, but it delays specifying the type of object to create until runtime. This is useful if a routine must decide at runtime what object it will create.

OLE Servers in C++

Now that you've seen how easily OLE servers can be created in Visual Basic, why do it in C++? Well, it turns out that Netscape defines some OLE server methods that protocol handlers and viewers must implement. Unfortunately, some of these methods use names that are keywords in Visual Basic! Thus, the appropriate class method names will not compile. Of course, depending on what the functions are, they may be better suited for implementation in C++ anyway. This is particularly true in instances where existing classes, libraries, or frameworks are used, or where inheritance or other specific C++ advantages over Visual Basic are required.

We will write our own set of C++ classes to create both in-process and local servers. A reasonable question to ask at this point is why not use some automatic OLE server generation code from Visual C++ (see the recent ActiveX Template Library from Microsoft) or use the Borland ObjectComponents library?

> First, I believe it is useful to see what is going on at the OLE API level in order to understand how to use and extend it effectively. Second, I do not like to depend heavily on a single manufacturer's compiler or library. Third, the standard OLE tools rely on C macros to hide C++ declarations so that C programmers are not left out. At the same time, most authors also point out that C++ is the most appropriate language for defining OLE objects. I strongly dislike this macro-ridden approach to OLE, and I felt that C++ templates and runtime type identification could eliminate the need for macros. Besides, if C++ is the most appropriate language, use it—do not try to force another language into a mode for which it is not well suited.

Finally, I should issue a warning here that the complexity and amount of code required for implementing OLE objects in C++ is considerably greater than for Visual Basic. However, in the next chapter we will build some tools to considerably simplify this coding task. We will use this tool throughout the book in constructing OLE servers in C++.

WinMain

Let's look at the C++ code required in a *WinMain* function for a local server. This server example implements an OLE object named Simple2.Shell. First, the main program needs to determine if the object is being created or the executable is being run directly by a user (which should fail). This is done by testing the command line for the presence of an "Embedding" argument.

Next, COM is initialized and *initWindow* is called. The *initWindow* function creates a window using the *ShellWndProc* window function. The class name used in the WNDCLASS structure and in the call to *CreateWindow* is *Shell*, the last part of the object name.

We will see why later when we develop a code generation tool to automate the C++ OLE server creation.

ShellWndProc only exists to trap the WM_DESTROY message, which is posted when it is safe for the OLE server to end. This happens when there are no more objects and no more class factory objects being referenced by client applications.

The *testForShutdown* function determines when the reference count for objects created by the server goes to zero and when the class factory count reaches one. The class factory which creates OLE server objects always has one instance declared as a static variable at the top of the module. When these conditions are satisfied, a WM_CLOSE method is posted to the window. The *objectFactory* and *windowHandle* variables are declared static at the top of the module to make them available to *testForShutdown*.

Before the message loop is started, a call to *CoRegisterClassObject* is made to register the class factory for the object's class with OLE so other applications can access the factory.

```
// exefuncs.C - main routine for Simple2.Shell OLE
//              local server
#define STRICT
#include <windows.h>
#include <stdio.h>
#include <string.h>

#include "tolefact.h"     // for TOLEFactoryFor
                          // template class
#include "objimpl.h"      // for the object
                          // implementation

// *************************************************

// the object factory instance that is returned to
// clients
static TOLEFactoryFor<myImplOfShell> objectFactory;
```

```
// the window handle
static HWND windowHandle = 0;

// *********************************************

// window callback
extern "C" LRESULT APIENTRY ShellWndProc(HWND hWnd,
   UINT iMsg, WPARAM wParam, LPARAM lParam)
{
    switch (iMsg) {
        case WM_DESTROY:
            PostQuitMessage(0);
            return 0L;

        default:
            return DefWindowProc(hWnd, iMsg, wParam,
                                 lParam);
    }
}

//  ----------------------------------------------

// initWindow - creates and initializes the
//              application window
BOOL initWindow(HINSTANCE hInst,
                HINSTANCE hInstPrev,
                LPSTR, int)
{
    // test for previous instance
    WNDCLASS wc;

    if (!hInstPrev) {
        // register the window class
        wc.style          = CS_HREDRAW | CS_VREDRAW;
        wc.lpfnWndProc    = ShellWndProc;
        wc.cbClsExtra     = 0;
        wc.cbWndExtra     = 0;
        wc.hInstance      = hInst;
```

```
        wc.hIcon          = 0;
        wc.hCursor        = 0;
        wc.hbrBackground  = (HBRUSH)(COLOR_WINDOW + 1);
        wc.lpszMenuName   = 0;
        wc.lpszClassName  = "Shell";

        if ( !RegisterClass(&wc) )
            return FALSE;
    }

    // create the window
    windowHandle = CreateWindow("Shell",
        "Shell Local Server", WS_OVERLAPPEDWINDOW, 0,
        0, 100, 100, 0, 0, hInst, 0);
    if (!windowHandle)
        return FALSE;

    return TRUE;
}

// -----------------------------------------------

// program entry point
extern "C" int PASCAL WinMain(HINSTANCE hInst,
                              HINSTANCE hInstPrev,
                              LPSTR pszCmdLine,
                              int nCmdShow)
{
    // if this is run outside of CoGetClassObject,
    // then fail
    if ( lstrcmpiA(pszCmdLine, "-Embedding") &&
         lstrcmpiA(pszCmdLine, "/Embedding") )
        return 1;

    // initialize COM
    if ( FAILED( CoInitialize(0) ) )
        return 2;
```

```
    // initialize the window
    if ( !initWindow(hInst, hInstPrev, pszCmdLine,
                      nCmdShow) )
        return 3;

    // register the class factory
    DWORD registered = 0;
    HRESULT hr = CoRegisterClassObject(getGUID(tCLSID),
       &objectFactory, CLSCTX_LOCAL_SERVER,
       REGCLS_MULTIPLEUSE, &registered);
    if ( FAILED(hr) )
        return 4;

    // event loop
    MSG msg;

    while ( GetMessage(&msg, 0, 0, 0) ) {
        TranslateMessage(&msg);
        DispatchMessage(&msg);
    }

    // terminate COM and exit
    if (registered)
        CoRevokeClassObject(registered);

    CoUninitialize();
    return msg.wParam;
}

// ----------------------------------------------
// testForShutdown - determines if the executable
// can be terminated
void testForShutdown()
{
    if ( (OLEFactoryObjectCounter::count() == 0L) &&
          (objectFactory.refCount() == 1L) &&
          IsWindow(windowHandle) )
        PostMessage(windowHandle, WM_CLOSE, 0, 0L);
        // closes the app
}
```

When the WM_DESTROY message is received, the server exits the message loop. A call to *CoRevokeClassObject* de-registers the class factory. *CoUninitialize* then terminates COM, and the program exits.

Interface Identifiers

You probably noticed in the call to *CoRegisterClassObject* the argument *getGUID(tCLSID)*. This function is defined in a separate header file, myguid.h (included by the tolefact.h header file). It returns *CLSID_Shell,* a Globally Unique Identifier (GUID) that uniquely identifies our object's class. GUIDs are required for providing uniqueness within the same system and across a network. Visual Basic also creates and uses GUIDs for OLE objects, but they are effectively hidden by the development environment.

Each of our objects will declare four unique GUIDs, which are outlined in the following table:

GUID Name	Example	Refers to
`CLSID_x`	`CLSID_Shell`	object class
`IID_Ix`	`IID_IShell`	object's interface
`DIID_DIx`	`DIID_DIShell`	dispatch interface
`LIBID_xTypeLibrary`	`LIBID_ShellTypeLibrary`	object's type library

IID_IShell refers to the *IShell* interface class we will define shortly for our OLE server. *DIID_DIShell* is a dispatch interface identifier used by an automation controller to invoke object methods and access properties using runtime type information. This information is provided at runtime by the object's type library (accessed via *LIBID_ShellTypeLibrary*). The type library provides the names of interfaces, function names, required and optional arguments, and function return types. OLE's standard *IDispatch* interface, referred to by the *DIID_DIx* identifier, maps function and property names to their corresponding function calls using this type information.

```
// myguid.h — declares GUIDs based on the object
// name
#ifndef MODULE_myguidh
#define MODULE_myguidh

#define INITGUID
#include <compobj.h>
#include <initguid.h>

// ************************************************

// GUIDs — use guidgen or a similar program to make
// new ids
DEFINE_GUID(LIBID_ShellTypeLibrary, 0x60eeef40,
            0x6559, 0x11cf, 0xb1, 0xeb, 0x48, 0xdc,
            0x04, 0xc1, 0x00, 0x00);
DEFINE_GUID(IID_IShell, 0x60eeef41, 0x6559, 0x11cf,
            0xb1, 0xeb, 0x48, 0xdc, 0x04, 0xc1,
            0x00, 0x00);
DEFINE_GUID(DIID_DIShell, 0x60eeef42, 0x6559,
            0x11cf, 0xb1, 0xeb, 0x48, 0xdc, 0x04,
            0xc1, 0x00, 0x00);
DEFINE_GUID(CLSID_Shell, 0x60eeef43, 0x6559, 0x11cf,
            0xb1, 0xeb, 0x48, 0xdc, 0x04, 0xc1,
            0x00, 0x00);

// ------------------------------------------------

// type used in function to retrieve a particular
// GUID
enum GUIDType { tLIBID = 0,          // library id
                tIID = 1,            // interface id
                tDIID = 2,           // dispatch id
                tCLSID = 3           // class id
};
```

```
// -------------------------------------------

// getGUID - returns a GUID
GUID getGUID(GUIDType t)
{
    if (t == tLIBID)
        return LIBID_ShellTypeLibrary;
    else if (t == tIID)
        return IID_IShell;
    else if (t == tDIID)
        return DIID_DIShell;
    else
        return CLSID_Shell;
}

#endif
```

The *getGUID* function just returns one of the four identifiers declared at the top of myguid.h using the DEFINE_GUID macro. The numeric identifiers can be obtained by running the guidgen.exe program that comes with Borland C++, or by using the uuidgen.exe tool in Visual C++. We will see later how to get GUIDs programmatically when we build a code generation tool.

The TOLEFactory Template

The *objectFactory* variable declared at the top of exefuncs.C is based on a template class defined in tolefact.h. The template class *TOLEFactoryFor<OLEObject>* acts as an object factory for the class used in the template argument, which in this case is *myImplOfShell*. We will define the object class in the next section. For now, just recognize that the factory object creates instances of the object class interface for OLE clients. Clients subsequently use the interface to invoke the object methods and access properties.

Here is the code from the tolefact.h header file. There is some supporting code for the factory that is included in the file. First, there is a extern declaration for the *testForShutdown* method defined in exefuncs.C. The factory calls this function to determine if it is okay to shut down the server.

```
// tolefact.h - OLE support classes
#ifndef MODULE_TOLEFactoryForh
#define MODULE_TOLEFactoryForh

#include <ole2.h>
#include <olectl.h>

#include "myguid.h"

extern void testForShutdown();    // defined in
                                  // exefuncs.C
```

The next declaration in tolefact.h is a counter class that keeps track of the number of objects created and in use by clients. If you refer to the implementation of *testForShutdown*, you can see a call to the static method *OLEFactoryObjectCounter::count*, which returns the current object count.

```
class OLEFactoryObjectCounter {
public:
    // increments and decrements object counter
    // (called by the object's constructor and
    // destructor)
    static void increment() { numberOfObjects += 1L; }
    static void decrement() { numberOfObjects -= 1L; }

    // returns the object count
    static unsigned long count()
    { return number-OfObjects; }

private:
    static unsigned long numberOfObjects;
};
```

```
// -----------------------------------------------

// initialize the static variable
unsigned long OLEFactoryObjectCounter::
numberOfObjects = 0L;
```

The actual template class declaration follows. Note that the template factory is derived from OLE's *IClassFactory*. The private variable *referenceCount* maintains a count of actual factory objects, which is initialized by the constructor and returned by the *refCount* member function. The *IUnknown* interface functions *AddRef* and *Release* increment and decrement the count.

```
template <class OLEObject>
class TOLEFactoryFor : public IClassFactory {
public:
   // constructor and destructor
   TOLEFactoryFor() { referenceCount = 0; }
   virtual ~TOLEFactoryFor() {}

   // returns the reference count
   unsigned long refCount() const { return
                                    referenceCount; }

   // IUnknown methods
   virtual HRESULT STDMETHODCALLTYPE QueryInterface
                                     (REFIID riid,
                                      LPVOID *ppv);
   virtual ULONG STDMETHODCALLTYPE AddRef()
   { return ++referenceCount; }
   virtual ULONG STDMETHODCALLTYPE Release()
   {
      if ( -- referenceCount == 0)
         return 0;
      return referenceCount;
   }

   // IClassFactory methods
```

```
    virtual HRESULT STDMETHODCALLTYPE CreateInstance
       (LPUNKNOWN pUnkOuter, REFIID riid,
        LPVOID *ppv);
    virtual HRESULT STDMETHODCALLTYPE LockServer
            (BOOL fLock);

private:
    unsigned long referenceCount;
};
```

The factory template's *QueryInterface* function calls *AddRef* to increment the reference count of the factory, and then returns a pointer to itself. The caller can use the returned pointer as an *IClass-Factory* to create a new instance of the object.

```
template <class OLEObject>
HRESULT STDMETHODCALLTYPE TOLEFactoryFor<OLEObject>::
QueryInterface(REFIID riid, LPVOID *ppv)
{
    // check the interface request
    if ( (riid == IID_IUnknown) ||
         (riid == IID_IClassFactory) ) {
        *ppv = this;
        ((LPUNKNOWN)(*ppv))->AddRef();

        return NOERROR;
    }

    // interface is not supported
    *ppv = 0;
    return ResultFromScode(E_NOINTERFACE);
}
```

CreateInstance is the factory object's implementation of an *IClassFactory* method, which accepts a request for a new instance of the template argument class. A test is made upon entering the function to ensure that the object is not being created for aggregation with another object. Aggregation of interfaces requires writing the object implementation differently, and we do not consider it in this book. Brockschmidt[1] discusses aggregation concepts in more detail.

The object instance is created using the C++ *new* operator. If the object was created successfully, the newly created object's *Init* method is called to carry out any initialization tasks. Then the object's *QueryInterface* function is used to set the return interface pointer for the caller to use.

```
template <class OLEObject>
HRESULT STDMETHODCALLTYPE TOLEFactoryFor<OLEObject>
    ::CreateInstance(LPUNKNOWN pUnkOuter,
                     REFIID riid, LPVOID *ppv)
{
    // initialize the return pointer
    *ppv = 0;

    // object will not support aggregation
    if ( pUnkOuter && (riid != IID_IUnknown) )
        return ResultFromScode(CLASS_E_NOAGGREGATION);

    // allocate a new object and initialize it
    OLEObject *p = new OLEObject(pUnkOuter);
    if (!p) {
        testForShutdown();
        return ResultFromScode(E_OUTOFMEMORY);
    }

    if ( p->Init() ) {
        // initialized ok, so query for the
        // requested interface
        HRESULT rc = p->QueryInterface(riid, ppv);
        if ( FAILED( GetScode(rc) ) ) {
            delete p;
            *ppv = 0;
```

```
            testForShutdown();
            return rc;
        }
    } else {
        // initialization failed
        delete p;
        *ppv = 0;
        testForShutdown();
        return ResultFromScode(E_OUTOFMEMORY);
    }

    return NOERROR;         // success!
}
```

If *Init* fails, the object is deleted and an error is returned.

Finally, the *IClassFactory*'s *LockServer* increments or decrements the object counter if called with an *fLock* argument of TRUE or FALSE, respectively. This method might be called by an application with special performance requirements—locking the server keeps it in memory for more rapid creation of objects.

```
template <class OLEObject>
HRESULT STDMETHODCALLTYPE TOLEFactoryFor
   <OLEObject>::LockServer(BOOL fLock)
{
    if (fLock)
        OLEFactoryObjectCounter::increment();
    else {
        OLEFactoryObjectCounter::decrement();
        testForShutdown();
    }

    return NOERROR;
}

#endif/* MODULE_TOLEFactoryForh */
```

The Object Classes

Now that all of the support code is defined, we need to specify an interface for our *Shell* object, so we derive a new class from the standard OLE interface class *IUnknown*, and call it *IShell*. This interface base class has no implementation methods defined, so we only need a header file (iobject.h) to define it:

```
// iobject.h - interface base class declaration
#ifndef MODULE_IShellh
#define MODULE_IShellh

#include <ole2.h>

// class declaration
class IShell : public IUnknown {
public:
    // IUnknown methods
    virtual HRESULT STDMETHODCALLTYPE
    QueryInterface(REFIID riid, LPVOID *ppv) = 0;
    virtual ULONG STDMETHODCALLTYPE AddRef() = 0;
    virtual ULONG STDMETHODCALLTYPE Release() = 0;

    // IShell methods
    virtual short STDMETHODCALLTYPE
    run(LPCTSTR filename) = 0;
};
#endif
```

There are three pure virtual functions that are part of the *IUnknown* interface, and one pure virtual function (*run*) that we declare for our object interface. Our *run* method will be used by OLE clients to execute a program specified by the *filename* argument.

Now we declare a derived class, *myImplOfShell*, from this interface base class. The derived class declaration is defined in the header file objimpl.h, and this new header file is included in the exefuncs.C module above. This class is used as the template argument to *TOLEFactoryFor<>*, and will be the actual class used by the factory to create instances for each OLE client that requests an *IShell* interface.

```
// objimpl.h
#ifndef MODULE_myImplOfShellh
#define MODULE_myImplOfShellh

#include "iobject.h"

// class declaration
class myImplOfShell : public IShell {
public:

    // constructor and destructor
    myImplOfShell(LPUNKNOWN outer);
    virtual ~myImplOfShell();

    // initializes the object
    BOOL Init();

    // IUnknown methods
    virtual HRESULT STDMETHODCALLTYPE QueryInterface(
    REFIID riid, LPVOID *ppv);
    virtual ULONG STDMETHODCALLTYPE AddRef();
    virtual ULONG STDMETHODCALLTYPE Release();

    // IShell methods
    virtual short STDMETHODCALLTYPE run
    (LPCTSTR filename);

protected:
    unsigned long refCount;     // reference counter
    LPUNKNOWN outerUnknown;     // controlling unknown
    ITypeInfo *typeInfo;        // type information
    IUnknown *pStdDispatch;     // StdDispatch object
};

#endif
```

Note that the *IUnknown* and *IShell* methods are declared in the derived class, and implementations of each function are supplied inside objimpl.C. There is also a declaration for an *Init* method which, as we saw in the last section, is called by the *TOLEFactory-For<OLEObject>::CreateInstance* method.

The constructor initializes all of the private pointers to dispatch and type information. It also increments the object count when a new object is created.

```
myImplOfShell::myImplOfShell(LPUNKNOWN outer)
{

    // init instance variables
    refCount = 0L;
    outerUnknown = outer;
    typeInfo = 0;
    pStdDispatch = 0;

    // increment the object factory's object counter
    OLEFactoryObjectCounter::increment();
}
```

The destructor releases the dispatch and type information interface pointers, and then decreases the object count. A call to *testForShutdown* checks to see if the server can be shut down.

```
myImplOfShell::~myImplOfShell()
{
    if (pStdDispatch)
        pStdDispatch->Release();
    if (typeInfo)
        typeInfo->Release();

    // decrement the object factory counter
    OLEFactoryObjectCounter::decrement();
    testForShutdown();
}
```

QueryInterface provides a means for callers of an object to determine what interfaces that object supports. In this case, either a pointer to the object is returned (for *IUnknown* or *IID_IShell* requests) or a pointer to the dispatch interface is returned (for *IDispatch* or *IID_DIShell* requests).

```
// QueryInterface - returns the object interface
HRESULT STDMETHODCALLTYPE myImplOfShell::
   QueryInterface(REFIID riid, LPVOID *ppv)

{
    // set the return pointer
    *ppv = 0;

    // check the interface request
    if ( (riid == IID_IUnknown) ||
         (riid == IID_IShell) )
         *ppv = this;

    // convert object dispinterface requests into
    // IID_IDispatch
    if ( (riid == IID_IDispatch) ||
        (riid == DIID_DIShell) )
        return pStdDispatch->QueryInterface(
        IID_IDispatch, ppv);

    // increment the reference count
    if (*ppv) {
        ((LPUNKNOWN)(*ppv))->AddRef();
        return NOERROR;
    }

    return ResultFromScode(E_NOINTERFACE);
}
```

AddRef increments the reference count of the object and *Release* decrements it. If the object reference count reaches zero, the object deletes itself by using the “delete this” statement:

```
ULONG STDMETHODCALLTYPE myImplOfShell::AddRef()
{
    return ++refCount;
}

ULONG STDMETHODCALLTYPE myImplOfShell::Release()
{
    if (--refCount == 0) {
        delete this;
        return 0;
    }

    return refCount;
}
```

Recall that after the object factory creates this object inside the *CreateInstance* method, a call to the *Init* method is made. This is where the private pointers declared in the objimpl.h header file are initialized. If this function fails, it returns FALSE and *CreateInstance* deletes the object rather than returning it to the caller. Here is the code for *Init*:

```
BOOL myImplOfShell::Init()
{
    // initialize the unknown interface pointer
    LPUNKNOWN pIUnknown = this;

    if (outerUnknown)
        pIUnknown = outerUnknown;

    // load the type library
    ITypeLib *pITypeLib;

    if ( FAILED( LoadRegTypeLib(
         LIBID_ShellTypeLibrary,
         1, 0, LANG_NEUTRAL, &pITypeLib) ) )
        return FALSE;
```

```
    // get the type information out of the type
    // library
    HRESULT hr = pITypeLib->GetTypeInfoOfGuid
                    (DIID_DIShell, &typeInfo);
    pITypeLib->Release();

    if ( FAILED(hr) )
        return FALSE;

    // create the standard dispatch interface
    hr = CreateStdDispatch(pIUnknown, (IShell *)this,
                              typeInfo, &pStdDispatch);
    if ( FAILED(hr) )
        return FALSE;

    return TRUE;
}
```

Init tries to load the type library information from the system registry using *LoadRegTypeLib* with the *LIBID_ShellTypeLibrary* GUID argument. The type information is then obtained from *GetTypeInfoOfGuid*, and a standard implementation of the *IDispatch* interface for the object is created. This standard implementation is used in the object's *QueryInterface* method to return the *IDispatch* pointer for the object to the caller. The advantage of doing this is so the object does not have to supply its own implementation of *IDispatch*.

The IShell Interface Method

Finally, we provide the last method, which is our implementation of the *run* method for the object. All of the other code serves as a wrapper around this function to allow it to be called by OLE Automation controllers.

```
short STDMETHODCALLTYPE myImplOfShell::run(LPCTSTR
                                              filename)
{
```

```
    // get a single byte representation of the file
    // name
    char exec[256];
    if ( !wstrcpy(exec, filename) )
        return 1;

    // execute the program
    WinExec(exec, SW_SHOW);
    return 0;
}
```

The filename is passed through by OLE using multibyte characters, so a *wstrcpy* method is defined and placed in tolefact.h to convert the argument to a single byte string. Then *WinExec* is called to launch the program.

```
// wstrcpy - copies a wide character string into a
// single byte string
char *wstrcpy(char *dest, LPCTSTR src)
{
    // make sure src and dest are specified
    if (!dest || !src)
        return 0;

    // copy the source string, skipping every other
    // byte
    char *sb = (char *)src;

    while (*sb) {
        *dest++ = *sb;
        sb += 2;
    }
    *dest = '\0';    // null terminate the destination
                     // string

    return dest;
}
```

Compiling the Server

You can compile these modules using a Borland C++ project, setting the TargetExpert to compile an application (.exe) for the Win32 platform, using a GUI target model, and including the run-time and OLE 2 libraries. The module definition file for the project is:

```
; win95exe.def
NAME Shell
DESCRIPTION 'Simple2.Shell OLE Automation object'

CODE PRELOAD DISCARDABLE
DATA PRELOAD MULTIPLE
```

Making a Type Library

We must now create a type library for our server. This is done by running a tool called mktyplib.exe (starting with NT 4.0, mktyplib is obsoleted by midl). The input to mktyplib is a file written in Object Description Language (ODL). I will not cover the details of ODL here, because a description is available from the OLE documentation. The following ODL statements (in the file simple2.odl) for the Simple2.Shell server are sufficient for our purposes.

```
// LIBID_Shell
[
    uuid(60eeef40-6559-11cf-b1eb-48dc04c10000),
    helpstring("Shell Type Library"),
    lcid(0x0000),
    version(1.0)
]

library ShellTypeLibrary
{
    importlib("stdole32.tlb");

    // IID_IShell
    [
```

```
        uuid(60eeef41-6559-11cf-b1eb-48dc04c10000),
        helpstring("Definition of interface IShell"),
        odl
    ]

    interface IShell : IUnknown
    {
        // methods
        [
            helpstring("executes program given by
                        filename"),
            id(1)
        ]
        short run([in] BSTR filename);
    };

    // DIID_DIShell
    [
        uuid(60eeef42-6559-11cf-b1eb-48dc04c10000),
        helpstring("Definition of dispinterface")
    ]

    dispinterface DIShell
    {
        interface IShell;
    };

    // CLSID_Shell
    [
        uuid(60eeef43-6559-11cf-b1eb-48dc04c10000),
        helpstring("Shell Object Type Information")
    ]

    coclass Shell
    {
        dispinterface DIShell;
        interface IShell;
    };
};
```

Note that the object definition includes the same GUIDs specified in myguid.h (although expressed in a different format). The methods defined for the *IShell* interface must also be defined here, as shown in the interface definition for the *run* method. Any additional methods added to our server must be added here, as well as added to the files iobject.h, objimpl.h, and objimpl.C.

Once we have an object description file, a type library can be generated using the following command:

```
mktyplib simple2.odl /nocpp
```

This creates the simple2.tlb type library, which you should distribute along with your OLE server.

Registering a C++ Server

Unfortunately, this is not the end of the story. We must now register the object in the system registry. An old method of doing this was to write a .reg file which included all of the registry entries. Then running regedit.exe with the .reg filename as an argument would make the appropriate object registry entries. You can see simple2.reg included on the example disk.

The recommended approach to register OLE servers today is to use the regsvr32.exe program when registering an in-process server. As we will see later, this will call an exported function in the in-process server DLL to add the appropriate entries to the Windows 95 registration database. With local servers, however, we need to provide command line switches to register and unregister the server. This will make our server registration compatible with Visual Basic's local server registration method.

Add the following code to exefuncs.C as the first statements in *WinMain*:

```
// see if the object is to be registered or
// unregistered
if ( (lstrcmpiA(pszCmdLine, "-R") == 0) ||
     (lstrcmpiA(pszCmdLine, "/R") == 0) ) {
```

```
    registerObject();
    return 0;
} else if ( (lstrcmpiA(pszCmdLine, "-U") == 0) ||
            (lstrcmpiA(pszCmdLine, "/U") == 0) ) {
    unregisterObject();
    return 0;
}
```

Now add an include statement for ospace\string.h (or wherever your favorite C++ ANSI string implementation is defined) to the exefuncs.C module. Then add the following functions that enter and remove the required entries in the system registry.

```
// setKeyAndValue - helper function that creates a
//                  key and sets its value

static void setKeyAndValue(LPTSTR pszKey,
                           LPTSTR pszSubkey,
                           LPTSTR pszValue)
{
    TCHAR szKey[256];

    lstrcpy(szKey, pszKey);
    if (pszSubkey) {
        lstrcat( szKey, TEXT("\\") );
        lstrcat(szKey, pszSubkey);
    }

    HKEY hKey;
    if (RegCreateKeyEx(HKEY_CLASSES_ROOT, szKey, 0, 0,
                       REG_OPTION_NON_VOLATILE,
                       KEY_ALL_ACCESS, 0, &hKey, 0)
                       != ERROR_SUCCESS)
        return;

    if (pszValue)
        RegSetValueEx( hKey, 0, 0, REG_SZ,
                       (BYTE *)pszValue,
                       (lstrlen(pszValue) + 1)*
                       sizeof(TCHAR) );
```

```
    RegCloseKey(hKey);
}

// ------------------------------------------------

// registerObject - put entries into registration
//                  database
void registerObject(HINSTANCE hInst)
{
    setKeyAndValue("Simple2.Shell", 0,
                   "Shell OLE automation object");
    setKeyAndValue("Simple2.Shell", "CLSID",
        "{60eeef43-6559-11cf-b1eb-48dc04c10000}");
    setKeyAndValue("Simple2.Shell", "CurVer",
        "Simple2.Shell.1");
    setKeyAndValue("Simple2.Shell", "NotInsertable",
        0);

    setKeyAndValue("Simple2.Shell.1", 0,
        "Shell OLE automation object (Ver 1.0)");
    setKeyAndValue("Simple2.Shell.1", "CLSID",
        "{60eeef43-6559-11cf-b1eb-48dc04c10000}");
    setKeyAndValue("Simple2.Shell.1",
        "NotInsertable", 0);

    // get the full pathname of the object
    char fullpath[512];
    GetModuleFileName( (HMODULE)hInst, fullpath, 512 );

    // strip off the filename
    string pathonly(fullpath);
    size_t index = pathonly.find_last_of('\\');
    if (index != os_npos)
        pathonly.resize(index);

    // get the type library full pathname
    string tlbfile(fullpath);
    index = tlbfile.find_last_of('.');
```

```
    if (index != os_npos)
        tlbfile.resize(index);
    tlbfile += string(".tlb");

    setKeyAndValue("CLSID\\{60eeef43-6559-11cf-b1eb-"
       48dc04c10000}", 0,
       "Shell OLE automation object (Ver 1.0)");
    setKeyAndValue("CLSID\\{60eeef43-6559-11cf-b1eb-"
       "48dc04c10000}","LocalServer32", fullpath);
    setKeyAndValue("CLSID\\{60eeef43-6559-11cf-b1eb-"
       "48dc04c10000}", "ProgID", "Simple2.Shell.1");
    setKeyAndValue("CLSID\\{60eeef43-6559-11cf-b1eb-"
                   48dc04c10000}",
                   "VersionIndependentProgID",
                   "Simple2.Shell");
    setKeyAndValue("CLSID\\{60eeef43-6559-11cf-b1eb-"
       "48dc04c10000}", "TypeLib", "{60eeef40-6559-"
       "11cf-b1eb-48dc04c10000}");
    setKeyAndValue("CLSID\\{60eeef43-6559-11cf-b1eb-"
       "48dc04c10000}", "Programmable", 0);
    setKeyAndValue("CLSID\\{60eeef43-6559-11cf-b1eb-"
       "48dc04c10000}", "NotInsertable", 0);
    setKeyAndValue( "TypeLib\\{60eeef40-6559-11cf-"
       "b1eb-48dc04c10000}", 0, "Shell Type Library"
       );
    setKeyAndValue( "TypeLib\\{60eeef40-6559-11cf-"
       "b1eb-48dc04c10000}", "DIR", (char *)
       pathonly.c_str() );
    setKeyAndValue( "TypeLib\\{60eeef40-6559-11cf-"
       "b1eb-48dc04c10000}", "HELPDIR", (char *)
       pathonly.c_str() );
    setKeyAndValue( "TypeLib\\{60eeef40-6559-11cf-"
       "b1eb-48dc04c10000}", "1.0",
       "Shell OLE automation object"
       " (Ver 1.0) Type Library" );
    setKeyAndValue( "TypeLib\\{60eeef40-6559-11cf-"
       "b1eb-48dc04c10000}", "1.0\\0\\win32", (char *)
       tlbfile.c_str() );
}
```

```
// -----------------------------------------------------

// unregisterObject - remove entries from
//                    registration database
void unregisterObject()
{
    RegDeleteKey(HKEY_CLASSES_ROOT,
    "Simple2.Shell\\CLSID");
    RegDeleteKey(HKEY_CLASSES_ROOT,
    "Simple2.Shell\\CurVer");
    RegDeleteKey(HKEY_CLASSES_ROOT,
                 "Simple2.Shell\\NotInsertable");
    RegDeleteKey(HKEY_CLASSES_ROOT, "Simple2.Shell");

    RegDeleteKey(HKEY_CLASSES_ROOT,
    "Simple2.Shell.1\\CLSID");
    RegDeleteKey(HKEY_CLASSES_ROOT,
    "Simple2.Shell.1\\NotInsertable");
    RegDeleteKey(HKEY_CLASSES_ROOT,
    "Simple2.Shell.1");

    RegDeleteKey(HKEY_CLASSES_ROOT, "CLSID\\"
        "{60eeef43-6559-11cf-b1eb-48dc04c10000}"
        "\\LocalServer32");
    RegDeleteKey(HKEY_CLASSES_ROOT, "CLSID\\"
        "{60eeef43-6559-11cf-b1eb-
        48dc04c10000}\\ProgID");
    RegDeleteKey(HKEY_CLASSES_ROOT, "CLSID\\"
        "{60eeef43-6559-11cf-b1eb-48dc04c10000}\\"
        "VersionIndependentProgID");
    RegDeleteKey(HKEY_CLASSES_ROOT, "CLSID\\"
        "{60eeef43-6559-11cf-b1eb-48dc04c10000}\\"
        "TypeLib");
    RegDeleteKey(HKEY_CLASSES_ROOT, "CLSID\\"
        "{60eeef43-6559-11cf-b1eb-48dc04c10000}\\"
        "Programmable");
    RegDeleteKey(HKEY_CLASSES_ROOT, "CLSID\\"
        "{60eeef43-6559-11cf-b1eb-48dc04c10000}\\"
        "NotInsertable");
    RegDeleteKey(HKEY_CLASSES_ROOT, "CLSID\\"
        "{60eeef43-6559-11cf-b1eb-48dc04c10000}");
```

```
    RegDeleteKey(HKEY_CLASSES_ROOT,
        "TypeLib\\{60eeef40-6559-11cf-b1eb-"
        "48dc04c10000}\\DIR");
    RegDeleteKey(HKEY_CLASSES_ROOT,
        "TypeLib\\{60eeef40-6559-11cf-b1eb-"
        "48dc04c10000}\\HELPDIR");
    RegDeleteKey(HKEY_CLASSES_ROOT,
        "TypeLib\\{60eeef40-6559-11cf-b1eb-"
        "48dc04c10000}\\1.0");
    RegDeleteKey(HKEY_CLASSES_ROOT,
        "TypeLib\\{60eeef40-6559-11cf-b1eb-"
        "48dc04c10000}\\1.0\\0\\win32");
    RegDeleteKey(HKEY_CLASSES_ROOT,
        "TypeLib\\{60eeef40-6559-11cf-b1eb-"
        "48dc04c10000}");
}
```

This code follows the pattern shown in code examples from reference 1. *setKeyAndValue* puts entries into the registry, and *RegDeleteKey* deletes the entries. Entries should be removed in the order of most nested keys first.

Running the server from the command line with a "/r" argument will now register our server so clients can use it. The *registerObject* method includes code that uses *GetModuleFileName* to obtain the full path of the server and its type library. The full pathnames are written into the registry so other applications can find them. The construction of the path and file names also illustrates the ANSI string class methods *find_last_of*, *resize*, and *operator+*.

Testing the C++ Server

To test our C++ local server, we'll create a small Visual Basic project (test2.vbp). This program has a form that contains an entry-field for specifying a program name (*txtProgramName*), and two buttons for running the program (*pbRun*) and exiting (*pbCancel*), respectively.

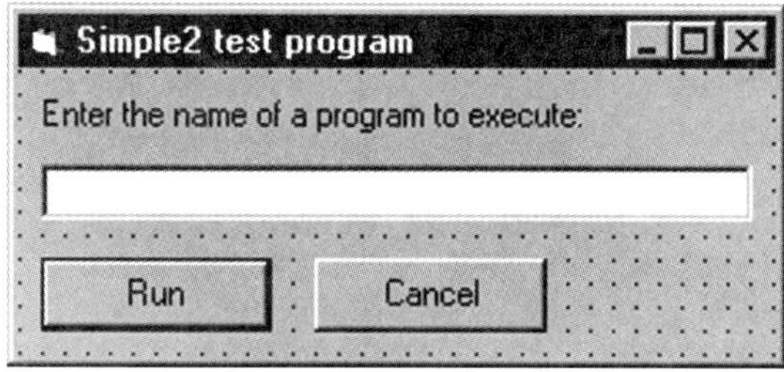

Figure 2.2. Form for test2.vbp project.

When the form loads, it is centered on the screen:

```
Private Sub Form_Load()
     Top = (Screen.Height—Height) / 2
     Left = (Screen.Width—Width) / 2
End Sub
```

Pressing the Cancel button ends the program:

```
Private Sub pbCancel_Click()
     End
End Sub
```

The *pbRun_Click* event is where the OLE client application creates an instance of our C++ server.

```
Private Sub pbRun_Click()
     Dim exec As Object

     ' make sure program name is specified
     If Len(txtProgramName.Text) = 0 Then
        MsgBox "You must specify a program name", _
        vbOKOnly, Caption
        Exit Sub
     End If
```

```
    ' create the OLE object
    On Error Resume Next
    Set exec = CreateObject("Simple2.Shell.1")
    If exec Is Nothing Then
         MsgBox "Could not create OLE object", _
         vbOKOnly, Caption
         Exit Sub
    End If

    ' call the run method on the object, passing
    ' it the filename specified by the user
    exec.run txtProgramName.Text

    ' clean up and exit
    Set exec = Nothing
    End
End Sub
```

We use late binding, so the *exec* variable is declared as an *Object* type, and *CreateObject* is called to create an instance of the C++ OLE server object, using the server's ProgId, or textual name. Visual Basic uses this name to look up the server information in the system registry.

Once the object has been created, the server's *run* method is called with the program name argument obtained from the *txtProgramName* entryfield. This server then launches the program using the code in *myImplOfShell::run*.

In-Process Servers

Now that we have created local servers using both Visual Basic and C++, we can focus on writing in-process servers. As stated previously, in-process servers perform faster because they are DLLs loaded into the client's process. Thus, no interprocess communication messages are required to invoke methods or access properties.

An In-Process VB Server

Visual Basic 4.0 comes in both 16 and 32 bit flavors. The 16 bit version does not support the creation of DLLs, so in-process servers can only be created with the 32 bit version. Let's create a new OLE server that pops up a file dialog box to retrieve a filename.

Our new project is stored in vbdll.vbp, and its startup options are set as for a Visual Basic local server. The Startup Form is *Sub Main*, it is marked as an OLE server, and the project name is SimpleVBDLL. As before, we create a modMain.bas code module with an empty main subroutine:

```
Sub Main()
    ' OLE startup code
End Sub
```

We define a simple form named *frmMain* with the property *Visible=False*. A single CommonDialog control is added to the form and named *dlgFileOpen*.

We then create a class module named *clsFileDialog*, mark the class as public, and set its *Instancing* property to 2 (Creatable MultiUse). This class should handle displaying the file dialog and return the selected filename to the user. We declare two private variables to store the filename and an instance of the form, and define a *Property Get* function to retrieve the filename.

```
Private myFilename As String
Private myform As New frmMain

Property Get selection() As String
    selection = myFilename
End Property
```

When the class is created, the private variables should be initialized:

```
Private Sub Class_Initialize()
    myFilename = ""
    Load myform
End Sub
```

Deleting the class should unload the form:

```
Private Sub Class_Terminate()
    Unload myform
End Sub
```

We need one more method that displays the dialog box using the *dlgFileOpen* control on the invisible form. This *showDialog* method displays the dialog and saves the resulting filename in the private variable so it may be returned by the *Property Get* function.

```
Public Sub showDialog()
    ' make sure form is loaded
    If myform Is Nothing Then Exit Sub

    ' set the default extension and show the dialog
    myform.dlgFileOpen.DefaultExt = ".exe"
    myform.dlgFileOpen.ShowOpen

    ' save the selected filename
    myFilename = myform.dlgFileOpen.filename
End Sub
```

Compile the project by selecting the File, Make OLE DLL file menu option to create the new in-process server. Using REGEDIT.EXE, you can then see the registry entry for SimpleVBDLL.clsFileDialog. If you want to install the entry manually, you should run the REGSVR32.EXE program, giving it the vbdll.dll name as an argument:

```
regsvr32 vbdll.dll
```

You can specify a "/u" switch to regsvr32 to remove the registry entries.

Testing clsFileDialog

The test3.vbp project contains a simple test program. This project contains no forms, as it simply uses the in-process server to display a dialog box from the Sub Main function. The selected program filename is then retrieved through the property function and run by a call to Visual Basic's *Shell* function.

```
Sub main()
     Dim fname As String

     ' create an instance of the in-process server
     Dim filedialog As Object

     On Error Resume Next
     Set filedialog = CreateObject(
        "SimpleVBDLL.clsFileDialog")
     If filedialog Is Nothing Then
          MsgBox
          "Could not create clsFileDialog", _
               vbOKOnly, "Test3"
          End
     End If

     ' show the File Open dialog box and get the
     ' filename selected by the user
     filedialog.showDialog
     fname = filedialog.selection

     ' run the program, clean up and end
     Shell fname, vbNormalFocus

     Set filedialog = Nothing
     End
End Sub
```

C++ In-Process Servers

We conclude this chapter with a look at the changes necessary to our local server code to create in-process servers in C++. The class structures defined for the local server do not change, but there are a few method implementations that must be modified, and four standard functions that must be defined and exported from the DLL.

First, we need new GUIDs for our new object (SimpleCPP-DLL.Shell). The four GUIDs are declared at the top of myguid.h as:

```
DEFINE_GUID(LIBID_ShellTypeLibrary, 0xa934ba20,
            0x6a1b, 0x11cf, 0xb1, 0xeb, 0x48, 0xdc,
            0x04, 0xc1, 0x00, 0x00);
DEFINE_GUID(IID_IShell, 0xa934ba21, 0x6a1b, 0x11cf,
            0xb1, 0xeb, 0x48, 0xdc, 0x04, 0xc1,
            0x00, 0x00);
DEFINE_GUID(DIID_DIShell, 0xa934ba22, 0x6a1b,
            0x11cf, 0xb1, 0xeb, 0x48, 0xdc, 0x04,
            0xc1, 0x00, 0x00);
DEFINE_GUID(CLSID_Shell, 0xa934ba23, 0x6a1b,
            0x11cf,0xb1, 0xeb, 0x48, 0xdc, 0x04,
            0xc1, 0x00, 0x00);
```

The remainder of myguid.h remains unchanged. The iobject.h and objimpl.h header files also do not change. We are defining the *IShell* interface for this in-process OLE server with the same *run* method used in the local server example.

The only modification to the objimpl.C file is the removal of a call to *testForShutdown* in the object destructor. Inside the tolefact.h header file, we also remove the extern declaration and calls to *testForShutdown*. We will see why this function is not needed shortly.

Next, the exefuncs.C module is renamed to dllfuncs.C, and we remove the *WinMain*, *initWindow*, and *ShellWndProc* functions. These functions are not needed because the server will be loaded by another application, and therefore does not need to create its own window or message queue to process messages. We also replace the static window handle declaration at the top of the module with one that holds the instance handle of the module.

A new function, *DLLEntryPoint*, is required to save the handle of the DLL module in the new static variable *hInstance*. This handle can be used to get the filename of the DLL for use in creating the system registry entries.

```
BOOL WINAPI DllEntryPoint(HINSTANCE handle, DWORD,
                          LPVOID)
{
   if (!hInstance)
      hInstance = handle; // saves the module
                          // handle

   return 1;
}
```

The first of our four required exported functions is now defined. *DllGetClassObject* is called by OLE clients to get a pointer to the object factory, which is subsequently used for creating *IShell* objects.

```
STDAPI DllGetClassObject(REFCLSID rclsid, REFIID
                         riid, LPVOID FAR *ppv)

{
   // initialize the return pointer (which should
   // contain the factory object)
   *ppv = 0;

   // make sure the class id is correct
   if ( rclsid != getGUID(tCLSID) )
      return ResultFromScode(E_FAIL);

   // check the interface request
   if ( (riid != IID_IUnknown) &&
       (riid != IID_IClassFactory) )
      return ResultFromScode(E_NOINTERFACE);
```

```
    // return a pointer to the object factory
    *ppv = &objectFactory;
    objectFactory.AddRef();
    return NOERROR;
}
```

The second function is *DllCanUnloadNow*, and it is called to check if the OLE server can be shutdown. It uses the object counter and reference count of the factory to determine when the DLL can be unloaded.

```
STDAPI DllCanUnloadNow()
{
    if ( (OLEFactoryObjectCounter::count() == 0L) &&
         (objectFactory.refCount() == 0L) )
        return ResultFromScode(S_OK);
    else
        return ResultFromScode(S_FALSE);
}
```

The last two functions are *DLLRegisterServer* and *DLLUnregisterServer*. These functions are used to enter and remove entries from the system registry, and are the DLL analogues of the /r and /u switches we defined for the local server command line arguments.

```
STDAPI DllRegisterServer()
{
    registerObject(hInstance);
    return NOERROR;
}

STDAPI DllUnregisterServer()
{
    unregisterObject();
    return NOERROR;
}
```

These functions simply call the registration functions developed earlier for the local server. The handle passed to *registerObject* is the DLL module handle declared at the top of dllfuncs.C and set by *DLLEntryPoint*.

The *registerObject* and *unregisterObject* functions are modified to use new GUIDs. We also need to make one additional change to these registration functions. The key **LocalServer32** should be changed to **InprocServer32**:

```
// change LocalServer32 in registerObject
setKeyAndValue("CLSID\\{60eeef43-6559-11cf-b1eb-
   48dc04c10000}", "InprocServer32", fullpath);

// change LocalServer32 in unregisterObject
RegDeleteKey(HKEY_CLASSES_ROOT,
    "CLSID\\{60eeef43-6559-11cf-b1eb-48dc04c10000}
    "\\InprocServer32");
```

Testing SimpleCPPDLL.Shell

To test the server, compile it as a Win32 DLL using the following module definition file:

```
LIBRARY cppdll
DESCRIPTION 'SimpleCPPDLL.Shell OLE object'

CODE PRELOAD DISCARDABLE
DATA PRELOAD SINGLE

EXPORTS
    DllGetClassObject     @2
    DllCanUnloadNow       @3
    DllRegisterServer     @4
    DllUnregisterServer   @5
```

Generate a type library by setting up an object description file (cppdll.odl) with the same statements as in the Simple2.Shell example. Be sure to change the GUIDs in the ODL file to the ones defined in the new myguid.h header file. Then run:

```
mytyplib cppdll.odl /nocpp
```

and also execute the following statement to register the new object:

```
regsvr32 cppdll.dll
```

It should be obvious that all the regsvr32 program does is load the DLL and call the exported routine *DLLRegisterServer* (or *DLLUnregisterServer* if the command line switch /u is used).

We can use almost exactly the same test program as in the Simple2.Shell example. On the disk, the test program is named test4.vbp. The only change from the test2 project is the type of object being created, which is specified in the *pbRun_Click* method by the statement:

```
Set exec = CreateObject("SimpleCPPDLL.Shell.1")
```

Summary

We have learned how to create OLE servers using Visual Basic and C++. Both languages can be used to create either local or in-process servers, and we have demonstrated some simple OLE clients written in Visual Basic to exercise the OLE objects.

In the next chapter, we continue the discussion of creating OLE objects. The result is a tool for generation of OLE source code in C++. We also discover how to write OLE Automation controllers in C++, so we can use C++ code in conjunction with OLE objects written in Visual Basic. Then we will be ready to apply these tools to extend the Netscape browser in some interesting directions.

References

1. K. Brockschmidt, "Inside OLE," 2nd edition, Microsoft Press, Redmond, WA, 1995.
2. "Creating OLE Servers," Visual Basic Professional Edition 4.0, Microsoft Corportion, Redmond, WA, 1995.

Chapter 3

OLE Automation Tools

The last chapter described the creation of OLE objects, and it was clear that creating these objects in C++ involves much more code than is required in the Visual Basic development environment. In this chapter, we will construct our own code generation tool to automate the creation of C++ OLE servers. This tool will be quite handy in later chapters, where we create OLE servers according to Netscape specifications. These servers will allow us to define our own protocols and custom viewers for the browser.

We also introduce an additional class and helper functions in this chapter to facilitate the construction of automation controllers in C++. All of our test programs for using OLE server objects, whether local or in-process, were written in Visual Basic. We would like to be able to use these OLE objects from C++ too.

Our OLE Automation class will be written as an abstract base class with some associated template functions that make the actual derived classes easy to write. These derived classes allow C++

to interface directly with OLE objects written in any language. We will use this technique often in later chapters to link the Netscape browser and our own custom objects together to create component-based application environments.

OLE Server Code Structure

Figure 3.1 shows the class diagram for the C++ server code developed in Chapter 2.

The *IShell* interface is declared in iobject.h as an abstract base class (or interface base class). All of the OLE interfaces are derived from *IUnknown*. The *TOLEFactoryFor* template class is derived from *IClassFactory*, and the server code uses the derived class *myImplOfShell* as the template argument. The objects delivered by the factory to OLE clients are instances of *myImplOfShell*, defined by objimpl.h and objimpl.C. Finally, the static *OLEFactoryObjectCounter* class keeps track of the number of objects created.

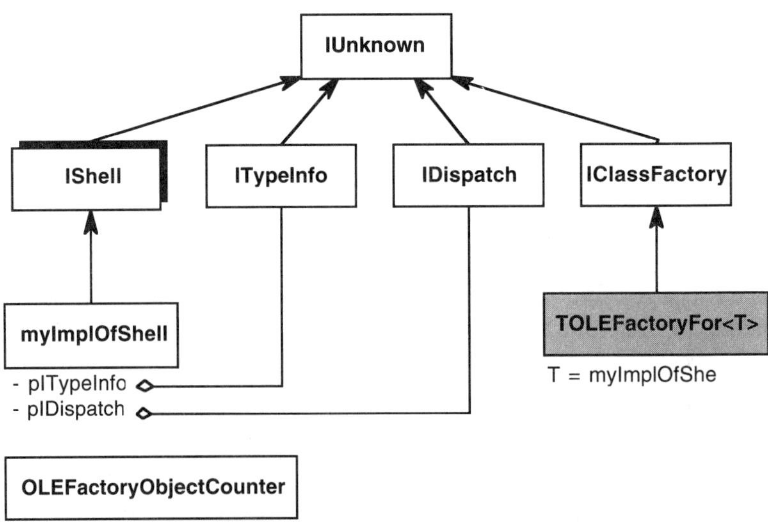

Figure 3.1 Layout of OLE server classes for the ***IShell*** interface.

If you examine this diagram and source code, it is clear that all of the classes except *IShell* and *myImplOfShell* are reusable. Of course, the actual object interface and implementation will change for each OLE object you wish to create. But, all of our other classes can be used with no changes. This potential reuse was provided for when the classes were developed in Chapter 2 by eliminating any direct references to *IShell* or *myImplOfShell* in the factory or counter classes. This was also the reasoning behind making a function (*getGUID*) in myguid.h to retrieve a specific interface or class identifier. Using this function in tolefact.h eliminates the dependency on the *IShell*-specific GUIDs.

Unfortunately, the reusability of the classes is not sufficient, because there are references to GUIDs and to the ProgId (i.e., name) of the OLE object embedded in other places. References to specific GUID values exist in the ODL file, objimpl.C, exefuncs.C, and dllfuncs.C files. The GUIDs must be generated by another program. They are even expressed with a different syntax, depending on whether it is used in a C++ or ODL file:

```
// ODL definition of LIBID_ShellTypeLibrary
uuid(60eeef40-6559-11cf-b1eb-48dc04c10000)

// myguid.h definition of LIBID_ShellTypeLibrary
DEFINE_GUID(LIBID_ShellTypeLibrary, 0x60eeef40,
            0x6559, 0x11cf, 0xb1, 0xeb, 0x48, 0xdc,
            0x04, 0xc1, 0x00, 0x00);
```

We can also examine the *IUnknown* functions and the implementation of the *Init* method in *myImplOfShell*. Factoring the references to specific GUIDs in these methods into the appropriate *getGUID* function call, the implementation of these functions is invariant with respect to the other interface methods (e.g., *IShell*).

Note that the template argument to the object factory is also declared at the top of the exefuncs.C and dllfuncs.C modules. When a new object is created, this argument will need to be changed to the new object's class name.

Thus, there is plenty of opportunity here for creating a code generation tool that automatically writes out the files for creating an OLE server. We can combine both local and in-process server types into a single set of code modules and specify which one we want using a command line switch. Let's first examine how to combine our two server examples.

Integrating the Server Code

We start with the local server code modules. We need no changes to myguid.h, iobject.h, tolefact.h, or the objimpl.h and .C modules. The exefuncs.C module is renamed to server.C, and a declaration at the top of the module is made to hold the instance handle of the DLL. We use the Borland __DLL__ predefined macro to detect whether the module is being compiled as an executable or a DLL:

```
#ifndef __DLL__
// the window handle for the local server
static HWND windowHandle = 0;
#else
// the module handle for the DLL
static HINSTANCE hInstance = 0;
#endif
```

The *registerObject* function needs to be changed to register either the **LocalServer32** or **InprocServer32** key:

```
#ifndef __DLL__
    setKeyAndValue("CLSID\\{60eeef43-6559-11cf-b1eb-"
                   "48dc04c10000}", "LocalServer32",
                   fullpath);
#else
    setKeyAndValue("CLSID\\{60eeef43-6559-11cf-b1eb-"
                   "48dc04c10000}", "InprocServer32",
                   fullpath);
#endif
```

Similarly, *unregisterObject* removes the appropriate key:

```
#ifndef __DLL__
    RegDeleteKey(HKEY_CLASSES_ROOT,
        "CLSID\\{60eeef43-6559-11cf-b1eb-
        48dc04c10000}\\LocalServer32");
#else
    RegDeleteKey(HKEY_CLASSES_ROOT,
        "CLSID\\{60eeef43-6559-11cf-b1eb-
        48dc04c10000}\\InprocServer32");
#endif
```

Next, the *ShellWndProc*, *initWindow*, and *WinMain* functions are wrapped in an #ifdef __DLL__/#endif pair.

The *testForShutdown* function is not used in the in-process server, but it is still called from the object factory template class. To avoid littering #ifdef statements throughout the template class, we just leave an empty implementation for the DLL:

```
void testForShutdown()
{
#ifndef __DLL__
    if ( (OLEFactoryObjectCounter::count() == 0L) &&
          (objectFactory.refCount() == 1L) &&
          IsWindow(windowHandle) )
        PostMessage(windowHandle, WM_CLOSE, 0, 0L);
    // closes the app
#endif
}
```

Finally, we append the *DLLEntryPoint* function and the four exported functions from the in-process server to the server.C module. We wrap all of these function definitions in a #ifdef __DLL__/#endif pair so they will be automatically compiled when an in-process server is created.

The combined server code is included in the simple2 subdirectory of the example code for this chapter. The enclosed Borland project files enable you to compile the project as either simpexe.exe or simpdll.dll. You should also create a type library from the enclosed ODL file, and copy the type library to simpexe.tlb and simpdll.tlb. Note that if you do not have the same base name for the server and its associated type library, you will get an object creation error. The type library will not be found because the type library is registered (through *registerObject*) with the same base name as the server.

To test the simpexe.exe OLE server, use the test2.vbp project (copied from Chapter 2). Remember to register the object (simpexe /r) before testing, and deregister the object (simpexe /u) afterwards. Deregistering the object enables you to register the simpdll.dll OLE server with regsvr32, which has the same ProgId as the local server. After testing the in-process server, you can deregister it also.

Writing a Code Generator

Our tool to automatically write C++ source code for OLE servers must generate the following modules:

- myguid.h
- iobject.h
- objimpl.h
- objimpl.C
- server.C
- iobject.odl
- win95exe.def or win95dll.def

The tolefact.h module remains unchanged, and can be placed in a standard include directory. It is located in the book CD-ROM's /include subdirectory.

The code generation tool, mkoleobj, is contained in the chap03\mkoleobj subdirectory. The strategy for generating the code is simple—we construct a data file that contains the source code modules concatenated together. A comment line in the data file separates each module and specifies the module name. In the data file, there are substitution markers embedded in each code module that mark where object-specific declarations, names, values, or code must be inserted.

The tool simply reads the data file, makes the appropriate substitutions (e.g., for new GUIDs, object names, etc.), and writes the new files to the current subdirectory. The value specified on the command line represents the name of the object.

Up to now, we have been naming our OLE objects rather arbitrarily. However, the recommended ProgId for an object is CompanyName.Object.Version (or sometimes ApplicationName.Object.Version). Thus, company XYZ's OLE server that provides a version 2 Widget class would be named XYZ.Widget.2. For the remainder of this book, we will use NPG (for Netscape Programmer's Guide) as the company name. Thus, you can easily find all of the OLE objects associated with the following chapters of the book by searching for NPG in the Registry Editor (using regedit).

It will make the tool more useful if we also parameterize the company name by including it in the data file. Then, by specifying a class name such as Shell on the command line, code for NPG.Shell.1 will be generated. We can also add an author name to place in a comment block at the top of the generated code module. You can further extend the entries to include things such as a copyright notice or version number.

Suggested exercise 3–1 Modify the source code of the tool to embed the data file directly into a resource file rather than keeping it separate from the executable.

Suggested exercise 3–2 Use the OLE structured storage model to store the code modules as separate streams in a compound document file.[1]

The Module Data File

We need a comment character sequence for the data file that is easy to detect and not normally encountered as the first two characters of a line in a C++ or ODL module. We will use "!!", so the first two lines of the mkoleobj.dat file are:

```
!!Author = Dick Lam
!!Company = NPG
```

We now need to define a substitution table to use in marking up the code modules. The following table should be adequate for the tool based on the contents of the modules we are generating.

Table Index	Marker	Description
0	%01	Type library id LIBID_x (C++ format)
1	%02	Interface id IID_Ix (C++ format)
2	%03	Dispatch interface id DIID_DIx (C++ format)
3	%04	Class id CLSID_x (C++ format)
4	%05	LIBID_x (ODL format)
5	%06	IID_Ix (ODL format)
6	%07	DIID_DIx (ODL format)
7	%08	CLSID_x (ODL format)
8	%09	Author name (from data file)
9	%10	Company name (from data file)
10	%11	Object name (from command line)

Once we have the substitution table, we begin substituting the markers into each module. For example, the next few lines in the mkoleobj.dat file are for the myguid.h header file:

```
!!StartFile = myguid.h
// ************************************************
//
// Module:   myguid.h
// Author:   %09
//
// Purpose: C++ class header file for GUIDs.
//
// Notes: This module defines four unique GUIDs
// based on the object
//          name. The GUIDs are:
//              LIBID_%11TypeLibrary  : %05
//              IID_I%11              : %06
//              DIID_DI%11            : %07
//              CLSID_%11             : %08
//
// ************************************************

#ifndef MODULE_myguidh
#define MODULE_myguidh

#define INITGUID
#include <compobj.h>
#include <initguid.h>

// ************************************************

// GUIDs - use guidgen or a similar program to make
//         new ids for each project
DEFINE_GUID(LIBID_%11TypeLibrary, %01);
DEFINE_GUID(IID_I%11, %02);
DEFINE_GUID(DIID_DI%11, %03);
DEFINE_GUID(CLSID_%11, %04);
```

```
// -----------------------------------------------

// type used in function to retrieve a particular
// GUID
enum GUIDType { tLIBID = 0,    // library id
                tIID = 1,      // interface id
                tDIID = 2,     // dispatch id
                tCLSID = 3     // class id
};

// -----------------------------------------------

// getGUID - returns a GUID

GUID getGUID(GUIDType t)

{
   if (t == tLIBID)
      return LIBID_%11TypeLibrary;
   else if (t == tIID)
      return IID_I%11;
   else if (t == tDIID)
      return DIID_DI%11;
   else
      return CLSID_%11;
}

#endif

// ***********************************************

// end of myguid.h
```

The “!!StartFile” key denotes the filename to use for storing the generated source code after making the appropriate substitutions from the table. You can examine the mkoleobj.dat file to see the other modules and their embedded substitution markers.

The OLE Server Generator

Now that the data file and substitution table are set up, we can start writing the code generation tool itself. The complete source code is in mkoleobj.C, which contains the following include files and global declarations:

```
#define __MINMAX_DEFINED

#include <fstream.h>
#include <strstrea.h>
#include <iomanip.h>
#include <dir.h>
#include <vector.h>
#include <ospace\string.h>
#include <iterator.h>
#include <ole2.h>

// ************************************************

// declare the program version
const int majorVersion = 1;
const int minorVersion = 0;

// declare the table used to substitute the %N
// (N = 01 - 11) strings:
//
// %N      Table entry                     Description
// ——  ——————————————————————————  ——————————
// %01 substitutionTable[0]    LIBID_x (GUIDs in C++
//     format)
// %02 substitutionTable[1]    IID_Ix
// %03 substitutionTable[2]    DIID_DIx
// %04 substitutionTable[3]    CLSID_x
// %05 substitutionTable[4]    LIBID_x  (GUIDs in
//                                       ODL format)
// %06 substitutionTable[5]    IID_Ix
// %07 substitutionTable[6]    DIID_DIx
// %08 substitutionTable[7]    CLSID_x
```

```
// %09 substitutionTable[8]    author (from data
//                                     file)
// %10 substitutionTable[9]    company name (from
//                             data file)
// %11 substitutionTable[10]   object name (from the
//                             command line)
vector<string> substitutionTable(11, "");
```

The program uses C++ file (*fstream*) and memory (*strstream*) streams extensively, and also relies on the ANSI C++ string class. The substitution table itself is declared as a vector of strings, using the Standard Template Library (STL) vector template class. The table is initialized with eleven entries, and each entry is assigned an empty string.

The main program starts by displaying a banner that includes the version number of the tool. A check is then made for the required command line argument specifying the name of the OLE object. If the argument is missing, help is displayed and the program exits. If the argument is present, it is entered into the substitution table.

```
// showTitle—displays the program title
void showTitle()
{
    cout << "mkoleobj - OLE automation object source"
         << " code generator"
         << endl
          << "Version " << majorVersion << "."
          << minorVersion << endl
          << "Written by Dick Lam, IBM Research"
          << endl << endl;
}

// ------------------------------------------------
```

```
// showHelp - displays help for the program
void showHelp()
{
    // see the disk for the help text
}

// -----------------------------------------------

int main(int argc, char *argv[])
{
    // display the program title
    showTitle();

    // check for a command line argument specifying
    // the object name
    if (argc != 2) {
        showHelp();
        return 1;
    }
    substitutionTable[10] = string(argv[1]);

    // create four new GUIDs
    if ( !createGUIDs() ) {
        cout << "An OLE error prevented generation "
             << "of unique GUIDs"
             << endl;
        return 2;
    }

    // open the input file
    ifstream fin( getPathname(argv[0],
                  "mkoleobj.dat").c_str() );
    if (!fin) {
        cout << "The code data file could not be read"
             << endl;
        return 3;
    }
```

```
    // generate the source code modules from the
    // input file, display a message to the user,
    // and end
    process(fin);
    cout   << "Source code for OLE object "
           << substitutionTable[9].c_str() << "."
           << substitutionTable[10].c_str()
           << " has been generated!" << endl;

    return 0;
}
```

The next step is to fill in the globally unique identifiers for the four interface identifiers. We need to generate these GUIDs and write them, in two formats each, into the first eight entries of the substitution table. The trick to doing this is in the *createGUIDs* function, which returns a *bool* (a new C++ data type) with a value of *false* if the function fails and *true* if it succeeds.

```
bool createGUIDs()
{
    // init COM
    if ( FAILED( CoInitialize(0) ) )
        return false;

    GUID guid;

    for (int i = 0; i < 4; i++) {
        // generate a new GUID
        CoCreateGuid(&guid);

        // make the C++ representation of the GUID
        // to insert into the
        // DEFINE_GUID macro
        strstream oscpp;
```

```
    oscpp.fill('0');
    oscpp << hex
        << "0x" << setw(8) << guid.Data1 << ", "
        << "0x" << setw(4) << guid.Data2 << ", "
        << "0x" << setw(4) << guid.Data3;

    for (int j = 0; j < 8; j++)
        oscpp << ", 0x" << setw(2)
               << (0xff & guid.Data4[j]);
    oscpp << ends;

    // put stream contents into the table
    substitutionTable[i] = string( oscpp.str() );
    delete oscpp.str();

    // make the ODL representation of the GUID
    strstream osodl;

    osodl.fill('0');
    osodl << hex
           << setw(8) << guid.Data1 << "-"
           << setw(4) << guid.Data2 << "-"
           << setw(4) << guid.Data3 << "-"
           << setw(2) << (0xff & guid.Data4[0])
           << setw(2) << (0xff & guid.Data4[1])
           << "-";

    for (j = 2; j < 8; j++)
        osodl << setw(2)
               << (0xff & guid.Data4[j]);
    osodl << ends;

    // put stream contents into the table
    substitutionTable[i + 4] = string(
                                    osodl.str() );
    delete osodl.str();
}
```

```
    // uninitialize COM and return
    CoUninitialize();
    return true;
}
```

GUIDs are created with an algorithm that uses a unique identifier obtained from a network card, if one is present. If it is not, some features of the local machine state and clock are used. Regardless, the chances of the algorithm generating a duplicate identifier are deemed microscopic. Here is the definition for the GUID data elements (defined in compobj.h):

```
struct GUID {
    DWORD Data1;
    WORD Data2;
    WORD Data3;
    BYTE Data4[8];
};
```

The unique GUIDs are obtained by calling the COM function *CoCreateGuid*. However, we cannot call this function without first initializing COM. Thus, our *createGUIDs* function needs to call *CoInitialize* at the beginning and *CoUninitialize* at the end. If we required COM or OLE support in other functions, we would move these initialization and termination calls to the main program (or as one reviewer points out, under Win32 we could avoid using these functions and simply call *UuidCreate*, which does not depend on COM at all).

We create our four unique GUIDs sequentially inside a *for* loop. We then set up the *oscpp* stream and put the data elements of the GUID structure into the stream using the following format:

```
0x88d2c020,0x6ae2,0x11cf,0xb1,0xeb,0x48,0xdc,0x04,
0xc1,0x00,0x00
```

Once the stream contents are set, the oscpp.str method returns the string for assignment to the appropriate substitution table entry. The program will substitute this format into the DEFINE_GUID macro in myguid.h for a C++ declaration of the GUID:

```
DEFINE_GUID(LIBID_ShellTypeLibrary, 0x88d2c020,
            0x6ae2, 0x11cf, 0xb1, 0xeb, 0x48, 0xdc,
            0x04, 0xc1, 0x00, 0x00);
```

Similarly, the *osodl* stream is used to construct the following GUID representation, which is also stored in *substitutionTable*:

```
88d2c020-6ae2-11cf-b1eb-48dc04c10000
```

The next step is to open the data file containing the parameterized source code. An *ifstream* is used to open the file with the full pathname of the data file. The full pathname is constructed by a call to *getPathName*:

```
string getPathname(const char *programPath,
                   const char *dataFile)
{
   // first determine the path to the data file by
   // extracting the mkoleobj.exe path from the
   // first argument
   string dataPath(programPath);

   size_t index = dataPath.find_last_of('\\');
   dataPath.resize(index + 1);

   // append the data filename to the path and
   // return the full pathname
   dataPath += dataFile;
   return dataPath;
}
```

The data file resides in the same directory as the executable, so the executable's path is extracted by finding the last path delimiter character (i.e., backslash) in *programPath*. The path string is then resized to include the backslash character, and the string's *operator+* method concatenates the data file name to the string.

After checking to make sure the file was opened, the *process* function is called to complete the source code generation. The code generation starts by reading the contents of the data file into a vector of strings, using the iostream *getline* method and the STL *vector<string>::push_back* method.

```
void process(istream& input)
{
    // separate the data into a vector of character
    // strings, 1 string per line
    vector<string> lines;
    char buf[256], cwd[256];

    while ( !input.eof() ) {
        // read a line and insert it into the vector
        input.getline(buf, 256);
        lines.push_back( string(buf) );
    }
```

Next, the current directory is obtained to determine where to write the code modules:

```
    // get the current working directory (where the
    // files will be written)
    getcwd(cwd, 255);
```

An output file stream is declared but not opened. A boolean variable then keeps track of whether the output file is open or not. The vector of strings is processed one at a time in a loop using an STL iterator:

```
    // process the vector of lines
    ofstream fout;
    bool fileOpened = false;
```

```
for (vector<string>::iterator i = lines.begin();
      i != lines.end(); i++) {
```

Dereferencing the iterator (**i*) gives the next string in the array. The string is checked to see if it represents one of the control statements that starts with "!!": If the line is not a control line, the substitution table is applied to the string through a call to *doSubstitutions*, and the line is written to the current file.

For each control line, a check is made to see if the line contains an Author, Company, or filename specification. The value of the control field is extracted by calling *getControlValue*. The Author and Company values are written to the substitution table, and the filename specification causes any currently open file to be closed. The new filename is then appended to the current directory, and a new output file stream is opened.

```
// see if the line is a special control line
// (line starts with "!!")
string curLine(*i);

if ( (curLine.size() >= 2) &&
     (curLine[0] == '!') &&
      (curLine[1] == '!') ) {
   // close the output file if open
   if (fileOpened)
      fout.close();

   // see if the control line is for Author,
   // Company, or a new file
   if ( curLine.find("Author") <
         curLine.size() ) {
      // Author
      substitutionTable[8] =
      getControlValue(curLine);
   } else if ( curLine.find("Company") <
               curLine.size() ) {
```

```
                // Company
                substitutionTable[9] =
                getControlValue(curLine);
            } else {
                // new file—form the full pathname
                string name = string(cwd) +
                              string("\\") +
                              getControlValue(curLine);
                fout.open( name.c_str() );
                fileOpened = true;
            }
        } else {
            // carry out any string substitutions and
            // then write out the line
            doSubstitutions(curLine);
            fout << curLine.c_str() << endl;
        }
    }
```

Finally, the last file that was written to is closed and the function ends.

```
    // close the output file if open
    if (fileOpened)
        fout.close();
}
```

The *getControlValue* function accepts a line such as "Company=NPG" and extracts the "NPG" value as a substring past the equals sign.

```
string getControlValue(const string& line)
{
    // look for the '=' character
    size_t pos = line.find('=');
    pos += 1;
    if ( pos == line.size() )
        return string("");
```

```
    // skip white space past the '=' sign
    while (line[pos] == ' ')
        pos += 1;

    // get the value string and return it
    string value = line.substr(pos);
    return value;
}
```

Of course, the real work is in the function *doSubstitutions*, where the embedded "%0n" values in the string are substituted for the table entries.

```
void doSubstitutions(string& line)
{
    // look for %01, %02, ..., %11 and substitute
    // the appropriate table entry
    static char *index[] = {"%01", "%02", "%03",
                            "%04", "%05", "%06",
                            "%07", "%08", "%09",
                            "%10", "%11"};
    size_t pos;
    char *p;

    for (int i = 0; i < 11; i++) {
        p = index[i];

      while ( ( pos = line.find(p) ) < line.size() )
            line.replace(pos, 3, substitutionTable[i]);
    }
}
```

Testing the Code Generator

Once our OLE Automation source code generator has been written, it is easy to test. Make a new directory and change to it—then run mkoleobj with a command line argument of an object name (e.g., Shell). The eight code modules needed to build an OLE object are generated, including module definition files for either a local or in-process server.

If you examine the myguid.h and iobject.odl files generated by the program, you will see that the four appropriate GUIDs for an *IShell* interface are already declared. The modules objimpl.h and objimpl.C implement a new class—the name of the class is constructed from the command line argument (e.g., *myImplOfShell*). In server.C, the object's class factory is declared with the new class name:

```
static TOLEFactoryFor<myImplOfShell> objectFactory;
```

Note also that *registerObject* and *unregisterObject* are automatically declared with the appropriate ProgId (NPG.Shell.1) and GUIDs:

```
// some statements automatically generated in
// registerObject
setKeyAndValue("CLSID\\{88d2c023-6ae2-11cf-b1eb-"
               "48dc04c10000}", "ProgID",
               "NPG.Shell.1");
setKeyAndValue("CLSID\\{88d2c023-6ae2-11cf-b1eb-"
               "48dc04c10000}",
               "VersionIndependentProgID",
               "NPG.Shell");
setKeyAndValue("CLSID\\{88d2c023-6ae2-11cf-b1eb-"
               "48dc04c10000}", "TypeLib",
               "{88d2c020-6ae2-11cf-b1eb-"
               "48dc04c10000}");
// . . ., etc.
```

The generated code module iobject.h includes a declaration of a dummy method for the new interface (*IShell*). It is inherited by the implementation class and defined in objimpl.C. This method should be deleted and replaced by your own set of specific interface methods for the new object. Your methods need to be declared as pure virtual in iobject.h, and re-declared and implemented in objimpl.h and objimpl.C. You will also need to modify iobject.odl to include the new object interface methods.

Once you define all of your methods, you can compile the project files into either a local or in-process OLE server. This tool takes a lot of the tedium out of creating your own OLE servers, and we will use it several times in later chapters. It will be particularly useful in defining our own Netscape protocol handlers and viewers.

An Automation Controller Class

Let's review what we can do so far. First, we can create OLE servers that expose an interface other applications may use. These servers can be constructed either as a separate (local) process or as a DLL (in-process). Furthermore, we can create either type of server in two different languages, Visual Basic and C++. We also created a tool in the last section of this chapter to simplify the creation of OLE objects in C++. We can now create objects based on the native language advantages of either C++ or Visual Basic.

Note that we have always tested our OLE servers using simple Visual Basic automation controllers. To complete the circle, we should have a way to call Visual Basic or C++ servers from a C++ automation controller application. The goal here is to make it very easy to construct a C++ header file with inline method and property calls to any OLE server.

Some Caveats

There are some limitations in our implementation of OLE servers. For one thing, only one type of object is exposed by each server. This makes our server code simpler and is of no consequence for the objects we develop in this book. If you wish to have your own applications expose an OLE Automation interface with multiple classes, you will need to modify the server code accordingly.

Another limitation is arguably more serious—Microsoft recommends that OLE Automation objects support a dual interface, which is based on both *IDispatch* and virtual function tables (VTBL).[2] VTBLs have a slight speed advantage over *IDispatch* function calls. I have ignored the VTBL approach because it requires the object methods to return *HRESULT*—arguments returned from a method in a dual interface must be passed back through the method parameter list. I prefer to maintain the flexibility of defining my own object function signatures, including the type of return arguments.

As for the speed question, we are concentrating on network-centric applications based on the Netscape browser. The rate-limiting step probably is not going to depend on any extra function calls made through *IDispatch*, but rather will depend on the speed of the network connection and the type of request made.

This brings us to the implementation of a base class for calling other OLE server methods. Our base class will be designed so derived classes can easily create an OLE server object at run-time (late binding). The methods of the derived class will use some helper functions to invoke the OLE object methods and properties through the *IDispatch* mechanism.

The Base Class

Our base class will be called *OLEDispatchInterface*, and is defined in oledisp.h and oledisp.C. These files are included on the book CD-ROM in the oledisp subdirectory. Here is the class declaration:

```
// oledisp.h
#ifndef MODULE_OLEDispatchInterfaceh
#define MODULE_OLEDispatchInterfaceh

#include <ole2.h>
#include <typeinfo.h>

// class declaration
class OLEDispatchInterface {
public:
    // constructors and destructor
    OLEDispatchInterface(const char *progid);
    // use name if known
    OLEDispatchInterface(IDispatch *dispatch);
    // use dispatch interface
```

```
virtual ~OLEDispatchInterface();

// returns dispatch pointer and locale
IDispatch *getDispatch() const { return
                                pDispatch; }
LCID getLCID() const { return lcid; }

// initializes number of arguments
// (returns 0 if ok, 1 if error)
int setNumArgs(int num);
// returns number of arguments
int getNumArgs() const { return numArgs; }

// returns a pointer to the internal args array
VARIANTARG *getArgArray() const { return args; }

// gets id of a method
DISPID getMethodID(const char *methodname);

// invokes property get and set
void getProperty(const DISPID id,
                VARIANTARG *arg);
void setProperty(const DISPID id);

// calls a method taking no arguments and
// returning none
void invokeMethod(const DISPID id);
void invokeMethod(const char *methodname)
   {invokeMethod( getMethodID(methodname) ); }

// calls methods requiring arguments and
// returning a value
void method(const DISPID id, VARIANTARG *arg);

// converts string to wchar_t representation
wchar_t *towide(const char *src);
```

```
    // class version and object state data types
    enum version { MajorVersion = 1,
                   MinorVersion = 0 };
    enum state { good = 0, bad = 1 };

    // methods to get the object state
    inline int rdstate() const { return myState; }
    inline int operator!() const { return(myState !=
                                          good); }

protected:

    IDispatch *pDispatch;        // pointer to
                                 // IDispatch interface
    LCID lcid;                   // locale
    int numArgs;                 // number of arguments
                                 // for method() call
    VARIANTARG *args;            // argument(s)

    // initializes a DISPPARMS structure
    void initParms(DISPPARAMS& parms);

    // deletes the VARIANTARG array
    void deleteArray();

private:

    state myState;    // (object state (good, bad,)

    // private copy constructor and operator=
    // (define these and make them public
    // to enable copy and assignment of the
    // class)
    OLEDispatchInterface(const
        OLEDispatchInterface&);
    OLEDispatchInterface& operator=(const
        OLEDispatchInterface&);
```

```
};

#endif
```

The copy constructor and *operator=* method are declared private with no implementation. Any application that tries to use them will get a compile error. There is a private state variable that determines if the base class object was initialized properly or not. The *myState* variable is assigned one of the enumerated types from the public declaration section, and the state of the object can be checked through the inline *not* operator or *rdstate* methods.

There are two constructors. The first one takes a ProgId string that names the OLE object to be created. The locale (*lcid*) is set by calling *GetUserDefaultLCID*, and the CLSID of the requested object is obtained from *CLSIDFromProgID*. *CoCreateInstance* is then called with the retrieved CLSID to get a pointer to the *IDispatch* interface of the OLE object.

```
// oledisp.C
OLEDispatchInterface::OLEDispatchInterface(
const char *progid)
{
    // init instance variables
    pDispatch = 0;
    lcid = GetUserDefaultLCID();
    numArgs = 0;
    args = 0;
    myState = bad;

    // form a wide char string
    CLSID clsid;
    wchar_t *objectname = towide(progid);
    if (!objectname)
        return;

    // get CLSID from the object's name
    CLSIDFromProgID(objectname, &clsid);
    delete objectname;
```

```
    // create an instance of the object
    HRESULT hresult = CoCreateInstance(clsid, 0,
        CLSCTX_SERVER, IID_IDispatch,
        (void * *)&pDispatch);
    if ( FAILED(hresult) )
        myState = bad;
    else
        myState = good;
}
```

The *towide* method creates a wide character version of the object name:

```
wchar_t *OLEDispatchInterface::towide(
const char *src)
{
    // check input argument
    if ( !src || (strlen(src) == 0) )
        return 0;

    // get size of wide character array needed
    size_t len = strlen(src);
    size_t size = MultiByteToWideChar(CP_ACP, 0,
                                      src, len,
                                      0, 0);

    // allocate memory
    wchar_t *dest = new wchar_t[size + 1];
    if (!dest)
        return 0;

    // convert and null terminate the destination
    // string
    size = MultiByteToWideChar(CP_ACP, 0, src, len,
                               dest, size);
    dest[size] = 0;
```

```
    return dest;
}
```

The second constructor initializes the object with an *IDispatch* pointer of an OLE object. This constructor is used in cases where an OLE object method returns a pointer to another OLE Automation object. For example, Visual Basic returns OLE object instances as *IDispatch* pointers.

```
OLEDispatchInterface::OLEDispatchInterface(IDispatch
                                           *dispatch)
{
    // init instance variables
    pDispatch = dispatch;
    lcid = GetUserDefaultLCID();
    numArgs = 0;
    args = 0;
    myState = bad;

    // check pointer to IDispatch interface
    if (pDispatch)
        myState = good;
}
```

There are two inline methods to return the dispatch pointer and locale. We will see how these and the other base class methods we have not discussed are used shortly.

Invoking Methods Through IDispatch

An OLE object's *IDispatch* interface allows properties to be accessed and methods to be invoked by knowing the following about the property or method:

- The member type (property get, property put, or method)
- The *IDispatch* identifier of the member
- The member's calling parameter list

- The return type of the member

You can extract this information from the object's type library using the *ITypeInfo* interface provided by OLE. However, we often know at least some of this information because the object's interface is published, or the information can be obtained from the Visual Basic Object Browser or similar programming tool.

> **Suggested exercise 3–3** Use the OLE *ITypeLib* and *ITypeInfo* interfaces to construct a tool to enumerate the properties and method signatures of OLE objects from a type library.

For our purposes, we will assume the object interface is documented, so we know the name of each member, whether it is a property get, property put, or method, and its calling arguments and return type. The only other piece of information we need is the dispatch identifier (*DISPID*), which maps the name of an object method or property to its corresponding function pointer. The *DISPID* is obtained for a particular method by calling *IDispatch::GetIDsOfNames.*

```
DISPID OLEDispatchInterface::getMethodID(const char
                                          *methodname)
{
    // convert the ANSI string to wide characters
    wchar_t *buf = towide(methodname);

    // call the IDispatch method to get the id
    DISPID id;
    pDispatch->GetIDsOfNames(IID_NULL, &buf, 1, lcid,
                             &id);
    delete buf;
```

```
    return id;
}
```

Rather than calling this function every time we need a *DISPID*, it would be a good idea to cache all of the identifiers when the derived class is initialized. This would provide some relatively easy performance enhancement. However, we do not bother with this detail here, so it is left as an exercise.

> **Suggested exercise 3–4** Change the *OLEDispatchInterface* to include support for caching the *DISPIDs* of all the methods in the derived class (hint: use an STL associative array that maps a *DISPID* to a function name).

Once we have the information needed for a particular member, it can be invoked through a call to *IDispatch::Invoke*. This function uses a set of calling parameters that specify the locale, the *DISPID*, the type of property operation (get or put) or method, and the number, types, and values of calling arguments. These arguments and any return argument are specified through *DISPPARAMS* and *VARIANTARG* structures.

For example, to invoke a property get function, we define the following function:

```
void OLEDispatchInterface::getProperty(
   const DISPID id, VARIANTARG *arg)
{
    // invoke the method
    DISPPARAMS parms;
    EXCEPINFO xcpt;
    UINT err;

    initParms(parms);
    VariantInit(arg);
```

```
    pDispatch->Invoke(id, IID_NULL, lcid,
                      DISPATCH_PROPERTYGET, &parms,
                      arg, &xcpt, &err);
}
```

This base class method is called with the *DISPID* obtained for a particular property get function by using *getMethodID*. The actual property value is returned in a *VARIANTARG* structure passed as an argument to the method. Before calling the base class dispatch pointer's *Invoke* method, a *DISPPARAMS* structure is initialized by calling *initParms*, and the return argument structure is initialized with OLE's *VariantInit* function.

We will see how to use the *VARIANTARG* structure shortly.

```
void OLEDispatchInterface::initParms(DISPPARAMS&
                                     parms)
{
    parms.cArgs = 0;
    parms.rgvarg = 0;
    parms.cNamedArgs = 0;
    parms.rgdispidNamedArgs = 0;
}
```

The code for invoking an object method that takes no arguments and returns none (e.g., `void someObjectFunction();`) is nearly identical. The *invokeMethod* function is defined below—its main difference is that no *VARIANTARG* is passed to the function because it returns nothing. So a local *arg* variable is declared to pass to *Invoke* (be careful to pass *arg* by reference).

```
void OLEDispatchInterface::invokeMethod(
   const DISPID id)
{
    // invoke the method
    DISPPARAMS parms;
    VARIANTARG arg;
    EXCEPINFO xcpt;
    UINT err;
```

```
    initParms(parms);
    VariantInit(&arg);
    pDispatch->Invoke(id, IID_NULL, lcid,
                      DISPATCH_METHOD, &parms, &arg,
                      &xcpt, &err);
}
```

Once this form of the function is defined, it is easy to write an inline definition (appearing in oledisp.h) that takes a method name argument rather than a dispatch identifier:

```
void invokeMethod(const char *methodname)
{
    invokeMethod( getMethodID(methodname) );
}
```

Note that the fourth argument to *Invoke* is a flag that denotes the type of object method. The valid types are:

Value	Description
DISPATCH_PROPERTYGET	Retrieves a property value (VB Property Get)
DISPATCH_PROPERTYPUT	Sets a property to a new value (VB Property Let)
DISPATCH_METHOD	Invokes a method (with or without arguments)
DISPATCH_PROPERTYPUTREF	Sets a property reference (VB Property Set)

The *setProperty* method assigns a new value to a property, but instead of passing the argument value to set through the parameter list, it is placed into one element of a *VARIANTARG* array maintained by the base class.

```
void OLEDispatchInterface::setProperty(const
                                       DISPID id)
{
    // invoke the method
    DISPPARAMS parms;
    EXCEPINFO xcpt;
    UINT err;
    DISPID idParam = DISPID_PROPERTYPUT;

    parms.cArgs = 1;
    parms.rgvarg = args;
    parms.cNamedArgs = 1;
    parms.rgdispidNamedArgs = &idParam;
    pDispatch->Invoke(id, IID_NULL, lcid,
                      DISPATCH_PROPERTYPUT, &parms,
                      args, &xcpt, &err);
}
```

The *DISPPARAMS* structure is initialized with the number of arguments (*cArgs*) set to one, and with *rgvarg* pointing to the array of *VARIANTARG* structures. The *cNamedArgs* field is set to one and *rgdispidNamedArgs* points to a special dispatch identifier with a value of *DISPID_PROPERTYPUT*. This designates the parameter that contains the new value.

The array of variant arguments and the number of elements in the array are declared in the protected section of *OLEDispatchInterface* above. There are also two inline functions to access these members, and a method called *setNumArgs* that must be called before a call to *setProperty* is made:

```
int OLEDispatchInterface::setNumArgs(int num)
{
    deleteArray();     // deletes the VARIANTARG array

    // if number of arguments requested is 0, we're
    // done
    if (num == 0)
        return 0;
```

```
    // allocate space for new arguments
    args = new VARIANTARG[num];
    if (!args)
        return 1;

    // initialize the new structures
    for (int i = 0; i < num; i++)
        VariantInit(&args[i]);

    // set number of arguments and return
    numArgs = num;
    return 0;
}
```

This function cleans up any existing elements and deletes the array—then a new array is allocated and initialized to hold the value for *setProperty* to use. It returns one if an error occurs—otherwise the function returns zero.

Now that the handling of the array is apparent, the destructor can be written. It needs to clean up the array and release the *IDispatch* interface set by one of the constructors.

```
OLEDispatchInterface::~OLEDispatchInterface()
{
    deleteArray();    // deletes the VARIANTARG array

    // release the IDispatch interface
    if (pDispatch)
        pDispatch->Release();
}
```

The *VARIANTARG* array is also used in the definition of *OLEDispatchInterface::method*:

```
void OLEDispatchInterface::method(const DISPID id,
                                  VARIANTARG *arg)
```

```
{
    // invoke the method
    DISPPARAMS parms;
    EXCEPINFO xcpt;
    UINT err;

    parms.cArgs = numArgs;
    parms.rgvarg = args;
    parms.cNamedArgs = 0;
    parms.rgdispidNamedArgs = 0;
    VariantInit(arg);

    pDispatch->Invoke(id, IID_NULL, lcid,
                      DISPATCH_METHOD, &parms, arg,
                      &xcpt, &err);
}
```

This function is used to call OLE object methods that take one or more calling arguments, and that may or may not return a value. If a value is returned, it is returned through the *arg* variable supplied in the call to the function (just as we did in *getProperty* above).

We could now derive a class from *OLEDispatchInterface* and add methods to the class to get and set properties or call methods for any OLE Automation object. However, take a look at the code required to call an example method (say the *IShell::run* method from our earlier example OLE server). The header file is straightforward:

```
#include "oledisp.h"

class shellController : public OLEDispatchInterface
{
public:
    // constructors and destructor
    shellController(const char *progid =
                    "Simple2.Shell.1")
        : OLEDispatchInterface(progid) {}
    shellController(IDispatch *dispatch)
        : OLEDispatchInterface(dispatch) {}
```

```
    virtual ~shellController() {}

    // run method
    void run(const char *program);
};
```

And the *run* method would be defined as follows:

```
void shellController::run(const char *program)
{
    // set the number of arguments to pass to the
    // method
    setNumArgs(1);

    // get a reference to the first VARIANTARG array
    // element, and put the program name into the
    // element
    VARIANTARG& v = args[0];

    // we need to convert the argument to a
    // BSTR—first create a wide string
    wchar_t *s = towide(program);
    if (!s)
        return;

    // now allocate a BSTR (to be deleted by
    //                          OLEDispatchInterface
    BSTR bstr = SysAllocString(s);
    v.vt = VT_BSTR;
    v.bstrVal = bstr;
    delete s;    // clean up wide string

    // get the dispatch identifier and invoke the
    // method
    DISPID id = getMethodID("run");
    VARIANTARG arg;
    VariantInit(&arg);
```

```
    method(id, &arg);       // ignore the return argu-
                            // ment for a void method
}
```

The Simple2.Shell.1 object requires one argument in its *run* method to specify the program name. This argument is a string, which is first converted to a wide character version. It is passed to the object method as a *BSTR* datatype using the *VARIANTARG* structure. After calling the base class method to set the number of arguments to one, a reference to the first array element is obtained. Then a new *BSTR* is created by calling *SysAllocString*.

The variant structure specifies the type of argument to the receiving function by setting the *vt* member to VT_BSTR. The *bstrVal* member holds the value of the argument, and this is set to the binary string we just created. Other data types and their corresponding structure members (defined as part of a *union*) are shown in the following table:

Value	union member(s)	Description
VT_EMPTY	wReserved	nothing
VT_NULL	wReserved	SQL style NULL
VT_I2	iVal, piVal	short
VT_I4	lVal, plVal	long
VT_R4	fltVal, pfltVal	float
VT_R8	dblVal, pdblVal	double
VT_CY	cyVal, pcyVal	currency
VT_DATE	date, pdate	date
VT_BSTR	bstrVal, pbstrVal	binary string
VT_DISPATCH	pdispVal, ppdispVal	IDispatch *
VT_ERROR	scode, pscode	SCODE
VT_BOOL	bool, pbool	True = -1, False = 0
VT_VARIANT	pvarVal	VARIANT *

(continued)

Value	union member(s)	Description
VT_UNKNOWN	punkVal	IUnknown *
VT_UI1	iVal, piVal	unsigned char
VT_ARRAY	parray	SAFEARRAY *
VT_BYREF	byref	void *

Finally, the dispatch identifier for the method named "run" in the OLE object is obtained. The *OLEDispatchInterface::method* function actually invokes the object's *run* function.

The last thing to note is a definition for *deleteArray*, called by both the destructor of *OLEDispatchInterface* and the *setNumArgs* method.

```
void OLEDispatchInterface::deleteArray()
{
    // clean up any existing arguments
    if (numArgs > 0) {
        for (int i = 0; i < numArgs; i++)
            VariantClear(&args[i]);

        // now delete the whole array
        numArgs = 0;
        delete [] args;
    }
}
```

This clean up is required to clear the variant arguments of any allocated data (such as the *BSTR* in the above example) or to release any interface pointers.

The shellcon example program shows the code we have presented so far, with a main program that calls the above function. Make sure the OLE server object from the simple2 project is registered before running the test program.

Simplify, Simplify

If we had to code every function in a derived class to access OLE objects as we did the *run* method in the last section, it would prove very tedious. There must be an easier way. That is what we will construct now, using our base class as a starting point. C++ gives us some tools to greatly simplify the task of creating our OLE object controllers.

The problem is that every argument passed to an object method needs to be placed into a *VARIANTARG* structure. These arguments have flags based on their datatype, and their values are put into a specific structure field. Similarly, any return arguments from a property get or other method need to be extracted from a *VARIANTARG* structure. Of course, we could take the C language approach and use macros, but these are ugly (in my opinion) and not typesafe.

What C++ language feature can be used to apply the same general operation to different datatypes? Templates! Function templates will do what we require nicely, maintain type-safety, and provide a one-line function call that can be implemented inline in the derived class for an object controller. Writing a one-line function is better than writing code like that shown above in *shellController::run*, right?

Let's start by defining the following template function. We will place the definition in oledisp.h so the template is accessible to derived classes of *OLEDispatchInterface*. We need a template function called *method_onearg* that passes one argument to an OLE object's method and returns an argument of another type (which may be void):

```
template <class ReturnType, class Arg1>
ReturnType method_onearg(OLEDispatchInterface *i,
                         char *methodname,
                         ReturnType p, Arg1 arg1)
{
    // check interface pointer
    if (!i)
        return (ReturnType)0;
```

```
    // initialize the argument
    i->setNumArgs(1);
    set_arg(i, 0, arg1);

    // get method's id and set the property
    VARIANTARG arg;
    VariantInit(&arg);

    DISPID id = i->getMethodID(methodname);
    i->method(id, &arg);

    // return the property value using the correct
    // type
    return return_arg(arg, p);
}
```

The function is parameterized on two data types—one for the return type of the function (*ReturnType*) and one for the argument to pass to the OLE object method (*Arg1*). The other two arguments are a pointer to the base class instance, and the actual method name to call.

Why do we need to pass a pointer to the base class as the first argument to the function? Well, as of this writing, most C++ compilers cannot embed template functions in a class declaration. This will change as new compiler versions appear, but in the meantime our template functions will be defined outside the class. The template functions will be called from derived classes of *OLEDispatchInterface*, so it is a simple matter to pass the *this* pointer as the first argument.

Note the similarity of the function body to that of *shellController::run*. The number of arguments for the base class instance is set to one, the calling parameter and return arguments are initialized, and *method* is called to invoke the object function. Finally, the return argument is returned after extracting the *ReturnType* from *arg*.

Naturally, there is some work going on behind the scenes—namely in the two function calls *set_arg* and *return_arg*. The argument that is supplied to the object method needs to be placed in the first element of the variant array in the base class instance. This is accomplished by passing *set_arg* a pointer to the base class instance, the array index to use for setting up the parameter, and the parameter value itself. The datatype of the parameter is also required to initialize the appropriate flag in the *VARIANTARG*, so *set_arg* itself is a template function.

```
// set_arg - sets the value of an argument in the
//           args array
//           (returns 0 if ok, 1 if invalid interface
//            pointer,
//           2 if invalid index, 3 if argument is not
//           supported)
template <class Arg>
int set_arg(OLEDispatchInterface *i, int index, Arg
value)
{
    // check interface pointer
    if (!i)
        return 1;

    // make sure index is ok
    if ( (index < 0) ||
           ( index >= i->getNumArgs() ) )
        return 2;

    // set the argument value based on its type
    VARIANTARG& arg = i->getArgArray()[index];

    if ( ( typeid(value) == typeid(unsigned char) )
            ||
           ( typeid(value) == typeid(char) ) ) {
        arg.vt = VT_UI1;
        arg.bVal = (unsigned char)value;
    } else if ( typeid(value) == typeid(short) ) {
        arg.vt = VT_I2;
        arg.iVal = (short)value;
```

```
} else if ( typeid(value) == typeid(long) ) {
   arg.vt = VT_I4;
   arg.lVal = (long)value;
} else if ( typeid(value) == typeid(float) ) {
   arg.vt = VT_R4;
   arg.byref = (void *)value;
} else if ( typeid(value) == typeid(double) ) {
   arg.vt = VT_R8;
   arg.byref = (void *)value;
} else if ( ( typeid(value) == typeid(BSTR) ) ||
            ( typeid(value) == typeid(unsigned
              char *) ) ||
            ( typeid(value) == typeid(const
              unsigned
              char *) ) ||
            ( typeid(value) == typeid(char *) )
              ||
            ( typeid(value) == typeid(const
              char *) ) ) {
   // make a wide string
   wchar_t *s = i->towide( (char *)value );
   if (!s)
       return 3;

   // allocate a BSTR
   BSTR bstr = SysAllocString(s);
   arg.vt = VT_BSTR;
   arg.bstrVal = bstr;
   delete s;   // clean up wide string
} else if ( typeid(value) == typeid(IDispatch *)
            ) {
   arg.vt = VT_DISPATCH;
   arg.pdispVal = (IDispatch *)value;
} else if ( typeid(value) == typeid(short *) ) {
   arg.vt = VT_I2 | VT_BYREF;
   arg.piVal = (short *)value;
} else if ( typeid(value) == typeid(long *) ) {
   arg.vt = VT_I4 | VT_BYREF;
   arg.plVal = (long *)value;
```

```
    } else if ( typeid(value) == typeid(float *) ) {
        arg.vt = VT_R4 | VT_BYREF;
        arg.pfltVal = (float *)value;
    } else if ( typeid(value) == typeid(double *) ) {
        arg.vt = VT_R8 | VT_BYREF;
        arg.pdblVal = (double *)value;
    } else if ( typeid(value) == typeid(BSTR *) ) {
        // make a wide string
        wchar_t *s = i->towide( (char *)value );
        if (!s)
            return 3;

        // allocate a BSTR
        BSTR bstr = SysAllocString(s);
        arg.vt = VT_BSTR | VT_BYREF;
        arg.pbstrVal = &bstr;
        delete s;    // clean up wide string
    } else if ( typeid(value) ==
                typeid(IDispatch **) ) {
        arg.vt = VT_DISPATCH | VT_BYREF;
        arg.ppdispVal = (IDispatch **)value;
    } else {
        return 3;
    }

    return 0;
}
```

Once the input arguments are checked, the *OLEDispatchInterface::getArgArray* method is used to retrieve a reference to the requested *VARIANTARG* element. The problem then is deciding the actual datatype of the template argument so the appropriate flag and union member can be initialized. This is done with a series of conditional statements using the C++ run-time type identification (RTTI) function *typeid*.

Only the more common datatypes rather than all of the ones listed in the variant argument table are reflected in the code. The last thing we need to define for the functmpl example project is the *return_arg* function. It is also a template function that simply takes the *VARIANTARG* and extracts the value based on the datatype of the second parameter.

```
// return_arg - returns an argument value based on
//              the datatype
template <class Property>
Property return_arg(VARIANTARG& arg, Property p)
{
   // return the property value using the correct
   // type
   if ( ( typeid(p) == typeid(unsigned char) ) ||
        ( typeid(p) == typeid(char) ) )
      return (Property)arg.bVal;
   else if ( typeid(p) == typeid(short) )
      return (Property)arg.iVal;
   else if ( typeid(p) == typeid(long) )
      return (Property)arg.lVal;
   else if ( typeid(p) == typeid(float) )
      return (Property)arg.byref;
   else if ( typeid(p) == typeid(double) )
      return (Property)arg.byref;
   else if ( ( typeid(p) == typeid(unsigned char *)
             ) ||
            ( typeid(p) == typeid(const unsigned
              char *) ) ||
            ( typeid(p) == typeid(char *) ) ||
            ( typeid(p) == typeid(const char *)
              ) ) {
      char *s = frombstr(arg.bstrVal);
      return (Property)s;
   } else if ( typeid(p) == typeid(BSTR) )
      return (Property)arg.bstrVal;
   else if ( typeid(p) == typeid(IDispatch *) )
      return (Property)arg.pdispVal;
   else if ( typeid(p) == typeid(short *) )
      return (Property)arg.piVal;
   else if ( typeid(p) == typeid(long *) )
      return (Property)arg.plVal;
```

```
    else if ( typeid(p) == typeid(float *) )
        return (Property)arg.pfltVal;
    else if ( typeid(p) == typeid(double *) )
        return (Property)arg.pdblVal;
    else if ( typeid(p) == typeid(BSTR *) )
        return (Property)arg.pbstrVal;
    else if ( typeid(p) == typeid(IDispatch **) )
        return (Property)arg.ppdispVal;

    return (Property)arg.byref;
}
```

So far this doesn't look like we've simplified anything. But wait, let's now rewrite the *run* method we wrote in the last section. Only this time, (see the functmpl example project) we will use a template function to define *shellController2::run*:

```
void shellController2::run(const char *program)
{
    method_onearg(this, "run", (int)0, program);
}
```

Now that looks like something that could be written quickly and easily (or at least more easily than the first method). With the template functions doing all of the work, writing a number of these methods to access other OLE objects would not be a difficult chore.

The only real "trick" involved here is one borrowed from the STL. A template function must have its parameterized arguments (such as *ReturnType*) in the function's argument list. We do not have a value for the return type before calling the function, so how can we pass only the datatype itself (with no value)? The answer is to pass a value of zero for the return type, **casting** it to the actual return type.

We have not defined the *frombstr* function used in *return_arg*, so here it is:

```
static char *frombstr(BSTR src)
{
    // get the length of the binary string and
    // allocate space for new string
    int len = SysStringLen(src);
    char *dest = new char[len + 1];
    if (!dest)
        return 0;

    // copy the source string, skipping every other
    // byte
    char *sb = (char *)src;
    char *sd = dest;

    for (int i = 0; i < len; i++) {
        *sd++ = *sb;
        sb += 2;
    }
    *sd = '\0';    // null terminate the destination
                   // string

    return dest;
}
```

There are a few other functions we need to define to complete the picture. The *method_onearg* function takes care of calling methods that take a single argument and return some type. The following *void_method* function calls an object method which takes no arguments and returns nothing. As there are no arguments involved, this does not have to be a template function.

```
void void_method(OLEDispatchInterface *i,
                 char *methodname)
{
    // check interface pointer
    if (!i)
        return;
```

```
    // invoke the method
    i->invokeMethod(methodname);
}
```

We also need template functions for getting and setting property values, so here are the corresponding *get_property* and *set_property* definitions. These functions call our base class *getProperty* and *setProperty* functions after setting up the *VARIANTARG.*

```
// get_property - retrieves a property value through
//                IDispatch
template <class Property>
Property get_property(OLEDispatchInterface *i,
                      char *methodname, Property p)
{
    // check interface pointer
    if (!i)
        return (Property)0;

    // get method's id and get the property
    VARIANTARG arg;
    VariantInit(&arg);

    DISPID id = i->getMethodID(methodname);
    i->getProperty(id, &arg);

    // return the property value using the correct
    // type
    return return_arg(arg, p);
}

// ------------------------------------------------

// set_property - sets a property value through
//                IDispatch
template <class Property>
void set_property(OLEDispatchInterface *i, char
                  *methodname, Property value)
```

```
{
    // check interface pointer
    if (!i)
        return;

    // set the argument to pass to the method
    i->setNumArgs(1);
    set_arg(i, 0, value);

    // get method's id and set the property
    DISPID id = i->getMethodID(methodname);
    i->setProperty(id);
}
```

Other functions you may wish to define are ones similar to *method_onearg* that pass more than one argument to an OLE object method. Here is a definition for *method_twoargs* used to invoke functions that take two parameters. You must be aware that the calling parameters in this and other cases must be put into the base class array in **reverse order** from their appearance in the OLE function definition. Note that the template function is now parameterized on three datatypes, representing the return type and the two argument types:

```
template <class ReturnType, class Arg1, class Arg2>
ReturnType method_twoargs(OLEDispatchInterface *i,
char *methodname, ReturnType p, Arg1 arg1, Arg2
arg2)
{
    // check interface pointer
    if (!i)
        return (ReturnType)0;

    // initialize the arguments (remember to use
    //                            reverse calling
    //                            order!)
    i->setNumArgs(2);
    set_arg(i, 0, arg2);
    set_arg(i, 1, arg1);
```

```
    // get method's id and set the property
    VARIANTARG arg;
    VariantInit(&arg);

    DISPID id = i->getMethodID(methodname);
    i->method(id, &arg);

    // return the property value using the correct
    // type
    return return_arg(arg, p);
}
```

Another Controller Example

Before leaving this chapter, let's look at how to use *OLEDispatchInterface* to write another C++ class. In this case, we will write a controller class for the Visual Basic OLE object developed in Chapter 2, namely the Simple1.clsShowProgress dialog box.

Recall that this object displays a progress bar dialog, and it has three property functions to set the range of the progress bar and text of a message to display. It also includes a void method to increment the progress bar. Using our template functions, we can quickly write the controller class using only a header file and inline functions:

```
// progdlg.h
#include "oledisp.h"

class showProgressDialog : public
                           OLEDispatchInterface {
public:
    // constructors and destructors
    showProgressDialog(const char *progid =
                       "Simple1.clsShowProgress")
        : OLEDispatchInterface(progid) {}
    showProgressDialog(IDispatch *dispatch)
        : OLEDispatchInterface(dispatch) {}
```

```
    virtual ~showProgressDialog() {}

    // clsShowProgress interface
    void BarMinimum(short minvalue)
    { set_property(this, "BarMinimum", minvalue); }

    void BarMaximum(short maxvalue)
    { set_property(this, "BarMaximum", maxvalue); }

    void Message(const char *msg)
    { set_property(this, "Message", msg); }

    void IncrementProgress()
    { void_method(this, "IncrementProgress"); }
};
```

The progdlg project on the CD-ROM contains a C++ program to use the above class. It is analogous to the Visual Basic test program we wrote in Chapter 2. You can see how easy it is using *OLEDispatchInterface* and the template functions to create an OLE Automation controller class for any OLE server. We will use this class and template functions extensively in the rest of the book.

> **Suggested exercise 3–5** Modify the programming tool written in exercise 3–3 to automatically generate a header file based on the *OLEDispatchInterface* base class.

Summary

Two C++ tools have been created. The first one is a code generation tool for creating C++ source modules that can be compiled into either a local or an in-process OLE server. This tool will make it easy in later chapters to extend Netscape based on the browser's published OLE Automation interfaces. The second tool is a base class that enables us to use either C++ or Visual Basic OLE server methods and properties from any C++ program.

We can now build inter-language component applications in Visual Basic and C++. Adding Netscape to the picture will provide a network-centric component. In the next chapter, we begin to look at Netscape's dynamic data exchange (DDE) interface. We also apply our OLE knowledge and tools to construct some useful components for browser-based applications.

References

1. K. Brockschmidt, "Inside OLE," 2nd edition, Microsoft Press, Redmond, WA, 1995.
2. "OLE Automation Programmer's Reference," Microsoft Press, Redmond, WA, 1996.

Chapter 4

Using the DDE Interface

Up to now, we have been looking at the mechanics of constructing software components and connecting them together. OLE brings considerable power to bear in developing componentware, and we now begin to apply what we have learned. In this chapter, we explore the dynamic data exchange (DDE) support built into the Netscape browser. Some Visual Basic OLE servers will be built to handle DDE messaging with Netscape.

Recall that two applications converse through DDE when one application initiates communication with another program. The one that starts the conversation is called the destination application (or DDE client), while the receiving program is the source application (or DDE server). Programs can act as either a client or a server when talking with the Netscape browser, depending on what topics they want to use.

DDE Topics

When a DDE connection is made, both the application (or service) name and topic must be specified. The official service name for the browser is NETSCAPE. The following table lists the DDE topics supported by Netscape. We will not cover every function here, so we can concentrate on the most important topics. Refer to Appendix A and the references at the end of this chapter[1,2] for additional information on all of the supported DDE functions.

Visual Basic provides an easy interface to DDE, and thus makes a good choice for building applications that provide Netscape DDE support. The application name and topic are specified in a *LinkTopic* property string of a text box, picture box, or label control. For example, to call the *WWW_GetWindowInfo* topic through DDE using a text box named *txtDDE*, use the following statement:

```
txtDDE.LinkTopic = "NETSCAPE|WWW_GetWindowInfo"
```

For flexibility, our client links between Visual Basic and Netscape will be made at runtime. This is specified by setting the *LinkMode* property of the DDE control to *vbLinkManual*. The topic is then activated whenever a *LinkRequest* is made. Resetting the mode to *vbLinkNone* terminates the DDE conversation. The default time-out for a DDE request is five seconds, and this can be changed through the *LinkTimeout* property.

Arguments that need to be passed to a DDE function are set up in a *LinkItem* string. The arguments must be separated by commas, and there should be no white space following either a comma or parameter value. If an argument is optional and you decide to leave it out, there should still be a comma denoting the argument's position.

If a text box control is used to receive return arguments, it can receive either a string, a boolean value, or a double word value. Booleans are two byte integers with a value of 1 (true) or 0 (false). Double word values (such as window ids) are returned as four byte integers.

DDE Topic	Netscape acts as
WWW_Activate	Server
WWW_Alert	Client
WWW_BeginProgress	Client
WWW_CancelProgress	Server
WWW_EndProgress	Client
WWW_Exit	Server
WWW_GetWindowInfo	Server
WWW_ListWindows	Server
WWW_MakingProgress	Client
WWW_OpenURL	Client or Server
WWW_ParseAnchor	Server
WWW_QueryURLFile	Server
WWW_QueryViewer	Client
WWW_RegisterProtocol	Server
WWW_RegisterURLEcho	Server
WWW_RegisterViewer	Server
WWW_RegisterWindowChange	Server
WWW_SetProgressRange	Client
WWW_ShowFile	Server
WWW_UnRegisterProtocol	Server
WWW_UnRegisterURLEcho	Server
WWW_UnRegisterViewer	Server
WWW_UnRegisterWindowChange	Server
WWW_URLEcho	Client
WWW_ViewDocFile	Client
WWW_WindowChange	Client or Server

Activating and Controlling Netscape Windows

Let's build a simple DDE client application that activates the current Netscape browser window. We will use the *WWW_Activate* topic to activate the last active browser window (remember that you can open multiple browser windows simultaneously). Start by constructing a Visual Basic form like the following:

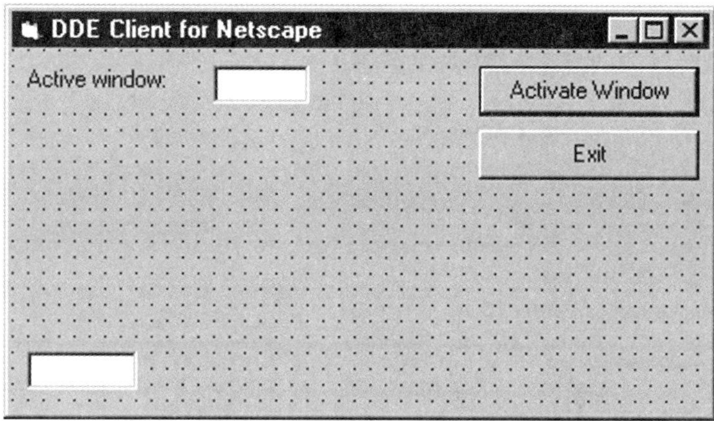

Figure 4.1.

This project is located in the chap04\activate subdirectory of the CD-ROM. There is a label control and a text control named *txtWindowID* that will contain the window id returned by the DDE function. The window id is used internally by Netscape to refer to the activated browser window, and can be used by clients to specify a particular browser window. Note that this id is **not** a Windows 95 standard window handle (HWND).

The text box control in the lower left corner of the window handles the conversation with Netscape. The control is named *txtDDE*, and its *Visible* property is set to *False*. The "Exit" button simply contains an *End* statement to exit the application. The code for the "Activate Window" button initiates the actual communication through DDE with Netscape.

```
Private Sub pbActivate_Click()
     Dim idstring As String
     Dim wid As Long

     ' set up DDE call
     txtDDE.Text = ""
     txtDDE.LinkTopic = "NETSCAPE|WWW_Activate"
     txtDDE.LinkItem = "0xFFFFFFFF,0"
     txtDDE.LinkMode = vbLinkManual
     txtDDE.LinkRequest
     txtDDE.LinkMode = vbLinkNone

     ' get return value and convert it to a long
     idstring = txtDDE.Text
     wid = ConvertToLong(idstring)

     ' show window id on form
     txtWindowID.Text = Str(wid)
End Sub
```

The *LinkItem* specifies the browser window id that should be activated. If we do not know the window id and just want to activate the last active window, we pass a value of 0xFFFFFFFF. Netscape will create a new window if a current window does not exist. The second argument is a reserved flag which is set to zero.

The window id of the now-active Netscape browser window is returned in *txtDDE*. This is converted to a long value using the following function:

```
Private Function ConvertToLong(s As String) As Long
     Dim v As Long, mult As Long
     Dim i As Integer
     Dim b As Byte

     ' loop to construct long value from bytes
     v = 0
     mult = 1
     For i = 1 To Len(s)
```

```
        b = Asc(Mid(s, i, 1))
        v = v + CLng(b) * mult
        If i < 4 Then mult = mult * 256
    Next i

    ConvertToLong = v
End Function
```

You can test this program by starting Netscape, minimizing the window, and running activate.exe. The browser window should then be restored and its window id will appear in the program's text box.

Moving and Sizing a Browser Window

Let's modify our activate program (see the chap04\activat2 project) to control the position and size of the browser window. We will add some controls to the form defined previously to allow specification of the position and size of the browser window in pixel units. We will also add another button to apply the position and size changes.

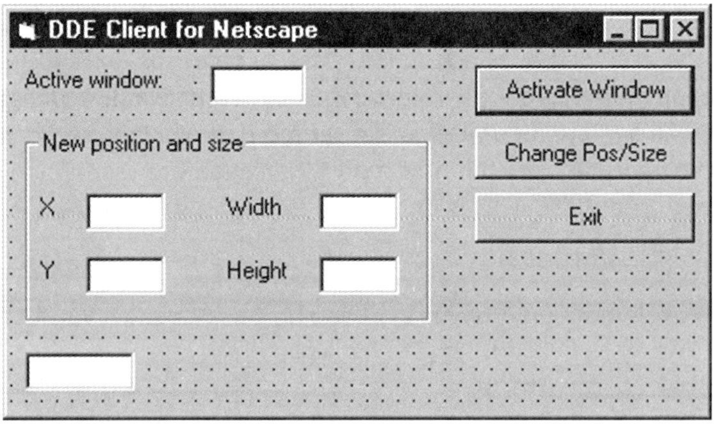

Figure 4.2.

Here is the source code for the new button, which uses the *WWW_WindowChange* topic with Netscape acting as a server:

```
Private Sub pbChange_Click()
    Dim args As String

    ' set up the argument string to pass—first get
    ' the window id
    If txtWindowID.Text = "" Then
        args = "0xFFFFFFFF"
    Else
        args = Trim(txtWindowID.Text)
    End If

    ' add flag to indicate position and size will
    ' change
    args = args & ",1"

    ' add the four arguments (X, Y, Width, and
    '                         Height)
    args = args & "," & Trim(newX.Text)
    args = args & "," & Trim(newY.Text)
    args = args & "," & Trim(newWidth.Text)
    args = args & "," & Trim(newHeight.Text)

    ' set up DDE call
    txtDDE.Text = ""
    txtDDE.LinkTopic = "NETSCAPE|WWW_WindowChange"
    txtDDE.LinkItem  = args
    txtDDE.LinkMode  = vbLinkManual
    txtDDE.LinkPoke
    txtDDE.LinkMode  = vbLinkNone
End Sub
```

This topic has two required and four optional arguments. The first required argument is the window id, which can be obtained from the *txtWindowID* control after pressing the "Activate Window" button. Alternatively, we just use 0xFFFFFFFF to indicate that the last active window should be used. The second argument is a flag that can take the following values:

Flag value	Meaning
0x0001	Change the window size and position
0x0002	Maximize the window
0x0004	Normalize the window
0x0008	Minimize the window
0x0010	Close the window

We add the other arguments to the *args* string after trimming any leading or trailing spaces. *LinkItem* is then set to the argument string and a *LinkPoke* is used to initiate the DDE topic. We do not expect anything back from Netscape in this case, and typical DDE transactions send data from the server to the destination. In this case, our destination application is providing data to Netscape, so a *LinkPoke* transaction type rather than a *LinkRequest* is used.

Querying Netscape Windows

There are some DDE topics that can provide useful information about the browser, such as the URL currently loaded in a browser window. The text of the browser's title bar can also be obtained—this text contains the document title specified in the <title></title> HTML tags of the current document.

In chap04\activat3, we will continue modifying the Visual Basic project in the last section. This time we will add another button, "Query URL." The *WWW_GetWindowInfo* topic is used to return both the currently loaded URL and the browser window title. We do not need any additional controls on the form, as the information will be displayed in a message box for the user. Here is the code for the button:

```
Private Sub pbQueryURL_Click()
    Dim args As String, retstr As String
```

```
    Dim url As String, title As String
    Dim pos As Integer, i As Integer

    ' get the window id
    If txtWindowID.Text = "" Then
        args = "0xFFFFFFFF"
    Else
        args = Trim(txtWindowID.Text)
    End If

    ' set up DDE call
    On Error Resume Next
    txtDDE.Text = ""
    txtDDE.LinkTopic = "NETSCAPE|WWW_GetWindowInfo"
    txtDDE.LinkItem = args
    txtDDE.LinkMode = vbLinkManual
    txtDDE.LinkRequest
    txtDDE.LinkMode = vbLinkNone

    ' get the return string and split it into the
    ' current URL and the browser window title
    retstr = txtDDE.Text
    If Len(retstr) = 0 Then Exit Sub

    ' find the comma
    pos = InStr(1, retstr, ",", 1)

    ' break string into two components—the first
    ' one is the current URL, and the second is
    ' the document title
    url = Mid(retstr, 1, pos—1)
    title = Right(retstr, Len(retstr)—pos)
    MsgBox url, vbOKOnly, title
End Sub
```

Once again, we start by specifying the window id in *LinkItem*. After the *WWW_GetWindowInfo* request is complete, the return string contains the URL and window title as comma-separated strings. A call to *InStr* finds the position of the separator character, and the *Mid* function extracts the two strings, which are then displayed in a message box.

Resolving URLs

Another useful function resolves a relative URL to an absolute URL. The *WWW_ParseAnchor* topic accepts an absolute (or fully qualified) URL, and a second URL that is relative to the first one. It returns a new fully qualified URL for the relative link. The project in chap04\anchor defines a form which has three text box controls: *txtAbsolute*, *txtRelative*, and *txtResult*. A pushbutton named *pbParse* is also defined, and the code that executes on the button click follows:

```
Private Sub pbParse_Click()
    Dim args As String

    ' clear the last result
    txtResult.Text = ""

    ' get absolute and relative URL arguments
    If (Len(txtAbsolute.Text) = 0) Or _
       (Len(txtRelative.Text) = 0) Then _
        MsgBox "Specify both an absolute and" & _
        "relative URL", vbOKOnly
        Exit Sub
    End If
    args = Trim(txtAbsolute.Text) & "," & _
           Trim(txtRelative.Text)

    ' set up DDE call
    txtResult.LinkTopic = "NETSCAPE|WWW_ParseAnchor"
    txtResult.LinkItem = args
    txtResult.LinkMode = vbLinkManual
    txtResult.LinkRequest
    txtResult.LinkMode = vbLinkNone
End Sub
```

Rather than defining a hidden text box for passing information back and forth to Netscape, we use the *txtResult* text box directly. The absolute and relative URLs are trimmed and concatenated together as arguments for the *LinkItem* property. Then the DDE request returns the combined URL back to the result text box.

Figure 4.3 shows an example run of the program, with the user providing a hypothetical fully qualified URL (http://www. example.com/home.html) in the *txtAbsolute* text box. The relative link is given in *txtRelative*, and the result of the DDE topic is returned automatically in the result text box.

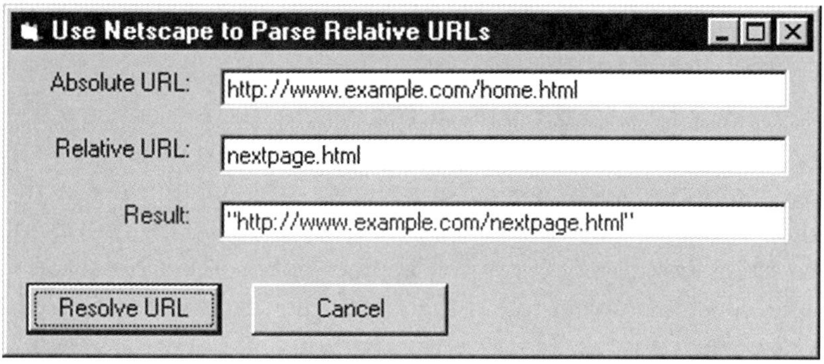

Figure 4.3.

Loading Documents

The *WWW_OpenURL* topic is probably the most useful one, allowing us to direct Netscape to load a particular URL from another program. We will incorporate this function into an OLE server to be built later in this chapter. For now, we will examine a simple program that exercises this function.

We start by defining the following form:

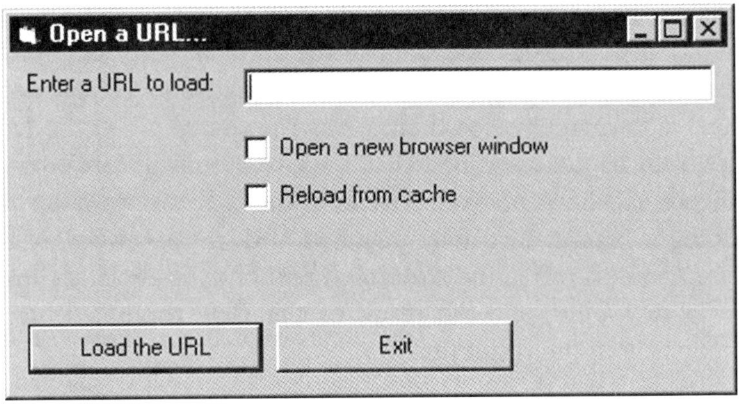

Figure 4.4.

There is a text box named *txtURL* where the user enters a specific URL, which the Netscape browser will be directed to load. The check box *chkNewWindow* specifies whether the last active window or a new window will be used to hold the new document. The check box *chkUseCache* can be checked to direct Netscape to reload a cached object rather than fetch the document from a network or file.

As in earlier projects, there is an invisible text box control named *txtDDE* that handles the DDE conversation. The pushbutton *pbLoadURL_Click* event sets up the DDE topic that tells Netscape to load the URL. There are seven arguments we need to specify in *LinkItem* in order to load a document. Only three of these are required. These are the URL to load, the id of the browser window to use, and a flag that denotes whether or not to use the document cache.

Here is the first part of the button click event where the argument string for *WWW_OpenURL* is defined:

```
Private Sub pbLoadURL_Click()
    Dim args As String, retstr As String
    Dim wid As Long
```

```
' get the URL to load
args = Trim(txtURL.Text)
If Len(args) = 0 Then Exit Sub

' see if user wants to open a new window or
' use the last active one
If chkNewWindow.Value = vbUnchecked Then
     args = args & ",,0xFFFFFFFF"     ' use last
                                      ' active
                                      ' one
Else
     args = args & ",,0"             ' open new
                                     ' window
End If

' see if document should be reloaded from the
' cache or the network
If chkUseCache.Value = vbUnchecked Then
     args = args & ",1,,,"            ' reload
                                      ' from
                                      ' network
Else
     args = args & ",0,,,"            ' use the
                                      ' cached
                                      ' version
End If
```

The first argument is the URL, trimmed to remove any leading or trailing spaces as usual. The next argument is optional—it provides a filename that Netscape can use for saving the URL data rather than displaying it. If you provide this filename and the topic succeeds, you are responsible for deleting the file.

The third argument is the window id to use for loading the document. If our user interface form's checkbox for opening a new window is not checked, a value of 0xFFFFFFFF is used. This directs Netscape to use the last active window. If the checkbox is checked, a value of zero tells Netscape to create a new instance of a browser window for holding the new URL.

The fourth argument is a flag which is set to zero if the cached version of the document should be used. If the flag is set to one, the document will be reloaded from the original source (the network or a file).

The last three arguments (which are not specified above) include:

- Form data that will be posted to the URL (using method="post")
- The MIME type the data will be posted with (defaults to application/x-www-form-urlencoded)
- Name of a DDE server that Netscape will use as a target for progress topics (if you want your application to receive *WWW_BeginProgress*, *WWW_SetProgressRange*, *WWW_MakingProgress*, and *WWW_EndProgress* topics)

After an error trap is set, the DDE request is made using the following code:

```
' set up the DDE call
On Error GoTo DDE_Error
txtDDE.Text = ""
txtDDE.LinkTopic = "NETSCAPE|WWW_OpenURL"
txtDDE.LinkItem = args
txtDDE.LinkMode = vbLinkManual
txtDDE.LinkTimeout = 300    ' set time-out to 30
                            ' seconds
txtDDE.LinkRequest
txtDDE.LinkMode = vbLinkNone
```

We set the DDE time-out to thirty seconds in case Netscape is busy. If an error does occur, the code after the *DDE_Error* label (see below) will be executed.

The return value should be the window id for the browser window that loaded the URL. A value of zero or 0xFFFFFFFF means the request failed.

```
    ' get return value and check it
    retstr = txtDDE.Text
    wid = ConvertToLong(retstr)

    Select Case wid
        Case 0
            MsgBox "Open URL request has failed", _
            vbOKOnly

        Case &HFFFFFFFF
            MsgBox "The Document MIME type is not
                    " & _ "recognized", vbOKOnly
    End Select
    Exit Sub

DDE_Error:
    MsgBox "A DDE Error occurred", vbOKOnly

End Sub
```

Using Netscape as a DDE Client

Visual Basic does not provide sufficient functionality to act as a DDE server for Netscape. The items sent by Netscape when it is acting as a DDE client contain variables such as browser window identifiers, filenames, URLs, etc. As Visual Basic handles items that have only specific names, we need to provide external DDE server support to Visual Basic. Hmmm, I think it's time for another OLE server.

We will write a general OLE object in C++ that intercepts DDE messages from Netscape. We can then create this OLE object from a Visual Basic program that is acting as a Netscape controller. The VB application will inform the DDE server of the messages from Netscape that it should intercept. Finally, the intercepted messages can be passed to yet another OLE object (this time written in Visual Basic) for final handling. Pictorially, the messages are passed among objects as in Figure 4.5:

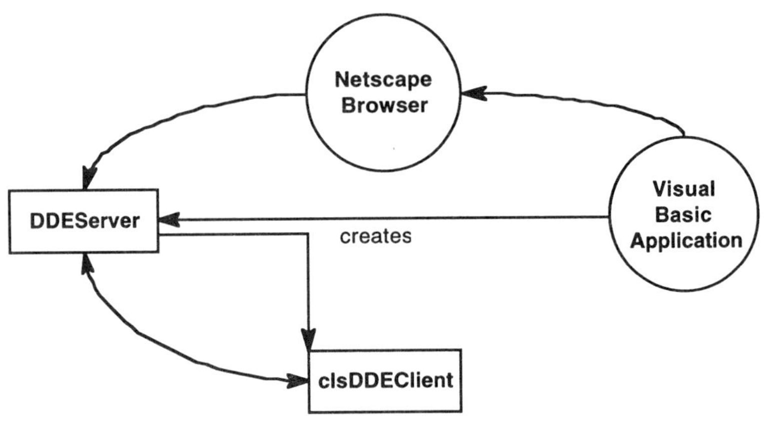

Figure 4.5 DDE message passing among Netscape, Visual Basic, and OLE objects.

When a controlling application creates an instance of *DDEServer*, it provides the name of an OLE object that will handle the DDE messages for the server. The application also calls functions in the server to set the service name and the topics that will be trapped. The server in turn creates an instance of the OLE object (e.g., *clsDDEClient*) and prepares to intercept messages from Netscape. Each intercepted message is handed off to an instance of the *clsDDEClient* for processing.

Writing a General Purpose DDE Server

Use the mkoleobj tool to set up the source code for a new C++ OLE server, and name it NPG.DDEServer. In the iobject.h file, set up the following interface methods:

```
// IDDEServer methods
virtual void STDMETHODCALLTYPE setNotifyObject
(LPCTSTR objectName) = 0;
virtual void STDMETHODCALLTYPE registerService
(LPCTSTR service) = 0;
```

```
virtual void STDMETHODCALLTYPE addTopic(LPCTSTR
topic) = 0;
```

We also include declarations for these methods in the object description file's interface section:

```
interface IDDEServer : IUnknown
{
    // methods
    [
    helpstring("Sets object to notify of DDE events"),
    id(1)
    ]
    void setNotifyObject([in] BSTR objectName);

    [
    helpstring("Registers a DDE service name"),
    id(2)
    ]
    void registerService([in] BSTR service);

    [
    helpstring("Adds a topic to this DDE service"),
    id(3)
    ]
    void addTopic([in]BSTR topic);
};
```

These declarations are also repeated in the objimpl.h file, along with some additional typedefs, methods, and properties. Here are the additional declarations for the implementation header file (omitting the standard declarations, which you can view in the chap04\ddeserv project files).

```
// objimpl.h
#include <stl.h>
#include "iobject.h"
```

```
// typedef for vector of topics to support
typedef vector<HSZ> topicarray_t;

// forward declaration
class clsDDEClient;

// class declaration
class myImplOfDDEServer : public IDDEServer {
public:
    // IDDEServer methods
    virtual void STDMETHODCALLTYPE setNotifyObject
    (LPCTSTR objectName);
    virtual void STDMETHODCALLTYPE registerService
    (LPCTSTR service);
    virtual void STDMETHODCALLTYPE addTopic(LPCTSTR
    topic);

    // helper methods
    HSZ getService() const { return service; }
    HCONV getConversation() const { return hconv; }
    void connect(HCONV h) { hconv = h; }
    void disconnect() { hconv = 0; }

    bool poke(HSZ topic, HSZ item, HDDEDATA data);
    HDDEDATA request(HSZ topic, HSZ item, WORD
                     wFmt);

protected:
    DWORD ddeInstance;              // DDE instance
                                    // handle
    HCONV hconv;                    // handle for
                                    // conversation
    HSZ service;                    // DDE service and
                                    // topic names
    topicarray_t topics;
    clsDDEClient *notifyObject;     // object to notify
                                    // of DDE events
};
```

Each instance of our general DDE server object will handle an unknown number of topics, so we define a new datatype, *topicarray_t*, as a vector of DDE topics (HSZ string handles) at the top of the module. We also forward declare a class named *clsDDEClient* that we will define shortly.

Our DDE server objects need to maintain a DDE instance handle and the current DDE conversation handle, so these are declared as members in the *protected* section. We also declare a string handle for the DDE service name, which will be set by a call to the *registerService* method. The *topics* vector is filled by successive calls to the *addTopic* method. Finally, the *notifyObject* pointer is initialized by creating an instance of *clsDDEClient* in response to a *setNotifyObject* call.

Some public helper methods are needed to return the current service and conversation handles, and to connect and disconnect from the current conversation. To handle XTYP_POKE and XTYP_REQUEST topics from a DDE client, *poke* and *request* methods are also declared.

In the objimpl.C module, the DDEML (Dynamic Data Exchange Management Library) is used for handling the DDE communications. This library uses the ddeml.h include file, and allows registration of a DDE callback method to handle DDE messages. Our callback method cannot be a C++ class member function, so we provide a way to map from the callback's messages to the corresponding OLE server class instance. At the top of the module, the following associative array, *ddemap*, is declared:

```
#include <ddeml.h>
#include "ddeclnt.h"

// ***********************************************

// the following map associates a DDE service with
// an instance of a myImplOfDDEServer object
```

```
typedef map< HSZ, myImplOfDDEServer *, less<HSZ> >
ddemap_t;
typedef pair<HSZ, myImplOfDDEServer *> ddepair_t;
ddemap_t ddemap;
```

Here is the DDE callback method included in objimpl.C:

```
HDDEDATA CALLBACK myDDEProc(WORD wType, WORD wFmt,
                            HCONV hConv, HSZ hsz1,
                            HSZ hsz2, HDDEDATA
                            hData, DWORD dwData1,
                            DWORD dwData2)
{
    switch (wType) {
        case XTYP_CONNECT:
            if ( getObject(hsz2) )
                return (HDDEDATA)TRUE;
            else
                return (HDDEDATA)FALSE;

        case XTYP_REQUEST:
            return request(hConv, hsz1, hsz2, wFmt);

        case XTYP_POKE:
            if ( poke(hConv, hsz1, hsz2, hData) )
                return (HDDEDATA)DDE_FACK;
            else
                return (HDDEDATA)0;

        case XTYP_CONNECT_CONFIRM:
            connect(hsz2, hConv);
            break;

        case XTYP_DISCONNECT:
            disconnect(hConv);
            break;
    }

    return (HDDEDATA)0;
}
```

In response to an XTYP_CONNECT, the function *getObject* is called. It returns 0 if the service is not recognized. Otherwise, it returns a pointer to the *DDEServer* instance obtained from the *ddemap*.

```
// getObject - returns pointer to object instance if
// the service is recognized
myImplOfDDEServer *getObject(HSZ service)
{
    // see if service is in the map
    if ( ddemap.find(service) == ddemap.end() )
        return 0;

    return ddemap[service];
}
```

If XTYP_CONNECT returns TRUE, an XTYP_CONNECT_CONFIRM message is sent, which establishes the conversation handle between the DDE client and server. An XTYP_DISCONNECT message terminates the conversation. These two messages are handled by the non-member *connect* and *disconnect* methods:

```
// connect - confirms the connection
void connect(HSZ service, HCONV hconv)
{
    // get the object
    myImplOfDDEServer *impl = getObject(service);
    if (!impl)
        return;

    impl->connect(hconv);     // connect
}

// -----------------------------------------------
```

```
// disconnect - terminates the conversation
void disconnect(HCONV hconv)
{
    // get the object based on the conversation
    // handle
    for (ddemap_t::iterator i = ddemap.begin(); i !=
          ddemap.end(); i++) {
        ddepair_t& entry = *i;
        myImplOfDDEServer *impl = entry.second;

        // see if conversation handle matches
        if (impl->getConversation() == hconv) {
            impl->disconnect();
            return;
        }
    }
}
```

The *connect* function simply calls *getObject* to retrieve the instance of the OLE object because it has the service handle to use to look up the instance in the *ddemap*. The *disconnect* function does not have access to the service handle, so an iterator is used to traverse the map to search for an object with a matching conversation handle. This is why we defined the inline method *getConversation* in the header file. Once the correct OLE object instance pointer is found, the corresponding member function is called to connect or disconnect the conversation.

XTYP_POKE messages are handled by passing them to the non-member *poke* function. This function again uses an iterator to search the map for the object with a matching conversation handle. The object's *poke* member function is then called to handle the message.

```
// poke - returns true if poke succeeds, false
//        otherwise
bool poke(HCONV hconv, HSZ topic, HSZ item, HDDEDATA
          data)
```

```
{
    // get the object based on the conversation
    // handle
    for (ddemap_t::iterator i = ddemap.begin();
         i != ddemap.end(); i++) {
        ddepair_t& entry = *i;
        myImplOfDDEServer *impl = entry.second;

        // see if conversation handle matches
        if (impl->getConversation() == hconv) {
            // a match!
            impl->poke(topic, item, data);
            return true;
        }
    }

    return false;
}
```

Finally, XTYP_REQUEST messages are handled similarly by the non-member *request* function:

```
// request - returns data associated with an
//             XTYP_REQUEST
HDDEDATA request(HCONV hconv, HSZ topic, HSZ item,
                 WORD wFmt)
{
    // get the object based on the conversation
    // handle
    for (ddemap_t::iterator i = ddemap.begin(); i !=
         ddemap.end(); i++) {
        ddepair_t& entry = *i;
        myImplOfDDEServer *impl = entry.second;

        // see if conversation handle matches
        if (impl->getConversation() == hconv) {
            // a match!
            return impl->request(topic, item, wFmt);
        }
```

```
    }
    return (HDDEDATA)0;
}
```

We now need to modify the constructor and destructor of the OLE object class to initialize and uninitialize the DDE library. In the constructor, we simply add initializations for the new member variables and call the following function:

```
ddeInstance = 0;
hconv = 0;
notifyObject = 0;
DdeInitialize(&ddeInstance, (PFNCALLBACK)myDDEProc,
                APPCLASS_STANDARD, 0L );
```

In the destructor, we need to disconnect from any ongoing conversation, delete the *notifyObject*, and clean up the string handles allocated in the vector of topics. We also need to remove this object from the *ddemap* and uninitialize DDEML.

```
// disconnect from any conversation
if (hconv) {
    DdeDisconnect(hconv);
    hconv = 0;
}
delete notifyObject;        // clean up notification
                            // object, if any

// free the string handles in the topic array
for (topicarray_t::iterator i = topics.begin();
      i != topics.end(); i++) {
    HSZ topic = *i;
    DdeFreeStringHandle(ddeInstance, topic);
}

// remove entry from the map and uninitialize DDE
ddemap.erase(service);
DdeUninitialize(ddeInstance);
```

The next step in finishing the definition of our general DDE server is to implement the three interface methods and the two helper methods, *poke* and *request*. The *setNotifyObject* method is called by the creator of the OLE server object to set the name of the OLE object that the server creates to notify it about DDE messages from Netscape.

```
// setNotifyObject - sets object to notify in poke
//                   and request events
void STDMETHODCALLTYPE myImplOfDDEServer::
setNotifyObject(LPCTSTR objectName)
{
    // get object name
    char s[256];
    if ( !wstrcpy(s, objectName) )
        return;

    // delete any previous object and create a new
    // notification object
    delete notifyObject;
    notifyObject = new clsDDEClient(s);
    if (notifyObject) {
        // check state of object
        if (notifyObject->rdstate()
        != OLEDispatchInterface::good) {
            delete notifyObject;
            notifyObject = 0;
        }
    }
}
```

This method creates a new instance of *clsDDEClient* based on the object name supplied in the calling argument.

The *registerService* method is called to create a string handle corresponding to the service name, and to register the new service with DDEML. It also adds the service handle and instance of *myImplOfDDEServer* to the *ddemap* so the lookup functions used in the callback routine will find the OLE server instance.

```
// registerService - registers a DDE service
void STDMETHODCALLTYPE myImplOfDDEServer::
registerService(LPCTSTR service)
{
    // get service name
    char s[256];
    if ( !wstrcpy(s, service) )
        return;

    // create the string handle
    HSZ hsz = DdeCreateStringHandle(ddeInstance, s,
                                    CP_WINANSI);

    // add this service name/object instance pair to
    // the ddemap and register the DDE service
    ddemap[hsz] = this;
    DdeNameService(ddeInstance, hsz, 0,
                    DNS_REGISTER);
}
```

Our VB application will call *addTopic* for each DDE topic we wish the OLE server to handle. This method creates a string handle for each new topic and puts it into the *topics* vector.

```
// addTopic - adds a topic to the list that this
//            server handles
void STDMETHODCALLTYPE
myImplOfDDEServer::addTopic(LPCTSTR topic)
{
    // get topic name
    char t[256];
    if ( !wstrcpy(t, topic) )
        return;
```

```
    // create the string handle and add it to vector
    // of topics
    HSZ hsz = DdeCreateStringHandle(ddeInstance, t,
                                    CP_WINANSI);
    topics.push_back(hsz);
}
```

Recall that XTYP_POKE messages trapped by our DDE server end up calling the *poke* member function. We could handle Netscape-specific requests here, but we want to keep this as a general purpose DDE server. So this method first checks that there is an object that can be notified about the message. The topic associated with the message is then checked against the vector of topics to see if it matches any that were registered through the *addTopic* method. When a match is found, the message data is extracted and passed to the *notifyObject* through its *DDEPoke* method.

```
// poke—handles XTYP_POKE messages
bool myImplOfDDEServer::poke(HSZ topic, HSZ item,
                             HDDEDATA data)
{
    // make sure there is an object to notify
    if (!notifyObject)
        return false;

    // look up topic in the array
    for (topicarray_t::iterator i = topics.begin();
         i != topics.end(); i++) {
        if (*i == topic) {
            // topic matches—get the string data
            char topicstring[256], itemstring[256],
            datastring[256];

            DdeQueryString(ddeInstance, topic,
                           topicstring, 256,
                           CP_WINANSI);
            DdeQueryString(ddeInstance, item,
                           itemstring, 256,
                           CP_WINANSI);
```

```
            DdeGetData(data, (LPBYTE)datastring, 256,
                       0);
            if (!datastring)
                return false;

            // notify the callback object
            notifyObject->DDEPoke(topicstring,
                                  itemstring,
                                  datastring);
            return true;
        }
    }

    return false;
}
```

The XTYP_REQUEST messages are handled in a similar manner. The differences are the calling arguments, and the need for a return argument. This is supplied by the *notifyObject*'s *DDERequest* function, which returns a string that is converted to a data handle using *DdeCreateDataHandle*.

```
// request—handles XTYP_REQUEST messages
HDDEDATA myImplOfDDEServer::request(HSZ topic,
                                    HSZ item,
                                    WORD wFmt)
{
    // make sure there is an object to notify
    if (!notifyObject)
        return (HDDEDATA)0;

    // look up topic in the array
    for (topicarray_t::iterator i = topics.begin();
         i != topics.end(); i++) {
        if (*i == topic) {
            // topic matches—get the string data
            char topicstring[256], itemstring[256];
```

```
            DdeQueryString(ddeInstance, topic,
                           topicstring, 256,
                           CP_WINANSI);
            DdeQueryString(ddeInstance, item,
                           itemstring, 256,
                           CP_WINANSI);

            // notify the callback object
            string datastring = notifyObject->
                                DDERequest
                                (topicstring,
                                itemstring);
            char *s = (char *)datastring.c_str();

            HDDEDATA hData = DdeCreateDataHandle
                             (ddeInstance, s,
                             datastring.size(),0,
                             item, wFmt, 0);
            return hData;
        }
    }

    return (HDDEDATA)0;
}
```

Defining clsDDEClient

The last thing we need to finish our general purpose DDE server object is a definition for *clsDDEClient*. Here is a general C++ header file based on the *OLEDispatchInterface* developed in Chapter 3:

```
class clsDDEClient : public OLEDispatchInterface {
public:
    // constructors and destructors
    clsDDEClient(const char *progid =
                 "NPG.clsDDEClient")
        : OLEDispatchInterface(progid) {}
    clsDDEClient(IDispatch *dispatch)
        : OLEDispatchInterface(dispatch) {}
```

```
    virtual ~clsDDEClient() {}

    // clsDDEClient interface
    void DDEPoke(const char *topic,
                 const char *item, const char *data)
    {
        method_threeargs(this, "DDEPoke", (int)0,
                         topic, item, data);
    }

    string DDERequest(const char *topic,
                      const char *item)
    {
        char *s = method_twoargs(this, "DDERequest",
                                 (char *)0,
                                 topic, item);
        string p(s);
        delete s;
        return p;
    }
};
```

You can now compile DDEServer as a local OLE server (remember to also create the type library using mktyplib), and register the server.

Note that the two methods *DDEPoke* and *DDERequest* are called internally by *DDEServer*. Therefore, any OLE object passed by name to *setNotifyObject* must implement these two methods. For example, let's set up a Visual Basic OLE object that handles the progress topics supported by Netscape.

A Netscape Progress Monitor

This project can be found in the chap04\ddeclnt directory. We first define a modMain.bas module with an empty *Sub Main* function. We then copy the progress bar dialog form, *frmMain*, from our very first Visual Basic OLE server project in Chapter 2. After changing the form title, the form looks like:

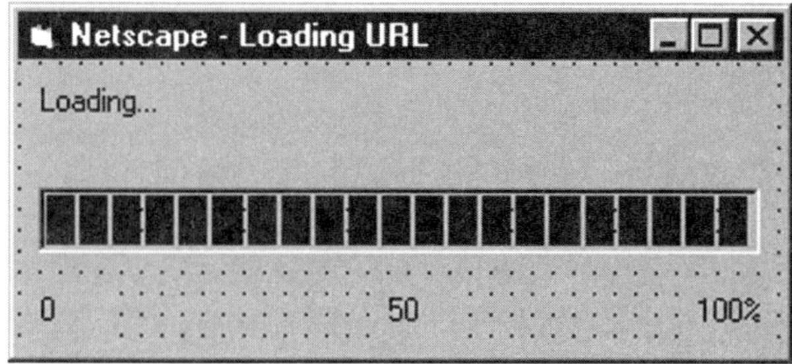

Figure 4.6.

The *clsShowProgress* class is basically the same as the code from Chapter 2. We do change the *Message* property so that only the *Caption* property is set, rather than both setting the caption and showing the form as we did previously. Separate methods are then defined for showing and hiding the form.

```
Property Let Message(msg As String)
    myform.lblMessage.Caption = msg    ' sets text
                                       ' to display
End Property

Public Sub ShowForm()
    myform.Show
End Sub

Public Sub HideForm()
    myform.Hide
End Sub
```

The old *IncrementProgress* method is replaced by a *Progress* property that lets us set the progress bar to any valid value between the allowed limits.

```
Property Let Progress(newvalue As Integer)
    ' sets a new progress value
    With myform.pbProgress
```

```
        If newvalue > .Max Then
            .Value = .Max
        ElseIf newvalue < .Min Then
            .Value = .Min
        Else
            .Value = newvalue
        End If
    End With
End Property
```

We now add one more class module, *clsDDEClient*, to this project. The module is marked Creatable SingleUse with its *Public* property set to True. The declarations section contains a private declaration for an instance of *clsShowProgress*, which is deleted in the *Class_Terminate* method:

```
Option Explicit
Private progressObject As New clsShowProgress

Private Sub Class_Terminate()
    Set progressObject = Nothing
End Sub
```

Now we define the *DDEPoke* and *DDERequest* methods. For this OLE object, we are only concerned with handling Netscape's four progress messages. These messages are:

1. *WWW_BeginProgress*
2. *WWW_SetProgressRange*
3. *WWW_MakingProgress*
4. *WWW_EndProgress*

Here is the definition for *DDEPoke*. The progress range message contains the transaction identifier followed by a comma and the maximum value to use. This value is extracted and stored in a static variable before using it to set the maximum of the form's progress bar control. The *WWW_EndProgress* topic signifies that Netscape's current load operation is complete, so we set the progress bar to its maximum value using the static *maxvalue* stored earlier. Then we hide the form.

```
Public Sub DDEPoke(topic As String, item As String,
                   data As String)
    Dim pos As Integer
    Dim msg As String
    Static maxvalue As Integer

    Select Case topic
        Case "WWW_SetProgressRange"
            ' get the maximum value for the
            ' progress range
            ' get the message to display from the
            ' item
            pos = InStr(1, item, ",", 1)
            msg = Mid$(item, pos + 1)
            maxvalue = CInt(msg)
            progressObject.BarMaximum = maxvalue

        Case "WWW_EndProgress"
            ' done displaying the form
            progressObject.Progress = maxvalue
            progressObject.HideForm
    End Select
End Sub
```

The *DDERequest* method handles the *WWW_BeginProgress* and *WWW_MakingProgress* topics. When the progress messages start, the function extracts the message to display and sets the progress form's *Message* property. The progress bar current, minimum, and maximum values are initialized, and *ShowForm* is called to display the progress dialog. The return value is a transaction id, which we will simply set to "1" for simplicity. You can use this return value to track multiple DDE transactions if desired.

One or more *WWW_MakingProgress* messages can be received during the progress conversation, and each one contains a transaction id, a message to display, and the current progress value. Both the message and the progress value are extracted and are used to set the corresponding properties for the form. The return value is set to true (1) if you want the browser to stop loading the document. Otherwise a return value of false (0) is used.

```
Public Function DDERequest(topic As String,
                           item As String) As String
    Dim pos As Integer
    Dim msg As String, tmp As String

    Select Case topic
        Case "WWW_BeginProgress"
            ' get the message to display from the
            ' item
            pos = InStr(1, item, ",", 1)
            msg = Mid$(item, pos + 1)

            ' set the progress properties
            progressObject.BarMinimum = 1
            progressObject.BarMaximum = 100
            progressObject.Progress = 1
            progressObject.Message = msg
            progressObject.ShowForm   ' show the
                                      ' form

        DDERequest = "1"

        Case "WWW_MakingProgress"
            ' get the message and value to
            ' display from the item
            pos = InStr(1, item, ",", 1)
            msg = Mid$(item, pos + 1)

            tmp = msg
            pos = InStr(1, msg, ",", 1)
```

```
            msg = Mid$(msg, 1, pos-1)
            ' extracts message
            tmp = Mid$(tmp, pos + 1)
            ' extracts value

            ' set new progress message and
            ' increment the value
            progressObject.Message = msg
            progressObject.Progress = CInt(tmp)
            DDERequest = "0"
    End Select
End Function
```

Connecting It All Together

We can now define a new project, chap04\receiver, that brings all of these pieces together. This Visual Basic application will use instances of NPG.DDEServer and NPG.clsDDEClient to track the progress of a browser window as a URL is being loaded. Start by defining a form that allows the user to type in a URL to load:

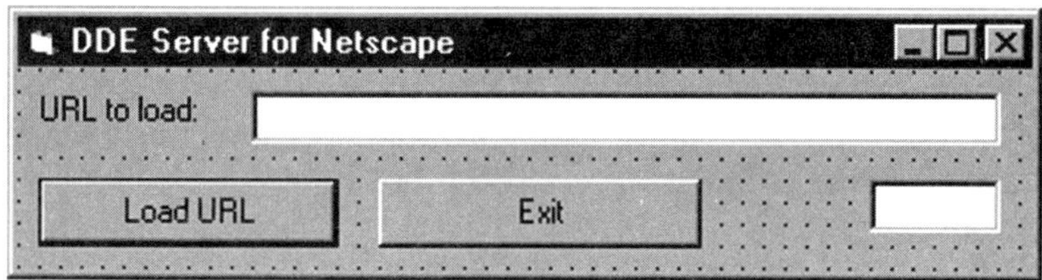

Figure 4.7.

The exit button simply ends the program. There is an invisible control, *txtDDE*, in the lower right corner of the window. This control handles the DDE messaging with Netscape acting as a server for the *WWW_OpenURL* topic. Here is the code for the *Form_Load* event, which creates an instance of our general purpose DDE server. The *Form_QueryUnload* event deletes the server object.

```
Option Explicit
Public ddeServer As Object          ' DDE server

Private Sub Form_Load()
    ' center the form
    Left = (Screen.Width-Width) / 2
    Top = (Screen.Height-Height) / 2

    ' create DDE server object
    On Error Resume Next
    Set ddeServer = CreateObject("NPG.DDEServer")
    If ddeServer Is Nothing Then
        ' error creating object
        MsgBox "Could not create DDE server"
        End
    End If

    ' set up object with service name and topics
    ' to handle
    ddeServer.setNotifyObject "NPG.clsDDEClient"
    ddeServer.addTopic "WWW_BeginProgress"
    ddeServer.addTopic "WWW_SetProgressRange"
    ddeServer.addTopic "WWW_MakingProgress"
    ddeServer.addTopic "WWW_EndProgress"
    ddeServer.registerService "DDESERV"
End Sub

Private Sub Form_QueryUnload(Cancel As Integer,
                             UnloadMode As Integer)
    Set ddeServer = Nothing
End Sub
```

The three *IDDEServer* interface methods are called to set up the object type to notify of DDE server events from Netscape (NPG.clsDDEClient), add the topics of interest to the list, and register the DDE service with a name of DDESERV.

Finally, the code for the pushbutton for loading a URL is

defined. This code is a simplified version of the same code we saw earlier in this chapter for communicating with Netscape.

```
Private Sub pbLoadURL_Click()
     Dim args As String, retstr As String
     Dim wid As Long

     ' get the URL to load
     args = Trim(txtURL.Text)
     If Len(args) = 0 Then Exit Sub

     ' use the last active window and reload from
     ' network - also specify
     ' the DDE server application that will receive
     ' progress updates
     args = args & ",,0xFFFFFFFF"
     args = args & ",1,,,DDESERV"

     ' set up the DDE call
     On Error GoTo DDE_Error
     MousePointer = 11
     txtDDE.Text = ""
     txtDDE.LinkTopic = "NETSCAPE|WWW_OpenURL"
     txtDDE.LinkItem = args
     txtDDE.LinkMode = vbLinkManual
     txtDDE.LinkTimeout = 300      ' set timeout to
                                   ' 30 seconds
     txtDDE.LinkRequest
     txtDDE.LinkMode = vbLinkNone
     MousePointer = 0

     ' get return value and check it
     retstr = txtDDE.Text
     wid = ConvertToLong(retstr)

     Select Case wid
          Case 0
               MsgBox "Open URL request has failed", _
               vbOKOnly
               LinkTopic = vbLinkNone
```

```
          Case &HFFFFFFFF
           MsgBox "The Document MIME type is not " _
                  & "recognized", vbOKOnly
           LinkMode = vbLinkNone
     End Select
     Exit Sub

DDE_Error:
     MousePointer = 0
     MsgBox "A DDE Error occurred", vbOKOnly
     LinkMode = vbLinkNone

End Sub
```

Note that we have specified DDESERV as the last argument in the string that gets put into *txtDDE.LinkItem*. Netscape will thus load the URL as before, but the progress messages during loading will be directed at our general purpose DDE server object. In turn, the DDE server directs those messages to an instance of our NPG.clsDDEClient OLE object. This object pops up our progress dialog, updates the progress bar, and deletes the dialog when Netscape is finished loading the URL. Try it!

A URL Monitor

Another topic that uses Netscape as a DDE client is *WWW_URLEcho*. This message is sent to a DDE server that registers itself to receive such topics. The purpose is to notify the server that Netscape is loading a URL. The server can do whatever it likes with the information, so we will use it to keep a history log of all URLs loaded by the browser.

We will create two VB projects for our monitor, in addition to reusing the general purpose DDE server. The first project is chap04\urlecho, which captures the *WWW_URLEcho* topics and writes the URL contained in the message to a history file. This project is a simple OLE server with a modMain.bas module containing an empty *Sub Main* function. As in the *clsDDEClient* server discussed in the last section, this server defines *DDEPoke* and *DDERequest* methods.

We name the class containing our DDE methods *clsURLMonitor,* and set the instancing property to Creatable SingleUse and *Public=True.* We do not need to process XTYP_REQUEST topics, so we simply define *DDERequest* as an empty function:

```
Public Function DDERequest(topic As String,
                                item As String) As String
     ' no request topics are handled by this object
     DDERequest = ""
End Function
```

There is only one topic that *DDEPoke* needs to process, namely *WWW_URLEcho.* Thus, the first statement in the method checks the topic string, exiting if it is not recognized.

```
Public Sub DDEPoke(topic As String, item As String,
                   data As String)
     Dim url As String
     Dim pos As Integer, filenum As Integer

     ' make sure this is a topic we are interested
     ' in
     If topic <> "WWW_URLEcho" Then Exit Sub

     ' extract the URL
     pos = InStr(1, item, ",", 1)
     url = Mid$(item, 2, pos-3)

     ' open the history list to append the current
     ' URL
     filenum = FreeFile
     Open "history.url" For Append As filenum
     Write #filenum, url
     Close #filenum
End Sub
```

If the topic is correct, the URL is extracted from the item string by looking for the first comma in the string. We then get the URL, ignoring the double quotes that enclose it. Finally, we open a history.url file and append the current URL to it. Of course, you may want to filter this list or even append the URL to a listbox or other control inside a dialog box that shows the current URL history.

Once the urlecho project has been built, we need to build the second project, chap04\regecho. This is a simple VB application that registers our URL monitor with Netscape through DDE. The form for this application is:

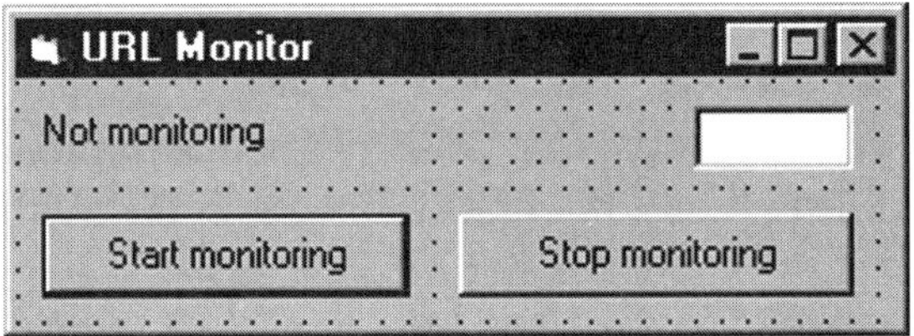

Figure 4.8.

The declarations section of this form declares an object variable to hold an instance of our *DDEServer.*

```
Option Explicit
Public ddeServer As Object          ' DDE server
```

The form's load event creates the instance of the server and calls our three methods. This time, the notification object will be an instance of the NPG.clsURLMonitor server we just created. The only topic we are interested in is *WWW_URLEcho*, and we will call the service URLMON.

```
Private Sub Form_Load()
     ' create DDE server object
     On Error Resume Next
     Set ddeServer = CreateObject("NPG.DDEServer")
     If ddeServer Is Nothing Then
```

```
        ' error creating object
        MsgBox "Could not create DDE server"
        End
    End If

    ' set up object with service name and topics
    ' to handle
    ddeServer.setNotifyObject "NPG.clsURLMonitor"
    ddeServer.addTopic "WWW_URLEcho"
    ddeServer.registerService "URLMON"
End Sub
```

When the form is unloaded, the pushbutton for stopping the URL monitoring is examined. If the button is enabled, the button's click event is called to turn off monitoring before the DDE server is destroyed.

```
Private Sub Form_QueryUnload(Cancel As Integer,
                              UnloadMode As Integer)
    If pbStopMonitor.Enabled Then Call _
    pbStopMonitor_Click
    Set ddeServer = Nothing
End Sub
```

The last two functions to write are the ones to tell Netscape to register and unregister the URL monitor. In the click event for the button that starts the monitoring operation, we set up a DDE conversation with Netscape using the *WWW_RegisterURLEcho* topic. This topic requires one argument that names the DDE service, which we set to URLMON in the load event when we called *registerService*. Note that this is an XTYP_POKE transaction, so the *LinkPoke* method is called.

```
Private Sub pbStartMonitor_Click()
    ' set up the DDE call
    On Error GoTo Register_Error
```

```
    txtDDE.Text = ""
    txtDDE.LinkTopic = "NETSCAPE|WWW_RegisterURLEcho"
    txtDDE.LinkItem = "URLMON"
    txtDDE.LinkMode = vbLinkManual
    txtDDE.LinkTimeout = 300      ' set timeout to
                                  ' 30 seconds
    txtDDE.LinkPoke
    txtDDE.LinkMode = vbLinkNone

    ' set the status message and enable buttons
    lblStatus.Caption = "Monitoring..."
    pbStartMonitor.Enabled = False
    pbStopMonitor.Enabled = True
    Exit Sub

Register_Error:
    MsgBox "A DDE Error occurred"
    LinkMode = vbLinkNone

End Sub
```

Once the monitor has been registered, we set the caption of the label above the buttons to indicate that the monitor is on. We also enable the stop button and disable the start button to prevent registering the monitor twice. Note that it is possible to register many monitors at once, all of which will be notified when Netscape loads a URL.

The code to stop monitoring uses another *LinkPoke* of the DDE server name (URLMON) with a topic of *WWW_UnRegisterURLEcho*. When the monitor is removed, the buttons are reset to their defaults and the status message is changed.

```
Private Sub pbStopMonitor_Click()
    ' set up the DDE call
    On Error GoTo Unregister_Error

    txtDDE.Text = ""
    txtDDE.LinkTopic = "NETSCAPE|WWW_UnRegisterURLEcho"
```

```
        txtDDE.LinkItem = "URLMON"
        txtDDE.LinkMode = vbLinkManual
        txtDDE.LinkTimeout = 300      ' set timeout to
                                      ' 30 seconds
        txtDDE.LinkPoke
        txtDDE.LinkMode = vbLinkNone

        ' set the status message and enable buttons
        lblStatus.Caption = "Not monitoring"
        pbStartMonitor.Enabled = True
        pbStopMonitor.Enabled = False
        Exit Sub

Unregister_Error:
        MsgBox "A DDE Error occurred"
        LinkMode = vbLinkNone
End Sub
```

Make sure the *DDEServer* and *clsURLMonitor* servers are registered before running this program. Then start Netscape and click the button to start monitoring URLs. When you have finished loading several pages in the browser, examine the history.url file to see the list of URLs that were loaded.

Summary

We have seen several example programs that demonstrate the remote programmatic control of the Netscape browser through DDE. You can now control the activation, size, and position of browser windows, tell the browser to load particular URLs, and resolve relative URLs. You can also intercept DDE messages when Netscape is acting as a DDE client using your own custom OLE object. Thus, you can monitor progress while Netscape is loading a file, or write your own history program that logs all sites visited by the browser.

In the next chapter, we look at the browser's OLE Automation interface. The OLE functionality can be used in place of or in addition to the DDE topics covered here for further control of Netscape.

References

1. Netscape Communications Corporation, http://home.netscape.com/newsref/std/ddeapi.html
2. Michiel De Bruijn, "Hook into Browsers for the Web," Visual Basic Programmer's Journal, Fawcett Technical Publications, Palo Alto, CA, February 1996, page 30.

Chapter 5

Accessing Netscape Through OLE

Netscape defines two OLE Automation objects you can use to directly access some of the browser's functionality for your own programs. The first, and the one we consider in this chapter, is the Netscape.Network OLE object. The functions available through this object allow setting and querying various properties of the browser, and allow use of Netscape's network functionality for loading URLs. Our applications then become independent of all the vagaries associated with Winsock, network protocols, SOCKS gateways, etc. We let the browser handle all of that complexity.

The second object, Netscape.Registry, allows the registration of custom OLE servers that you can write to extend Netscape's functionality. For example, you can define your own protocol (or service), analogous to http, ftp, gopher, etc. By writing an OLE server to handle the protocol, you can direct Netscape to use your server to handle requests based on your protocol. Similarly, you can write OLE servers which handle the viewing of specific MIME data types. When Netscape encounters data with that MIME type, it calls your server to handle it. We discuss the registry functions and write our own custom protocol handlers and viewers in Chapters 6, 7, and 8.

Appendix B summarizes the function calls available in Netscape.Network and Netscape.Registry. For additional information, also see the references at the end of this chapter.[1,2]

Differences Between DDE and OLE

Several differences are apparent in the Netscape DDE and OLE interfaces. The most obvious is that the browser must be running for DDE messaging to work. With OLE, Netscape does not have to be running, and yet the functionality is still available to your applications. This is advantageous when you want to do some operation in an application, such as getting a file from an FTP server. You can invoke Netscape's OLE functions to get the file and store it on disk without ever starting the browser.

Another difference is that there is not much overlap in the functionality of the two APIs. As we saw in the last chapter, DDE allows you to activate a particular browser window, control its size and position, and query information about the current document URL and title. You can also monitor the progress of a document being loaded and trap the URLs loaded by the browser to maintain a history list.

None of these functions are available through OLE.

In addition to opening a connection and reading URL data from a server, Netscape.Network functions basically provide properties you can set or query. For example, the object maintains a user name and password for accessing sites that implement access control. You can also set flags to control the display of FTP file information and newsgroups, and query the content type of a document.

Both APIs can be used to load URLs from a server, and to

resolve relative to absolute URLs. As we will see in later chapters, both APIs also allow the definition of DDE or OLE servers to handle custom protocols or act as a viewer for new MIME types. These similarities and differences allow us to write network-centric applications that effectively use both APIs.

Resolving URLs

Let's start using the OLE interface by rewriting a DDE application to use the corresponding OLE function. The chap05\anchor project uses exactly the same form as the anchor program we wrote in Chapter 4. Recall that this program used the *WWW_ParseAnchor* topic to resolve a relative to an absolute URL.

We simply need to replace the DDE calls in the *pbParse_Click* event handler with a call to the Netscape.Network.1 object's *Resolve* function. Here is the new version of this function:

```
Private Sub pbParse_Click()
    Dim ns As Object
    Dim url As String, base As String
    Dim relative As String

    ' clear the last result
    txtResult.Text = ""

    ' get absolute and relative URL arguments
    If (Len(txtAbsolute.Text) = 0) Or _
       (Len(txtRelative.Text) = 0) Then _
        MsgBox "Specify both an absolute and" & _
        "relative URL"
        Exit Sub
    End If

    ' create Netscape automation object
    Set ns = CreateObject("Netscape.Network.1")
    If ns Is Nothing Then
```

```
        MsgBox "Could not create Netscape.Network"
        Exit Sub
    End If

    ' call the Resolve method
    base = Trim(txtAbsolute.Text)
    relative = Trim(txtRelative.Text)
    url = ns.Resolve(base, relative)

    ' show the resolved URL and delete the Netscape
    ' object
    txtResult.Text = url
    Set ns = Nothing
End Sub
```

We first clear the *txtResult* control and make sure that both absolute and relative URLs have been input by the user. Then we set the *ns* object variable to a new instance of Netscape.Network.1 using *CreateObject*. If the object cannot be created, an error message will be displayed and we will exit the event handler. If the object is created with no errors, we will call the OLE *Resolve* function, which returns a string that is placed on the form's *txtResult* control. Before leaving the function, we will set *ns* to *Nothing* to delete the object.

Unlike the example in Chapter 4, you can run this application with or without starting the Netscape browser.

Setting and Querying Properties

There are three sets of properties that Netscape's OLE object maintains. We now write a Visual Basic application to get and set each of these properties. The form is shown below, and is defined in the frmMain.frm module of the chap05\props project.

Figure 5.1.

The three sets of properties relate to access control (user name and password), FTP file information (whether or not to show file size, file type, etc.), and newsgroup information (obtained through the news:// protocol). One news property controls whether all newsgroups are shown, or only those with descriptions. The second news property controls the showing of all articles, or only those articles which remain unread.

The form's declarations section contains a private declaration that will hold the Netscape.Network object:

```
Option Explicit
Private ns As Object
```

In the *Form_Load* event, the object is created—if it cannot be created, the application immediately exits.

```
Private Sub Form_Load()
    ' create the Netscape.Network object
```

```
    On Error Resume Next
    Set ns = CreateObject("Netscape.Network.1")
    If ns Is Nothing Then
        MsgBox "Could not create Netscape.Network.1"
        End
    End If
End Sub
```

When the application exits, *Form_QueryUnload* will be called. This is where the object created in *Form_Load* is deleted.

```
Private Sub Form_QueryUnload(Cancel As Integer,
                             UnloadMode As Integer)
    ' delete the object
    Set ns = Nothing
End Sub
```

Once we have the Netscape OLE object, we can access its properties. For example, the get and set buttons in the Access Control frame get and set the user name and password maintained by *ns*. Note that these are properties rather than methods, so they are not called using, for example, *GetUserName* and *SetUserName*.

```
Private Sub pbAccessGet_Click()
    ' get user name and password
    txtUsername.Text = ns.UserName
    txtPassword.Text = ns.Password
End Sub

Private Sub pbAccessSet_Click()
    ' set user name and password
    ns.UserName Trim(txtUsername.Text)
    ns.Password Trim(txtPassword.Text)
End Sub
```

For the FTP frame, the buttons use the *FlagFancyFTP* property, which returns a *Boolean* that is subsequently used to reflect the checkbox state.

```
Private Sub pbFTPGet_Click()
     Dim showInfo As Boolean

     ' get flag
     showInfo = ns.FlagFancyFTP

     ' set checkbox
     If showInfo Then chkShowInfo.Value = vbChecked: _
     Else chkShowInfo.Value = vbUnchecked
End Sub

Private Sub pbFTPSet_Click()
     ' set flag based on checkbox setting
     If chkShowInfo.Value = vbChecked Then _
     ns.FlagFancyFTP = True: _
     Else ns.FlagFancyFTP = False
End Sub
```

For the News frame, *FlagFancyNews* returns *False* if all groups will be shown. It returns *True* if only groups with descriptions are shown. *FlagShowAllNews* controls showing either all of the news articles (*True*), or only those articles that are unread (*False*).

```
Private Sub pbNewsGet_Click()
     Dim showGroups As Boolean
     Dim showArticles As Boolean

     ' get flags
     showGroups = ns.FlagFancyNews
     showArticles = ns.FlagShowAllNews

     ' set checkboxes
     If showGroups Then chkShowAllGroups.Value = _
     vbUnchecked: _
     Else chkShowAllGroups.Value = vbChecked

     If showArticles Then chkShowAllArticles.Value = _
     vbChecked: _
```

```
    Else chkShowAllArticles.Value = vbUnchecked
End Sub

Private Sub pbNewsSet_Click()
    ' set flags based on checkbox settings
    If chkShowAllGroups.Value = vbChecked _
    Then ns.FlagFancyNews = False: _
    Else ns.FlagFancyNews = True

    If chkShowAllArticles.Value = vbChecked _
    Then ns.FlagShowAllNews = True: _
    Else ns.FlagShowAllNews = False
End Sub
```

Opening URLs

The most useful of the OLE functions allows the capture of documents from the network through opening a URL. Of course, we can also do this using the DDE *WWW_OpenURL* topic. Recall that an optional argument of this topic allows saving of the data to a local file, rather than displaying it in the browser. However, Netscape must be running for this to work, and we cannot do anything to the data until the entire file is written.

With Netscape.Network's *Open*, *Read*, and *Close* functions, we can initiate the downloading of a document, write it to disk or dynamically display it in a window during the download, or stop the download before it is complete. Also note that a document downloaded through the OLE interface is not automatically displayed by a browser window—it is up to you to tell Netscape to load the document (e.g., using the DDE procedures we developed in the last chapter).

Loading a Document from VB

Let's explore the OLE functions necessary to download a document by writing a Visual Basic application. Our program will accept a URL from the user and download it through Netscape's

OLE Automation interface. The resulting document is then displayed in a message box. Here is the form, defined in the frmMain module of the chap05\vbopen project.

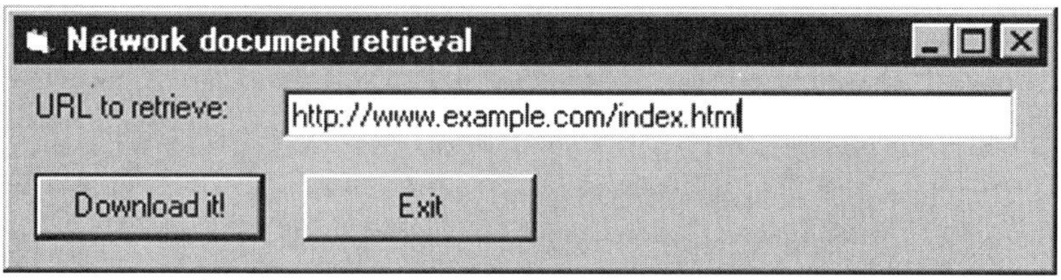

Figure 5.2.

The *pbExit* pushbutton simply terminates the application. The rest of the code is in the event handler for the *pbDownload* button. We start by declaring the variables needed, and make sure that the user has typed in a URL into the *txtURL* entryfield.

```
Private Sub pbDownload_Click()
     Dim ns As Object
     Dim url As String, data As String,
     Dim buffer As String * 8192
     Dim rc As Boolean, done As Boolean
     Dim numBytes As Integer, status As Integer

     ' make sure there is a URL specified
     url = txtURL.Text
     If Len(url) = 0 Then Exit Sub
```

Next, the Netscape OLE object is created using *CreateObject* just as we have done in the examples above. If the object cannot be created, this simple example just exits the event handler.

```
     ' create the network object
     On Error Resume Next
     Set ns = CreateObject("Netscape.Network.1")
     If ns Is Nothing Then Exit Sub
```

Now we call the OLE object's *Open* function, passing in the URL and specifying GET (0) as the retrieval method. We are not posting data to a URL, so the other arguments are ignored (see Appendix B for the definitions of the post arguments).

```
' open the URL and wait for the URL to be
' processed
rc = ns.Open(url, 0, "", 0, "")
While (Not ns.IsFinished) And _
      (Len(ns.GetContentType) = 0)
     DoEvents
Wend
```

We wait for Netscape to complete its processing of the URL by calling the *IsFinished* method, and waiting for *GetContentType* to return the MIME type of the requested URL. Once this *DoEvents loop* is done, we make sure *Open* returned *True*. If it is not *True*, a call to *GetStatus* is made to determine the cause of the problem. Then the *Close* method is called, *ns* is deleted, and the event handler is exited.

```
' check the return code
If Not rc Then
     ' get the status to find out why the Open
     ' call failed
     status = ns.GetStatus()
     MsgBox "Netscape error: status is " & _
             Str(status)

     ' clean up and end
     ns.Close
     Set ns = Nothing
     Exit Sub
End If
```

Note that you must call *Close* to reset the object state, even if *Open* failed.

The following loop reads in the data from the open connection. The *buffer* is declared as a *String*8192*, and it is passed to the OLE object's *Read* method along with its maximum length. The method returns the number of bytes actually retrieved.

The return value from *Read* is checked to see if it equals -1, which indicates that there is no more data. A value of zero indicates that there is currently no data available, but more data may be available later. Therefore, I have put in a *DoEvents* statement for this case. Any other return value represents the number of valid bytes in the *buffer*. These are extracted and appended to the *data* string that will hold the complete document.

```
' loop to read all of the data
done = False
data = ""

While Not done
     ' read data into a temporary buffer
     numBytes = ns.Read(buffer, 8192)
     Select Case numBytes
          Case -1       ' no more data to read
               done = True

          Case 0        ' no current data to read
               DoEvents

          Case Else     ' append buffer to data
               data = data & Left(buffer,
                                   numBytes)
     End Select
Wend
```

Finally, we close the connection, delete the object, and display the resulting data in a message box.

```
' clean up and end
ns.Close
Set ns = Nothing
```

```
    ' display the data
    MsgBox data
End Sub
```

Simplifying Again

Now that we see how easy it is to access the Netscape functionality from Visual Basic, we will write an in-process server to simplify the opening and reading of URL data. This will provide a higher level interface layer on the *Open* and *Read* functions so we can more easily use the Netscape interface in future VB or C++ projects. The code for this project can be found in chap05\nsoleapi.

Start by defining an empty *Sub Main* function in a module named modMain.bas. Then add a class module named *clsNetscape-OLEAPI*, and set its *Instancing* property to Creatable Multiuse and *Public=True*. Under the Visual Basic Tools, Project options, set the project name to NPG and mark the application as an OLE server.

In the declarations section of *clsNetscapeOLEAPI*, define the following private variables:

```
Option Explicit

Private ns As Object                  ' Netscape OLE
                                      ' interface
Private gotConnection As Boolean      ' True if
                                      ' OpenURL
                                      ' succeeded,
                                      ' False if not

Private currentURLData As String      ' string data
                                      ' read from a
                                      ' URL
Private currentURLSize As Long         ' length of
                                       ' data in the
                                       ' string

Private Const maxRetries = 3          ' max retries
                                      ' for opening a
                                      ' URL
```

The object variable, *ns*, will hold an instance of the Netscape interface, and the *gotConnection* flag will indicate that a connection has been opened successfully. The *currentURLData* string will hold the data read in by Netscape's *Read* method. Both the data and size (in bytes) of the string will be returned through *Property Get* functions.

```
Property Get URLData() As String
     ' return the data obtained by a call to Read
     ' URL
     URLData = currentURLData
End Property

Property Get URLSize() As Long
     ' return the size (in bytes) of the URL data
     URLSize = currentURLSize
End Property
```

In the *Class_Initialize* method for our OLE server, we first initialize all of these private variables to their default values. We then create the Netscape.Network.1 object.

```
Private Sub Class_Initialize()
     ' initialize the variables
     Set ns = Nothing
     gotConnection = False
     currentURLData = ""
     currentURLSize = 0

     ' create the Netscape interface
     On Error Resume Next
     Set ns = CreateObject("Netscape.Network.1")
End Sub
```

In the corresponding *Class_Terminate* method, we need to make sure that any open connections are closed (in case the user of our class inadvertently forgets). We check the *gotConnection* flag to see if it is necessary to call *Close*, and then we delete our private instance of *ns* created in *Class_Initialize*.

```
Private Sub Class_Terminate()
     ' make sure any open connection is closed
     If gotConnection Then ns.Close

     ' delete the Netscape interface
     Set ns = Nothing
End Sub
```

Our simplification (from the class user's point of view) of the *Open* function is implemented in our new *OpenURL* method. This method traps errors and checks the status of the connection without having to bother the user with calling *IsFinished*, *GetContentType*, etc. as we did in the last project. Our new method also checks the status and retries the connection automatically if Netscape reports that it is busy.

We start by defining *OpenURL* as a function that takes a single argument (the URL to open), and returns a *Long*. The return value is zero if the function succeeds, and is set equal to the combination of one or more flag values in case an error is found.

Next, the function exits if the Netscape interface was not created when the object was initialized, or if the URL passed in has a length of zero.

```
Public Function OpenURL(url As String) As Long
     Dim numRetries As Integer
     Dim status As Long
     Dim rc As Boolean

     ' make sure the Netscape interface is available
     On Error Resume Next
     If ns Is Nothing Then
          OpenURL = 4          ' interface not available
          Exit Function
     End If
```

```
' see if the URL is valid
If Len(url) = 0 Then
     OpenURL = 8        ' bad URL
     Exit Function
End If
```

Although we will define a *CloseURL* method shortly, there is no guarantee the user will actually call it before making another call to *OpenURL*. Therefore, we call a private method named *ResetNetscape* that closes any previously open connection on this interface object. We also initialize the number of retries to zero before entering a loop to try making the connection.

```
' reset the object and set the number of
' retries to 0
ResetNetscape
numRetries = 0

' now try opening the connection
While Not TryOpening(url)
     ' open failed—get the status
     status = ns.GetStatus()
```

The private function *TryOpening* returns *True* if the connection was opened. Otherwise, it returns *False* and Netscape's *GetStatus* function is called to find out what caused the failure.

We next check the number of times the connection has been tried. If the maximum number of retries (set by the private constant *maxRetries* defined in the declarations section) is reached, *Close* is called and the function exits.

```
     ' exit if the max number of retries has
     ' been reached
     If numRetries = maxRetries Then
          ns.Close
          OpenURL = status
          Exit Function
     End If
```

The *GetStatus* flag is set to 0x100 if Netscape was busy and could not honor the request. Thus, we check *status* and increment the retry counter. If there was another error, we again call *Close* and exit.

```
        ' if Netscape was busy, try again -
        ' otherwise exit with error
        If status And 256 Then
            numRetries = numRetries + 1
        Else
            ns.Close
            OpenURL = status
            Exit Function
        End If
    Wend
```

Finally, if the function succeeds, the boolean flag indicating a good connection is set and the function returns zero.

```
    ' the connection is open
    gotConnection = True
    OpenURL = 0
End Function
```

We finish the definition of our new method by providing the two private methods it uses. The function to close any previously open connection also re-initializes the object's private variables.

```
Private Sub ResetNetscape()
    ' re-initialize the variables
    gotConnection = False
    currentURLData = ""
    currentURLSize = 0

    ' make sure any previous open connection is
    ' closed
    ns.Close
End Sub
```

The *TryOpening* function hides the extra arguments of the *Open* function and the *DoEvents* loop that waits for the URL to be handled. As we noted above, it returns *True* if the connection was opened successfully.

```
Private Function TryOpening(url As String) As Boolean
     Dim rc As Boolean

     ' open the URL and wait for it to be processed
     On Error Resume Next
     rc = ns.Open(url, 0, "", 0, "")
     While (Not ns.IsFinished) And _
           (Len(ns.GetContentType) = 0)
          DoEvents
     Wend

     TryOpening = rc          ' True if opened ok,
                              ' False if not
End Function
```

The companion *CloseURL* function is simple by comparison. It simply checks that an interface object is available, resets the connection flag, and closes the connection. The data and size variables are not reset because the user may close the connection before accessing any data read from it.

```
Public Sub CloseURL()
     ' make sure the Netscape interface is available
     If ns Is Nothing Then Exit Sub

     ' close the connection
     gotConnection = False
     ns.Close
End Sub
```

The last high level function we need is one to read data from the connection and store it in the private string variable. The user can then access the complete data contents at once using the

Property Get function, thus avoiding the read loop that collects the data in chunks.

We basically repeat the *While . . . Wend* loop coded in the last section for calling *Read*. The differences are that the object variable and connection flag are checked first, and each data chunk we read is appended to the private data string.

```
Public Function ReadURL() As Boolean
     Dim done As Boolean
     Dim numBytes As Integer
     Dim buffer As String * 8192

     ' make sure the Netscape interface is available
     ' and the connection is open
     If (ns Is Nothing) Or (Not gotConnection) Then
          ReadURL = False
          Exit Function
     End If

     ' loop to read all of the data
     On Error Resume Next
     done = False

     While Not done
          ' read data into a temporary buffer
          numBytes = ns.Read(buffer, 8192)
          Select Case numBytes
               Case -1       ' no more data to read
                    done = True

               Case 0        ' no current data to read
                    DoEvents

               Case Else    ' append buffer to data
                  currentURLData = currentURLData & _
                  Left(buffer, numBytes)
                  currentURLSize = currentURLSize + _
                  numBytes
          End Select
     Wend
```

```
    ReadURL = True          ' success
End Function
```

You should compile this project as an OLE DLL (in-process server). You can then verify the functionality of the *clsNetscape-OLEAPI* object for yourself. In the next section, we access the functions in this DLL with a C++ program.

> **Suggested exercise 5–1** Write a Visual Basic test program that uses the nsoleapi.dll server to capture data from a web site.

Writing a WebCopy Tool in C++

In this section, we write a general purpose tool in C++ to copy a file from a network site to the local file system. The idea is to provide a network-to-local copy function similar to the DOS copy command. The difference is that the source object can be any http or ftp URL rather than a filename. Whatever file is pointed to by the URL will be copied as a new file on the local disk.

For simplicity, we will ignore relative path information, and only deal with complete pathnames. Thus, our WebCopy tool will handle copy operations such as:

```
WebCopy ftp://sample.ftp.site/pub/read.me
              c:\ftpfiles\read.me
```

but will not work on relative filenames:

```
WebCopy ftp://sample.ftp.site/pub/read.me
..\test\read.me
```

> **Suggested exercise 5–2** Modify the WebCopy tool developed in this section to work with relative pathnames.

A C++ Interface to clsNetscapeOLEAPI

Our starting point will be the OLE server we built to provide a simple interface to Netscape's OLE functions for retrieving URLs. As this project is being built in C++, we need to first define a class that accesses the public functions of *clsNetscapeOLEAPI*. As in previous chapters, we do this by deriving a new class from *OLEDispatchInterface*.

```
#include <ospace/stl.h>
#include <ospace/string.h>

#include "oledisp.h"

class NetscapeOLEAPI : public OLEDispatchInterface {
public:
    // constructors and destructors
    NetscapeOLEAPI(const char *progid =
                   "NPG.clsNetscapeOLEAPI")
        : OLEDispatchInterface(progid) {}
    NetscapeOLEAPI(IDispatch *dispatch)
        : OLEDispatchInterface(dispatch) {}

    virtual ~NetscapeOLEAPI() {}

    // NetscapeOLEAPI interface
```

The *OpenURL* function takes a URL character string argument and returns a *long*, so it can be implemented easily with the *method_onearg* template function defined in oledisp.h:

```
    long OpenURL(const char *url)
    {
        return method_onearg(this, "OpenURL",
        (long)0, url);
    }
```

ReadURL does not need any arguments, but it returns a *bool*, so it is implemented with the *method_noargs* template function.

```
    bool ReadURL() { return method_noargs
                     (this, "ReadURL", (bool)0); }
```

CloseURL is called by *void_method*:

```
    void CloseURL() { void_method(this, "CloseURL"); }
```

The last two public interface functions are the properties for accessing the URL data and its size:

```
    string URLData()
    {
        char *s = get_property(this, "URLData",
                               (char *)0);
        string p(s);
        delete s;
        return p;
    }

    long URLSize() { return get_property(this,
                     "URLSize", (long)0); }
};
```

The WebCopy Source Code

The main program for WebCopy is simple. We first check the command line arguments to make sure the first argument is a URL. We assume that if the second argument is not an ftp or http URL, it is a valid filename—you can add your own more sophisticated error checking code here. Next, OLE is initialized by calling *CoInitialize*. If there are no errors, a *process* function is called to do the network to local file copy, and *CoUninitialize* is called before the program ends.

```
int main(int argc, char *argv[])
{
    // check the arguments
    if ( (argc != 3) || badArgs(argv[1], argv[2]) ) {
```

```
        cout << "WebCopy performs a web URL-to-local
             << file copy. Specify"
             << endl
             << "a URL source document (using either
             << an http:// or"
             << endl
             << "ftp:// protocol), and a local
             << filename destination."
             << endl;
        return 1;
    }

    // init COM
    if ( FAILED( CoInitialize(0) ) ) {
        cerr << "Could not initialize COM!" << endl;
        return 2;
    }

    // process the request
    if ( !process(argv[1], argv[2]) )
        cerr << "Error copying " << argv[1]
             << " to " << argv[2] << endl;

    // uninitialize COM and return
    CoUninitialize();
    return 0;
}
```

Note that the function *badArgs* is where we check for valid command line arguments. It uses another function called *isURL* to determine if an argument is either an http or ftp URL. These two functions are defined at the top of the WebCopy.C module, along with the include files as follows:

```
// WebCopy.C
#define __MINMAX_DEFINED

#include <iostream.h>
```

```
#include <fstream.h>
#include <strstream.h>
#include <ospace/stl.h>
#include <ospace/string.h>

#include "nsoleapi.h"

// ***********************************************

// isURL - returns true if the argument is a URL,
// false otherwise

bool isURL(const char *arg)
{
   // see if the string contains "http://" or
   // "ftp://"
   string url(arg);
   if ( (url.find("ftp://") == os_npos) &&
        (url.find("http://") == os_npos) )
       return false;
   else
       return true;
}

// -----------------------------------------------

// badArgs - returns true if the arguments are bad,
//           false if ok
//           (the arguments are good if one is an
//           ftp URL and
//           the other is a regular file)

bool badArgs(const char *arg1, const char *arg2)
{
   if ( isURL(arg1) && !isURL(arg2) )
       return false;  // ok
```

```
    else
        return true;    // bad arguments
}
```

isURL does a very basic check by looking for the presence of "ftp://" or "http://" substrings in the argument. This is done using the ANSI string's *find* method. Again, you can add more complete error checking if you wish.

Of course, the *process* method is where the action takes place. It uses another function, *getURLData*, to obtain a string that holds the data obtained from the network connection. Once the data is obtained, an output file stream is opened using the name from the *arg2* command line argument. A call to the stream's *write* method copies the data to the local file. The file is automatically closed when the *ofstream* goes out of scope at the end of the function.

```
// process - handles the copy request (returns true
//           if ok, false if not)
bool process(const char *arg1, const char *arg2)
{
    // get the data from the URL
    bool success;
    string buffer = getURLData(arg1, success);
    if (!success)
        return false;

    // write the data to the output file
    ofstream fout(arg2);
    fout.write( buffer.c_str(), buffer.size() );

    return true;
}
```

The network data is retrieved using an instance of *Netscape-OLEAPI* that we defined in the last section. As you can see in the function's implementation below, we declare *ns* as an instance of the class, and then call *OpenURL*. If the return value is zero, we continue by calling the *ns.ReadURL* method. If this succeeds, the string holding the data just retrieved from the network is obtained through the *URLData* property.

```
// getURLData - retrieves data from a URL
string getURLData(const char *url, bool& success)
{
    // create an instance of the Netscape.Network.1
    // object
    success = false;
    NetscapeOLEAPI ns;
    if (!ns)
        return string("");

    // open the URL
    long status = ns.OpenURL(url);
    if (status)
        return string("");

    // read the data
    bool rc = ns.ReadURL();
    if (!rc)
        return string("");

    // get the data to return
    string data = ns.URLData();
    ns.CloseURL();

    success = true;
    return data;
}
```

Note that *CloseURL* is called before returning the string, which is good practice but not technically necessary in this case. We were careful in our class implementation above to make sure any open connections are automatically closed when the object is destroyed.

You can compile this project as a console mode application, including WebCopy.C and oledisp.C (from Chapter 3) as the source modules in the project. You will also need the appropriate STL library module.

Using WebCopy

You might use this tool rather than an FTP client to avoid logging in, changing to the appropriate directory, and doing an FTP get on a particular file. This is especially true if you know the exact file you want. For instance, say you wanted to retrieve the README.FTP file from the FTP server at software.watson.ibm.com. You could simply type the command:

```
WebCopy ftp://software.watson.ibm.com/pub/README.FTP
c:\myfiles\readme.ftp
```

Remember that upper and lower case can be important. If you are accessing an FTP server with your own account, you can use the URL format that includes your user id and password:

```
WebCopy ftp://userid:password@your.server/pub/whatev-
er.txt local.txt
```

Summary

We demonstrated the use of the Netscape.Network OLE Automation object interface functions. These functions are complementary to those provided in the DDE interface we examined in Chapter 4. We saw how a previous DDE example program could be rewritten to use an OLE function, and how to set and retrieve various properties maintained by Netscape's OLE interface. Finally, we wrote some programs to capture HTML and FTP data from Netscape using both Visual Basic and C++.

In the next chapter, we explore another aspect of Netscape OLE functions. We look at protocol handlers, and how to extend Netscape to work with your own custom protocols.

References

1. Netscape Communications Corporation, http://home.netscape.com/newsref/std/oleapi.html
2. Michiel De Bruijn, "*Hook into Browsers for the Web,*" Visual Basic Programmer's Journal, Fawcett Technical Publications, Palo Alto, CA, February 1996, page 30.

Chapter 6

Writing Protocol Handlers

So far, we have appropriated the Netscape browser's existing functionality for our own use. Both DDE and OLE interfaces allow other programs to access the networking capabilities of Netscape without even knowing anything about TCP/IP or Winsock programming.

Starting with this chapter, we start exploring how to actually enhance Netscape through our own extensions. There are several ways Netscape provides for extending the browser functionality. In the chapter on DDE, we saw an example of this where Netscape can act as a DDE client. We provided a DDE server, and the browser informed the server about some aspect of the current operation being performed.

Some DDE functions were not discussed in Chapter 4. For example, *WWW_RegisterProtocol* and *WWW_UnRegisterProtocol* are used to install and uninstall a DDE server that Netscape can pass particular URL types to for handling. That is, we can make up our own protocol, similar to http, ftp, etc. Then we write a DDE server that understands the URL based on our custom protocol and register it with Netscape. When Netscape encounters a URL with our protocol, it hands the URL off to our server for processing.

Netscape's OLE object Netscape.Registry also provides a protocol registration function. This function tells Netscape to hand off a custom protocol to an OLE server rather than a DDE server. In this chapter, we see how to use both DDE[1] and OLE[2] to write custom protocol handlers.

Specifying a Protocol Handler

We first need to specify our own protocol or service name and its intended function. The possibilities are wide open. For instance, you might define an odbc protocol that provides access to a relational database using the Open Database Connectivity API. The database name, user id, and password, along with an SQL query, could then be part of your odbc URL. Your protocol handler then becomes responsible for parsing the odbc URL and determining the database operation to carry out.

Once a particular operation is done, you may wish Netscape to display the results. Say you have extracted some data from a relational database in an odbc protocol handler and wish to display it in the browser. Your protocol handler can format the data and write it as a dynamic HTML document. The handler can then display the file by directing Netscape to load the new HTML file using the DDE functions we talked about in Chapter 4.

DDE Protocol Handlers

For now, we will start with something a little less ambitious (in the next chapter, we will define a protocol handler that accesses Lotus Notes databases). Let's begin with an example DDE protocol handler that simply executes a program on the local client machine. We will call our new protocol clientexec.

Now right away, astute readers will recognize that this opens up a serious security hole. After all, you may download HTML documents from anywhere in the world. If there is a link in any document to a clientexec protocol, Netscape will dutifully hand off the URL to your protocol handler. It in turn will execute the requested program. Clearly, you do not want to allow anyone to write a web page that may cause you to launch any program on your system whenever you happen to click on an innocent-looking link on that page.

However, our handler is just an example. Further, we will not define our URL so that it recognizes just any executable file. Rather, our clientexec protocol handler will accept specific URLs, and launch only certain (trusted) applications. This might be useful, especially in company or school intranets that maintain administrative or educational programs on a central server.

Let's set up a map between the URLs that our handler will recognize, and the applications that will be launched when one of the URLs is received. For illustrative purposes, we will use some standard Windows accessory applications. The following table lists the valid URLs our protocol will handle:

URL	Program to launch
clientexec://windows/calculator	Calculator (c:\windows\calc.exe)
clientexec://windows/editor	Notepad (c:\windows\notepad.exe)
clientexec://system/paint	Paint ("c:\Program Files\Accessories\MSPaint.exe")
clientexec://system/backup	Backup ("c:\Program Files\Accessories\backup.exe")

Registering a DDE Protocol Handler

We need a program that will register our new protocol and our DDE server for handling the protocol with Netscape. In chap06\ddeexec\ddereg, there is a standalone VB program that registers a DDE protocol handler. The form for this project is shown below:

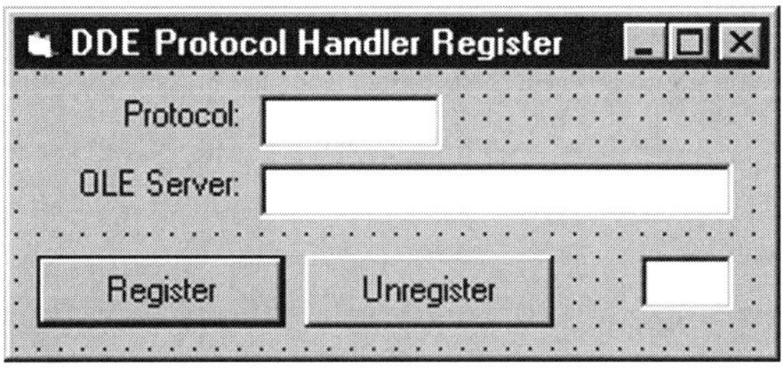

Figure 6.1.

There is an invisible text box control named *txtDDE* in the lower right corner of the window. The other two entryfields allow the user to specify the protocol name and the corresponding OLE server for the protocol. These controls are named *txtProtocol* and *txtServer*, respectively.

As we saw in a similar project in Chapter 4, the *Form_Load* event creates an instance of our C++ DDE server (NPG.DDEServer) that works with VB programs.

```
Option Explicit
Public ddeServer As Object          ' DDE server

Private Sub Form_Load()
     ' create DDE server object
     On Error Resume Next
     Set ddeServer = CreateObject("NPG.DDEServer")
     If ddeServer Is Nothing Then
          ' error creating object
          MsgBox "Could not create DDE server"
```

```
            End
        End If
End Sub
```

The two pushbuttons on the form are enabled and disabled depending on whether a protocol is registered. We can then manually register and unregister the protocol multiple times. When we exit the program however, we want to make sure the protocol handler is unregistered. Therefore, in *Form_QueryUnload*, the state of the *pbUnregister* button is checked. If the button is enabled, a protocol is currently registered. So, the click event of the button is called to unregister the handler before the program exits. We also delete the instance of NPG.DDEServer created in *Form_Load.*

```
Private Sub Form_QueryUnload(Cancel As Integer,
                             UnloadMode As Integer)
    If pbUnregister.Enabled Then _
    Call pbUnregister_Click
    Set ddeServer = Nothing
End Sub
```

The registration function is carried out in the *pbRegister* pushbutton's click event. We start by making sure the user has entered a protocol name and OLE server ProgId in the two entryfields.

```
Private Sub pbRegister_Click()
    Dim protocol As String, oleServer As String

    ' make sure there is a protocol and OLE server
    ' specified
    protocol = Trim(txtProtocol.Text)
    oleServer = Trim(txtServer.Text)
    If (Len(protocol) = 0) Or (Len(oleServer) = 0) _
    Then Exit Sub
```

Next, the ddeServer object must be initialized with the ProgId of the server that will receive DDE notification events. The only topic this DDE server needs to recognize for Netscape to use it as a protocol handler is *WWW_OpenURL*. Finally, the DDE server needs a name that Netscape can use as the service name (so the correct DDE server is called). We will use DDEClientexec as the service name for this example.

```
' set up object with service name and topics
' to handle
ddeServer.setNotifyObject oleServer
ddeServer.addTopic "WWW_OpenURL"
ddeServer.registerService "DDEClientexec"
```

The actual registration is done through a *WWW_RegisterProtocol* topic. The *LinkItem* holds the service name we just used in *registerService*, followed by the protocol name.

```
' set up the DDE call
On Error GoTo Register_Error

txtDDE.Text = ""
txtDDE.LinkTopic = "NETSCAPE|WWW_RegisterProtocol"
txtDDE.LinkItem = "DDEClientexec," & protocol
txtDDE.LinkMode = vbLinkManual
txtDDE.LinkTimeout = 300      ' set timeout to 30
                              ' seconds
txtDDE.LinkRequest
txtDDE.LinkMode = vbLinkNone
```

Once the registration is complete, we disable the *pbRegister* pushbutton and the entryfields. The *pbUnregister* button is then made active and the click event ends.

```
' enable controls
txtProtocol.Enabled = False
txtServer.Enabled = False
pbRegister.Enabled = False
pbUnregister.Enabled = True
Exit Sub
```

```
Register_Error:
     MsgBox "A DDE Error occurred"
     LinkMode = vbLinkNone
End Sub
```

The procedure for removing the protocol handler from Netscape is nearly identical. We use the *WWW_UnRegisterProtocol* topic with the same arguments used in the registration. The protocol is extracted from the *txtProtocol* entryfield (which was disabled so it could not be modified before unregistering the protocol). The controls are also reset to their default states.

```
Private Sub pbUnregister_Click()
     ' set up the DDE call
     On Error GoTo Unregister_Error

     txtDDE.Text = ""
     txtDDE.LinkTopic = _
        "NETSCAPE|WWW_UnRegisterProtocol"
     txtDDE.LinkItem = "DDEClientexec," & _
                       Trim(txtProtocol.Text)
     txtDDE.LinkMode = vbLinkManual
     txtDDE.LinkTimeout = 300       ' set timeout to
                                    ' 30 seconds
     txtDDE.LinkRequest
     txtDDE.LinkMode = vbLinkNone

     ' enable controls
     txtProtocol.Enabled = True
     txtServer.Enabled = True
     pbRegister.Enabled = True
     pbUnregister.Enabled = False
     Exit Sub

Unregister_Error:
     MsgBox "A DDE Error occurred"
     LinkMode = vbLinkNone
End Sub
```

Note that this ddereg program is general. Once you compile the project, you can use the registration application in conjunction with NPG.DDEServer and any other OLE server you define. You can thus easily install any DDE-based protocol handler for Netscape to use. If you want to define multiple protocols simultaneously, you will need to modify the code to register different service names for each *ddeServer* object.

Handling clientexec URLs

Now that we have a method for registering a new protocol with Netscape, we need to write an OLE server (in Visual Basic) that receives Netscape's *WWW_OpenURL* requests. In this case, the browser acts as a DDE client to tell protocol handlers to process the appropriate URLs.

Start by defining a new project (see the chap06\ddeexec\ddeph project) with an empty *Sub Main* procedure in a modMain.bas module. Then add a public class named *clsClientexec* as Creatable SingleUse. In the declarations section of the class, add the following constants:

```
Option Explicit

Const protocolString = "clientexec://"
Const wToken = "windows"
Const sToken = "system"
Const wPath = "c:\windows\"
Const sPath = "c:\Program Files\Accessories\"
```

This server will receive only protocol handler events (i.e., *WWW_OpenURL* topics). As there are no XTYP_POKE topics to handle, we just define an empty procedure for *DDEPoke*. This avoids any errors in case our NPG.DDEServer tried to call *DDE-Poke* on a *clsClientexec* object.

```
Public Sub DDEPoke(topic As String, item As String,
                    data As String)
```

```
    ' no poke topics for this server
End Sub
```

The only public function that will actually be invoked in processing clientexec requests is *DDERequest*. This function checks that the topic is indeed a *WWW_OpenURL* request. It then extracts the URL from the item string and hands it off to a private function, *parseURL*, for handling. If *parseURL* returns True, we set *DDERequest* to "1" to indicate success—otherwise the function returns a "0" string to NPG.DDEServer.

```
Public Function DDERequest(topic As String,
                            item As String) As String
    Dim url As String
    Dim pos As Integer
    Dim ok As Boolean

    ' make sure this is a topic we are interested
    ' in
    If topic <> "WWW_OpenURL" Then
        DDERequest = "0"      ' indicates failure
        Exit Function
    End If

    ' extract the URL
    pos = InStr(1, item, ",", 1)
    url = Mid$(item, 2, pos-3)

    ' handle the URL—return "1" if ok,
    ' "0" if failure
    ok = parseURL(url)
    If ok Then DDERequest = "1" _
    Else DDERequest = "0"
End Function
```

The handling of the clientexec URL from Netscape winds up in *parseURL*. Here, the "clientexec://" substring is removed from the URL first.

```
Private Function parseURL(url As String) As Boolean
     Dim pos As Integer
     Dim token As String, path As String,
     Dim prog As String

     ' strip off "clientexec://" string
     pos = InStr(1, url, protocolString, 1)
     If pos = 0 Then GoTo Parse_Error
     token = Mid$(url, Len(protocolString) + 1)
```

The *token* variable contains the remainder of the URL, so we look at the first part of this string (up to the first slash character). According to our table of valid URLs (see the table on page 183), this should match either the *wToken* or *sToken* constant strings we declared earlier. We therefore set the *path* variable to the corresponding path (*wPath* if the string matches *wToken*, and *sPath* if the string matches *sToken*).

```
     ' now look at the next token to see if it is
     ' "windows" or "system"
     pos = InStr(1, token, "/", 1)
     If pos = 0 Then GoTo Parse_Error
     Select Case Mid$(token, 1, pos-1)
          Case wToken
               path = wPath

          Case sToken
               path = sPath

          Case Else
               GoTo Parse_Error
     End Select
```

We now examine the last token, which will give us the program name. The *Select Case* statement maps the valid URL tokens to the appropriate program name.

```
     ' look at the last token to get the program
     ' name
```

```
    Select Case Mid$(token, pos + 1)
        Case "calculator"
            prog = "calc.exe"

        Case "editor"
            prog = "notepad.exe"

        Case "paint"
            prog = "MSPaint.exe"

        Case "backup"
            prog = "backup.exe"

        Case Else
            GoTo Parse_Error
    End Select
```

The final part of this function simply constructs the full pathname of the requested program, and uses the VB *Shell* statement to execute the program. Note that *parseURL* returns *False* if there is any error in parsing the URL.

```
    ' run the program
    Shell path & prog, vbNormalFocus
    parseURL = True
    Exit Function

Parse_Error:
    parseURL = False

End Function
```

Using the DDE Version of clientexec

Figure 6.2 shows a screen capture of the ddereg executable program, where the clientexec protocol is registered. We specify both the protocol name and the ProgId of our OLE server that actually handles the *WWW_OpenURL* messages from Netscape.

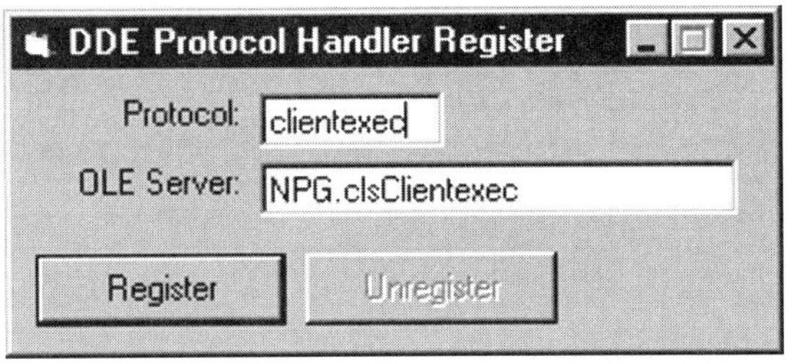

Figure 6.2. Registration of the clientexec protocol handler.

Of course, Netscape must be running before we push the Register button in this program, because the registration takes place using the *WWW_RegisterProtocol* DDE topic. Once the protocol is successfully registered, we can load HTML documents in Netscape that contain links to clientexec URLs. Here is an example HTML document that will launch any of the programs our protocol handler understands:

```
<html>
<head>
<title>DDE Protocol Handler Example</title>
</head>
<body>

<h1>Currently supported programs:</h1>

<ul>
<li><a href="clientexec://windows/calculator">
       Calculator</a>
<li><a href="clientexec://windows/editor">Editor</a>
<li><a href="clientexec://system/paint">
       Paint program</a>
<li><a href="clientexec://system/backup">
       Backup utility</a>
</ul>

</body>
</html>
```

This document is stored in the chap06\ddeexec directory as example.html. Here is a view of the document in a Netscape browser window. Clicking on any link launches the appropriate program by calling our clientexec server with the appropriate URL specified in the link's anchor.

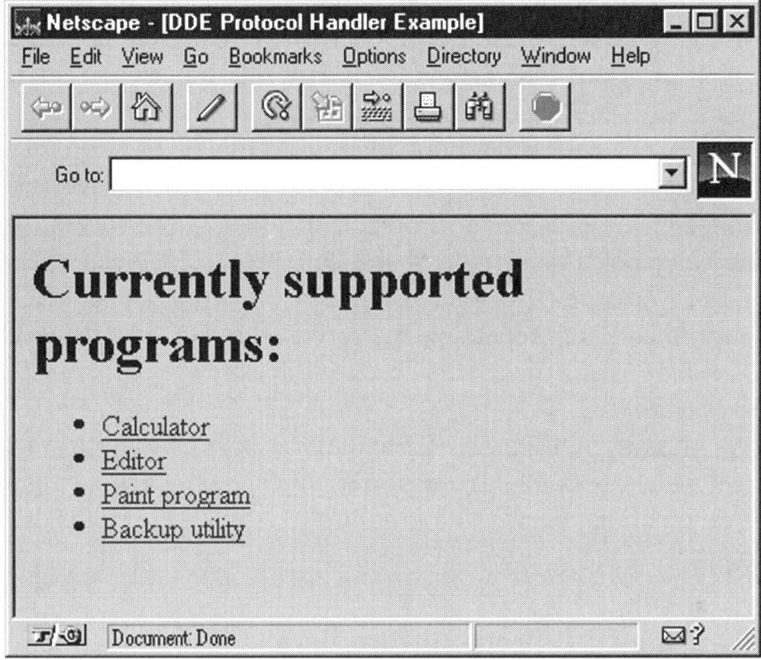

Figure 6.3.

OLE Protocol Handlers

Now that we understand protocol handling in DDE, we can note some disadvantages of the DDE interface. For one thing, there must be a DDE server running so that Netscape can communicate with it. This DDE server has to be started independently from the browser. Also, the server must register the protocols it services by registering them with Netscape. This registration must be done at runtime, so if the server is stopped and restarted, the registration must be repeated. Finally, you probably want to direct the browser to load another document when handling a custom protocol. Unfortunately, this is done through DDE, and your protocol handler is already in the middle of another DDE conversation.

The solution to all of these problems is to use the browser's Netscape.Registry interface. This interface includes a function to register an OLE server as a protocol handler. Once we have built and registered an OLE server, Netscape will launch the server automatically whenever a protocol is encountered that requires the server to handle it. Furthermore, the registration of an OLE protocol handler needs to be done only once. The system registry holds the name of the protocol or protocols handled by the server. The registry also holds the ProgId of the OLE protocol handler to create. Once Netscape creates an instance of the server and hands off the custom URL for processing, the server is free to use other OLE or DDE functions if necessary to direct the browser to carry out other operations.

We introduce OLE protocol handlers by mirroring the protocol handler we wrote in the last section using DDE. The first step is to write a program that handles registration of OLE servers with Netscape.

Registering OLE Protocol Handlers

We'll start by writing a Visual Basic program that associates a protocol name with an OLE server object as we did for DDE registration. The difference is that when we register a new protocol, it remains registered with Netscape across invocations of the browser.

Here is the form for our registration program, modified from the ddereg program defined earlier in this chapter. The project files for our olereg registration program can be found in chap06\oleexec\olereg.

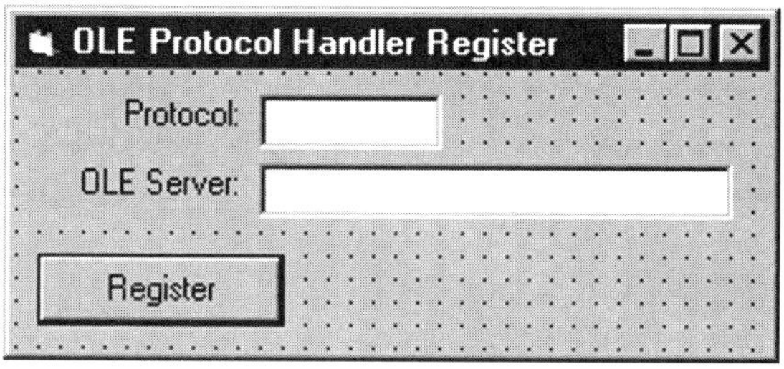

Figure 6.4.

Unlike the DDE registration program, we do not need any declarations or code for loading and unloading the form. We also do not require the *txtDDE* entryfield or the Unregister pushbutton. The only code in this project is associated with the *pbRegister* button's *Click* event:

```
Private Sub pbRegister_Click()
     Dim protocol As String, oleServer As String
     Dim ns As Object
     Dim rc As Boolean

     ' make sure there is a protocol and OLE server
     ' specified
     protocol = Trim(txtProtocol.Text)
     oleServer = Trim(txtServer.Text)
     If (Len(protocol) = 0) Or (Len(oleServer) = 0) _
     Then Exit Sub
```

Once the *protocol* and *oleServer* strings have been verified, an instance of the Netscape.Registry interface object is created.

```
     ' create the Netscape.Registry object
     On Error GoTo Register_Error
     Set ns = CreateObject("Netscape.Registry.1")
     If ns Is Nothing Then GoTo Register_Error
```

If the object was created, the *RegisterProtocol* method is called to set up an association between the protocol name and the OLE server that handles protocols of that type. A message is then displayed indicating whether or not the protocol was registered.

```
    ' register the protocol handler
    rc = ns.RegisterProtocol(protocol, oleServer)
    If Not rc Then GoTo Register_Error

    ' display message to user and end program
    MsgBox "The protocol was registered"
    Set ns = Nothing
    End

Register_Error:
    MsgBox "The protocol was not registered", _
    vbOKOnly + vbExclamation
    Set ns = Nothing

End Sub
```

Note that there is no *pbUnregister* pushbutton in olereg, because there is no Netscape.Registry OLE Automation function for unregistering an OLE protocol handler. However, you can remove a protocol handler by directly editing the system registry to remove the entry. The relevant registry entry can be found (using regedit.exe) in:

```
HKEY_CURRENT_USER/Software/Netscape/Netscape
Navigator/Automation Protocols
```

> **Suggested exercise 6–1** Write a program to unregister OLE protocol handlers by removing the key from the system registry (hint: use the *RegDeleteKey* function).

Writing an OLE Protocol Handler

When an OLE server is registered with Netscape as a custom protocol handler, it needs to expose methods that Netscape can call to communicate with the handler. There are only two methods an OLE protocol handler needs to implement. These methods are *Initialize* and *Open*. Their prototypes and functions are

- **short Initialize(LPCTSTR protocol, LPCTSTR url)**, called by Netscape to initialize an external protocol handler. The *protocol* argument contains the service name, and *url* contains the complete URL to handle. The function should return a "1" if the protocol will be handled, and "0" if it does not want to handle it,
- **void Open(LPCTSTR url)**, called by Netscape to initiate the handling of the URL by the external protocol handler.

Netscape's choice of the method name *Open* for one of the OLE object's interface functions was unfortunate. *Open* is a Visual Basic keyword, and therefore cannot be used as a method name in a VB class. This effectively precludes writing an OLE protocol handler for Netscape using only Visual Basic. But, we can easily write OLE servers in C++ using our mkoleobj tool. Thus, our OLE protocol handlers will be implemented in C++.

Start by running the mkoleobj tool, specifying the name of the OLE server as *Clientexec* (to distinguish it from the VB *clsClientexec* server defined earlier):

```
mkoleobj Clientexec
```

This creates the source code modules for NPG.Clientexec (see the chap06\oleexec\oleph project files). We then define the two OLE Automation methods in the ODL file, which we rename to oleph.odl. The interface section of the object description is changed to:

```
interface IClientexec : IUnknown
    {
        // methods
        [
         helpstring("Returns 1 if protocol is handled"),
         id(1)
        ]
        short Initialize([in] BSTR protocol, [in]
                            BSTR url);

        [
         helpstring("Handles the URL"),
         id(2)
        ]
        void Open([in] BSTR url);
    };
```

Note that *Initialize* is given a dispatch id of 1 and *Open* is given a dispatch id of 2. See the protocol.odl file shown in Reference 2 for another example.

Once the ODL file is completed, we can make the type library using the following command:

```
mktyplib oleph.odl /nocpp
```

We now replace the dummy method declaration in iobject.h with the following two pure virtual functions:

```
// IClientexec methods
virtual short STDMETHODCALLTYPE Initialize
(LPCTSTR protocol, LPCTSTR url) = 0;
virtual void STDMETHODCALLTYPE Open(LPCTSTR url) =
0;
```

We also do the same substitution in objimpl.h, except that the functions are no longer pure virtual:

```
// IClientexec methods
virtual short STDMETHODCALLTYPE Initialize
(LPCTSTR protocol, LPCTSTR url);
virtual void STDMETHODCALLTYPE Open(LPCTSTR url);
```

Finally, the implementations of our two OLE server methods are defined in objimpl.C (be sure to delete the implementation of the dummy function). We use the *wstrcpy* routine in tolefact.h we defined in Chapter three to convert the input strings from their *wchar_t* input types.

```
// Initialize - decides on whether to handle a
//              protocol and associated URL
short STDMETHODCALLTYPE myImplOfClientexec::
Initialize(LPCTSTR protocol, LPCTSTR url)
{
   // get protocol and URL from wide char inputs
   char myProtocol[256];
   char myURL[256];

   wstrcpy(myProtocol, protocol);
   wstrcpy(myURL, url);

   return 1;
}

// ----------------------------------------------

// Open - opens a URL
void STDMETHODCALLTYPE myImplOfClientexec::Open
(LPCTSTR url)
{
   // get URL from wide char input
   char myURL[256];
   wstrcpy(myURL, url);
}
```

Once these two methods are defined and the project is built, we have a completed OLE protocol handler that may be registered with Netscape. Of course, this protocol handler does not do anything so far, but I have purposely shown the steps above first so you can easily create your own protocol handlers.

We continue the current example by specializing this OLE protocol handler to match the functionality of our clientexec DDE protocol handler.

The C++ Version of clientexec

Start by putting the next two statements at the top of the objimpl.h module:

```
#define __MINMAX_DEFINED
#include <ospace/string.h>
```

Next, place the following declarations in the protected section of the class declaration in objimpl.h:

```
protected:
    string myPath;                  // pathname
    string myProgram;               // program name

    // helper method
    bool parseURL(string& url);
```

We use the same name for the *parseURL* helper method as we did in the VB example. In the C++ implementation, however, we are going to parse the URL when Netscape calls the *Initialize* method. This gives us a chance to make sure the URL is valid and if not, to tell Netscape that our server is not going to handle the request. To avoid parsing the same URL when Netscape calls *Open*, we save the path and program name obtained from *parseURL* in the two object member variables.

Here is our new definition for *Initialize*, which checks that the first argument matches the protocol our server handles. It then calls *parseURL* and checks the return value—if the function succeeds, *Initialize* returns a 1, telling Netscape that the server will handle the URL.

```
// Initialize - decides on whether to handle a
//              protocol and associated URL
short STDMETHODCALLTYPE myImplOfClientexec::
Initialize(LPCTSTR protocol, LPCTSTR url)
{
    // get protocol and URL from wide char inputs
    char myProtocol[256];
    char myURL[256];

    wstrcpy(myProtocol, protocol);
    wstrcpy(myURL, url);

    // make sure the protocol is clientexec
    if ( strcmp(myProtocol, "clientexec") )
        return 0;

    // if URL cannot be parsed, return an error
    if ( !parseURL( string(myURL) ) )
        return 0;

    return 1;
}
```

Once Netscape knows the server will handle the URL, the browser calls the OLE object's *Open* method. At that point, the browser is done handling the URL—it is up to the OLE object to carry out the URL request. In this case, our OLE object concatenates the path and program name set by *parseURL*, and then uses a *WinExec* call to start the program.

```
// Open – opens a URL
void STDMETHODCALLTYPE myImplOfClientexec::Open
(LPCTSTR url)
```

```
{
    // get URL from wide char input
    char myURL[256];
    wstrcpy(myURL, url);

    // execute the program (Initialize has already
    // parsed the URL)
    string fullpath = myPath + myProgram;
    WinExec(fullpath.c_str(), SW_SHOW);
}
```

The *parseURL* function is analogous to the one we implemented in Visual Basic. We strip off the "clientexec://" protocol string, leaving the rest of the URL in *tokenlist*. We then split the remainder of the URL into two parts using the slash character as a token delimiter.

```
// parseURL - returns true if URL can be parsed,
//            false otherwise (the result of
//            parsing the clientexec URL is stored
//            in myPath and myProgram)
bool myImplOfClientexec::parseURL(string& url)
{
    // strip off the clientexec protocol
    size_t pos = url.find("://");
    if (pos == os_npos)
        return false;

    string tokenlist(url, pos + 3);

    // get the path from the first token and the
    // program name from the second token
    pos = tokenlist.find('/');
    if (pos == os_npos)
        return false;

    string pathtoken(tokenlist, 0, pos);
    string progtoken(tokenlist, pos + 1);
```

We then compare *pathtoken* to the "windows" and "system" strings to set the appropriate value for *myPath*:

```
// decide on the actual path to use
if ( pathtoken == string("windows") )
    myPath = string("c:\\windows\\");
else if ( pathtoken == string("system") )
    myPath = string("c:\\Program Files\\"
                    "Accessories\\");
else
    return false;
```

We also compare *progtoken* to the four values we originally specified in the table of allowed URLs. This sets the correct executable filename in *myProgram*. If both *pathtoken* and *progtoken* are recognized, the function succeeds by returning "true."

```
    // set the actual program name to run
    if ( progtoken == string("calculator") )
        myProgram = string("calc.exe");
    else if ( progtoken == string("editor") )
        myProgram = string("notepad.exe");
    else if ( progtoken == string("paint") )
        myProgram = string("MSPaint.exe");
    else if ( progtoken == string("backup") )
        myProgram = string("backup.exe");
    else
        return false;

    return true;    // success!
}
```

You should compile this project as either an in-process or local server (the example provided on the CD-ROM is an in-process server). Then register the OLE server using regsvr32 or /r, depending on whether you have compiled it as a DLL or EXE. When the server is registered with Windows 95, you can then register it with Netscape using the olereg program. After that, you can use the clientexec protocol in your HTML documents to run these four "trusted" applications.

Be sure to stop running the DDE version of clientexec before you register and try out this protocol handler. You should also be aware that nothing prevents you from installing protocol handlers for protocols that Netscape already handles (such as http), but the results of doing this are in your hands.

Form Data and Custom URLs

There may be times when you want to process input from users through an HTML form. For example, the browser display below shows a sample form defined in HTML.

The sample form has two drop-down listboxes that select an editor program and document type to open. Once the selections are made, pressing the "Open" button submits a URL for processing. Normally, this URL would point to a Common Gateway Interface (CGI) program that runs on a web server. However, look at the HTML source for this form:

```
<html>
<head><title>Document Editor Form</title></head>
<body>

<h1>Open a Document</h1>

Fill in the requested information and press "Open".
<hr>
<form action="localexec://editor" method="GET">
   Select your preferred editor:
   <select name="program">
   <option selected>Notepad
   <option>WordPad
   <option>MS Word
   <option>Lotus WordPro
   </select>

   <p>
   Enter a document type:
```

```
    <select name="type">
    <option selected>Letter
    <option>Report
    <option>Memo
    <option>HW/SW Request
    </select>

    <p>
    <input type="submit" name="pb" value="Open">
</form>

</body>
</html>
```

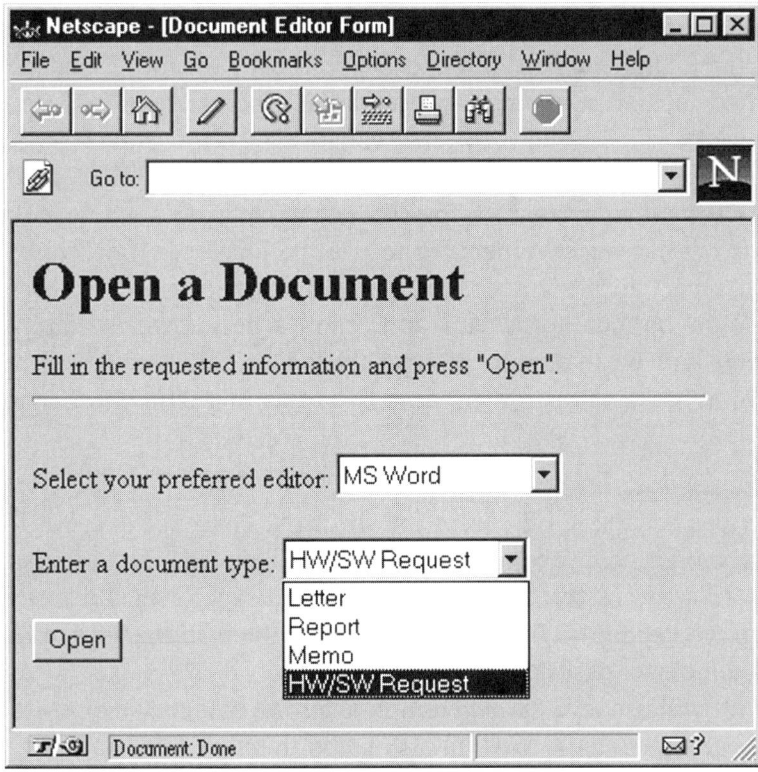

Figure 6.5.

Notice that in the <form> tag, the action is specified using a localexec URL. When the form is submitted using method="GET", the form data is collected into a set of name-value pairs. The data is then attached to the end of the URL, prepended with a question mark character. For example, if the selected editor is Notepad and the document type is Letter, the URL submitted to Netscape would be:

```
localexec://editor?program=Notepad&type=Letter&pb=
Open
```

We explore the concept of HTML forms further in Chapter 10. For now, it is sufficient to recognize that the user selections or input are encoded in a set of name-value pairs separated by the ampersand character. Also, any special characters (such as spaces or punctuation marks) in the user input are "escaped," or transformed into an alternate representation. For example, MS Word would be represented by the value MS+Word and HW/SW Request would be represented by HW%2FSW Request (note the hexadecimal equivalent for the slash character).

Now that we have decided to use the localexec protocol in a form, our OLE server needs to be modified. Specifically, it needs to parse the optional form data, and use it to decide which editor to launch and what document type the editor should open. While we're at it, we will parse the base URL data in a different manner.

Writing localexec

The files for this OLE server are in chap06\oleexec\oleph2. We start as we did above for the NPG.Clientexec server, using mkoleobj to create the source code modules for NPG.Localexec. Then we define the *Initialize* and *Open* methods in the source files and the object description file (oleph2.odl).

We will use an STL *map* template for the associative array that holds the form data. We will also parse the base URL data into a set of tokens that are stored in a queue. STL defines a container adaptor that implements the functionality of a queue, so we declare the following typedefs at the top of iobject.h:

```
#define __MINMAX_DEFINED
#include <ospace/stl.h>
#include <ospace/string.h>

// typedefs for queue and map to store URL and form
// data
typedef queue< list<string> > urlqueue_t;
typedef map< string, string, less<string> >
formdata_t;
typedef pair<string, string> namevalue_t;
```

We also define instances of the *urlqueue_t* and *formdata_t* types as protected members of our implementation class. There are also several helper methods we will need to implement.

```
protected:
    urlqueue_t myURLQueue;      // queue of URL tokens
    formdata_t myFormData;      // name-value pairs

    // helper methods
    bool parseURL(const string& url);
    void separateTokens(const string& tokens);
    void extractData(const string& formdata);
    void extractPair(const string& pairdata);
    string decode(const string& encoded);
    char unescaped(char h1, char h2);
```

The *Initialize* method is implemented exactly as before, except that it accepts localexec URLs.

```
#include <strstream.h>

// Initialize - decides whether to handle a
//              protocol and associated URL
short STDMETHODCALLTYPE myImplOfLocalexec::Initialize
(LPCTSTR protocol, LPCTSTR url)
```

```
{
    // get protocol and URL from wide char inputs
    char myProtocol[256];
    char myURL[256];

    wstrcpy(myProtocol, protocol);
    wstrcpy(myURL, url);

    // make sure the protocol is localexec
    if ( strcmp(myProtocol, "localexec") )
        return 0;

    // if URL cannot be parsed, return an error
    if ( !parseURL( string(myURL) ) )
        return 0;

    return 1;
}
```

This time, the *parseURL* function strips off the "localexec://" protocol string and then searches for a '?' that divides the remaining string into base and form data parts. Each part is then handled by separate functions.

```
// parseURL - returns true if URL can be parsed,
//            false otherwise
bool myImplOfLocalexec::parseURL(const string& url)
{
    // strip off the localexec protocol
    size_t pos = url.find("://");
    if (pos == os_npos)
        return false;

    string remainder(url, pos + 3);

    // separate the remainder of the URL into the
    // URL token list and the form data (if present)
```

```
    string tokenlist(remainder);
    string formdata("");

    pos = remainder.find('?');
    if (pos != os_npos) {
        // form data is present
        formdata = string(remainder, pos + 1);
        tokenlist.resize(pos);
    }

    // separate tokenlist into queue entries and
    // form data into map entries
    separateTokens(tokenlist);
    extractData(formdata);

    return true;
}
```

The *separateTokens* helper function gets each token from the base URL and places it into the queue using a call to the container adaptor's *push* method. Each token is found using the standard URL delimiter character ('/').

```
// separateTokens - separates tokens separated by
//                  '/' into queue entries
void myImplOfLocalexec::separateTokens(const string&
tokens)
{
    // make a local copy of the string to work on
    string path(tokens);
    size_t index;

    do {
        // find the delimiter
        index = path.find_first_of('/');
        string nexttoken(path, 0, index);

        // put token onto queue
```

```
        myURLQueue.push(nexttoken);
        path.remove(0, index + 1);
    } while ( (index != os_npos) &&
              (path.size() != 0) );
}
```

Parsing of the name-value pairs representing the form data requires a few more helper functions. We start with the function *extractData*, which divides the set of name-value pairs using the ampersand delimiter. It in turn calls the helper method *extractPair* to extract the name and value from the string.

```
// extractData - extracts name-value pair data and
//               stores in associative array
void myImplOfLocalexec::extractData
(const string& formdata)
{
    // see if there is any data
    if (formdata.size() == 0)
        return;

    // make a local copy of the string to work on
    string nvpairs(formdata);
    size_t index;

    do {
        // find the delimiter
        index = nvpairs.find_first_of('&');
        string nextpair(nvpairs, 0, index);

        // put pair into map
        extractPair(nextpair);
        nvpairs.remove(0, index + 1);
    } while ( (index != os_npos) &&
              (nvpairs.size() != 0) );
}
```

The name and value are separated by searching for the '=' sign in the string. The value that is extracted may be escaped, so it needs to be processed before storing it in *myURLData*. A call to *decode* converts any '+' signs in the string to spaces, and replaces any hex representations with their character equivalents.

```
// extractPair - extracts a name-value pair and
//               stores it
void myImplOfLocalexec::extractPair
(const string& pairdata)
{
    // see if there is any data
    if (pairdata.size() == 0)
        return;

    // make a local copy of the string to work on
    string p(pairdata);

    // find the delimiter
    size_t index = p.find_first_of('=');
    string nextname(p, 0, index);
    string nextvalue(p, index + 1);

    // put name value pair into map
    myFormData[nextname] = decode(nextvalue);
}

// ---------------------------------------------

// decode - unescapes an input string
string myImplOfLocalexec::decode(const string&
encoded)
{
    // see if there is any data
    if (encoded.size() == 0)
        return string("");
```

```
    // remove any escaped characters
    string decoded("");

    for (int i = 0; i < encoded.size(); i++) {
        if (encoded[i] == '%') {
            // convert escaped character
            decoded += unescaped(encoded[i + 1],
                                 encoded[i + 2]);
            i += 2;
        } else {
            // copy the regular character
            decoded += encoded[i];
        }
    }

    // change the '+' characters to spaces
    for (i = 0; i < decoded.size(); i++) {
        if (decoded[i] == '+')
            decoded[i] = ' ';
    }

    return decoded;
}

// ------------------------------------------------------

// unescaped - returns a character corresponding to
//             the hex value h1h2
char myImplOfLocalexec::unescaped(char h1, char h2)
{
    strstream ss;
    int i;

    ss << h1 << h2 << ends;
    ss >> hex >> i;

    return (char)i;
}
```

Once the base URL and form data are parsed and stored in the queue and map, respectively, the *Open* method can handle the URL. The following implementation looks at the first item in the queue. Note that in our form example, this will be the first token of the localexec URL. If this token matches "editor", *fullpath* is defaulted to the Notepad executable. Then the form data is checked to see if an alternate editor was chosen by looking for a "program" key. If found, the *fullpath* should be set to the correct path for executing the selected program specified by the key's corresponding value (you can fill in this code). The "type" key is also checked to see if a specific document type was requested. If so, that key's value is appended to *fullpath* as a command line argument before calling *WinExec*.

```
// Open - opens a URL
void STDMETHODCALLTYPE myImplOfLocalexec::Open
(LPCTSTR url)
{
    // get URL from wide char input
    char myURL[256];
    wstrcpy(myURL, url);

    // set the fullpath to the requested program
    // type from the base URL
    string program = myURLQueue.front();
    myURLQueue.pop();

    if ( program == string("editor") ) {
        string fullpath =
        string("c:\\windows\\notepad.exe");

        // see if there is an alternate editor and
        // document type to load
        // specified in the form data
        string progkey("program");
        string typekey("type");
```

```
        if ( myFormData.find(progkey) !=
              myFormData.end() )
            fullpath = myFormData[progkey];
        if ( myFormData.find(typekey) !=
              myFormData.end() )
            fullpath += string(" ") +
                        myFormData[typekey];

        // execute the program
        WinExec(fullpath.c_str(), SW_SHOW);
    }
}
```

Summary

In this chapter, we explored the definition and registration of custom protocols. We defined custom protocols using both the DDE and OLE functionality of Netscape, and wrote some general registration programs to communicate the protocol types and server names to Netscape. We also developed some functions to parse custom URLs and any associated form data they may contain.

Extending the browser through custom protocol handlers is a quite powerful and flexible technique. It enables us to use the browser interface for a variety of functions. In the next chapter, we investigate the possibility of using Netscape as an interface to Lotus Notes, using a custom protocol handler.

References

1. Netscape Communications Corporation, http://home.netscape.com/newsref/std/ddeapi.html
2. Netscape Communications Corporation, http://home.netscape.com/newsref/std/oleapi.html

Chapter 7

Interfacing to Lotus Notes

Lotus Notes is a powerful groupware product that enables collaborative work, document sharing, on-line discussions, and workflow applications in a network-centric environment. All of this is provided in a secure application that works over intranets or the Internet. Notes also provides a built-in web browser and a powerful application development environment using LotusScript, a scripting language having much in common with Visual Basic.

There are numerous products that enhance Notes capabilities even further. For example, NotesPump transfers data back and forth between relational databases and Notes document databases. InterNotes Web Publisher acts as a two-way conduit between a Notes server and a web server. Thus, data in a Notes database that is marked for public access can be published in HTML format and served up on the web. HTML forms (with the aid of some server scripts) can also use InterNotes to store data back into Notes.

Typically, all user interaction with Notes takes place by using the Notes client software. In this chapter, we explore how to hide the Notes client software from users. Instead, we want to use the Notes database capabilities and take advantage of Notes security features, but with Netscape as the user interface!

Secure Access to Notes

We already mentioned that InterNotes provides a web-based interface to Notes documents. So what are we doing here? Well notice, in the InterNotes description above, the words "public access." When you use Netscape or any other browser to access Notes documents published as web pages through InterNotes, there is no security check to validate that you have access to the data. There is no universal standard for WWW security yet. By contrast, if you try to access a Notes document through the Notes client, your permissions are checked before access to the data is granted. The Notes client requires you to log on to verify your identity, and the id is matched with the access control lists maintained for databases, documents, and even fields within documents.

What we're after is a way to gain access to Notes documents through Netscape without sacrificing Notes security. It turns out that we can do this and bypass the need for InterNotes altogether. The trick is to use a combination of Notes OLE objects (which are also used with LotusScript) and a custom Netscape protocol handler. We will develop our own protocol handler (as we did in the last chapter) that uses the Notes OLE interfaces to access Notes data as if we were going through the Notes client.

As this book was being written, Lotus introduced Domino, a combined web and Notes server that eliminates the need for InterNotes. Domino has a facility on the server side to check access control for Notes documents requested through a web browser. However, this requires additional administration on the server side, and can prompt you for a password multiple times. By contrast, the protocol handler we develop here is a client-side solution.

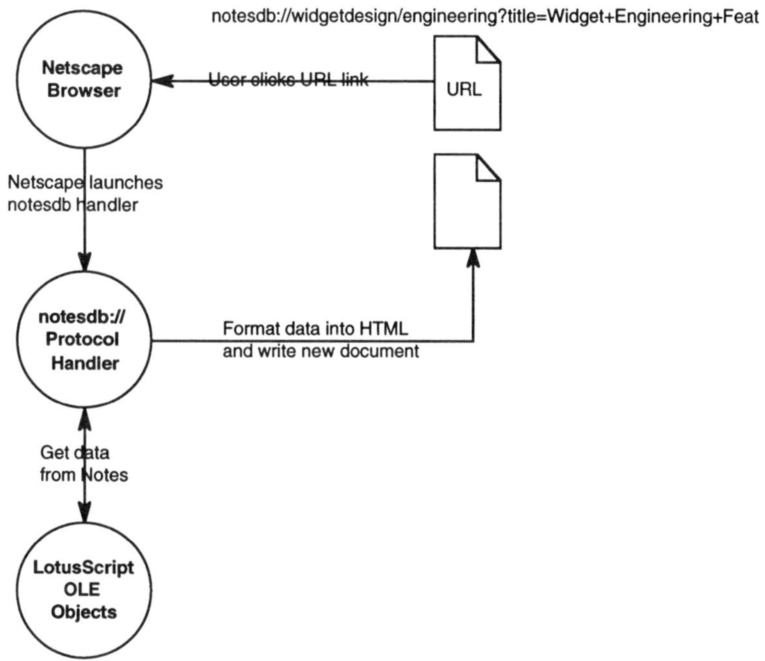

Figure 7.1.

Our custom protocol handler actually has a number of jobs. First, it must parse whatever URL we define for finding a particular document in a Notes database. Second, the handler needs to create some Notes OLE server objects to access the document data (either retrieving or storing the data). Once the Notes data is obtained, it must be formatted as an HTML document (if it isn't already) and loaded by Netscape.

For example, assume we have defined our own URL to access a Notes database named widgetdesign.nsf. Our hypothetical database might contain a number of engineering design documents. A particular document could be specified by having the user select a document title via an HTML form. Our URL for a custom notesdb protocol handler might look like:

```
notesdb://widgetdesign/engineering?title=
          Widget+Engineering+Features
```

The following figure shows the sequence of steps our protocol handler would carry out to format the contents of the document in a Netscape window. Once the data has been written as a local file, a DDE call can be made to Netscape to display the file.

Of course, this process involves some work to develop a custom URL, write the protocol handler, format the data, etc. But, secure access is inherently more complicated. To be fair, we should recognize that InterNotes automatically formats the contents of a document as HTML. The advantage to our approach, in addition to secure document access, is that you have control over the data presentation format. You are not bound as in the Notes client by the forms or views that were originally programmed by the database designer. This approach also does not load the Notes server with publishing tasks, but rather lets the client handle the formatting of the data.

Lotus Notes OLE Classes

Before proceeding with our example Notes application, we need to look at some of the available Notes OLE objects. We will only scratch the surface of LotusScript capabilities here, so refer to the manuals for a more complete description.[1] The OLE objects used in Notes programs (or agents) are typically accessed using LotusScript. However, we can also use these objects from other languages that support OLE. We will use Visual Basic to handle these Notes objects for the examples to follow.

The first class we need is *NotesSession*. It initializes communication with the Notes client and provides information on the Notes version (*NotesVersion* property), user name (*UserName* property), and methods to get and set environment variables. *NotesSession* also provides an *AddressBooks* property that returns a collection of address books recognized by the current session. This collection can be treated as a normal Visual Basic collection object.

NotesSession contains a method named *GetDatabase* that opens a database and returns an instance of another OLE object, *Notes-*

Database. The *Close* method should be called when you are done using the session object.

NotesDatabase provides properties and methods to handle a Notes database opened through the session's *GetDatabase* method. You can use this object to handle access control through a *NotesACL* object, and get information such as the database *FilePath*, *FileName*, *Server*, and *Title*. The *AllDocuments* property returns a collection of *NotesDocument* objects for working with individual documents within the database. A *Views* property returns a collection of *NotesView* objects to provide access to the views programmed by the database designer.

Each *NotesDocument* object contains a unique *NoteID* property that identifies the document. The items in the document may be accessed through a set of methods. *HasItem* checks if a document contains a particular item. *GetFirstItem* and *GetNextItem* allow iteration through the collection of items in the document, while *GetItemValue* and *ReplaceItemValue* get and set the contents of a particular item.

There are various other properties and methods associated with documents. For example, *IsResponse* detects if the document is a response to another document. Files attached to documents can be retrieved through *GetAttachment*, and a mail response to a document can be initiated by calling *CreateReplyMessage*.

The *NotesView* class provides access to documents in a database view, using the iterator functions *GetFirstDocument*, *GetNextDocument*, and *GetNthDocument*. To get the documents at the same level as another document, the *GetNextSibling* method is provided. You can also do a full text search on all documents in a view to retrieve only those documents matching a given query using *FTSearch*.

An Address Book Example

Let's write a simple standalone Visual Basic application that uses some of the Notes OLE objects to access a Notes address book. We first need to create an address book with some entries to view. A sample address book, NPGaddr.nsf, is included on the CD-ROM in chap07\nsf. The contents of the database are shown in Figure 7.2 for the Notes version 4.1 client:

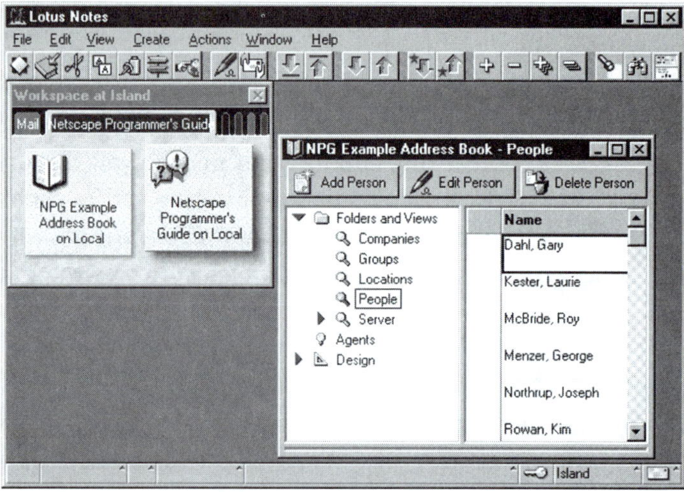

Figure 7.2. Contents of the example address book database.

The program to read the address book database and show the address entries is not an OLE object nor does it interface with Netscape. It merely illustrates the use of Notes OLE interfaces in preparation for writing a protocol handler later on in this chapter.

A logical starting point is to design a form in Visual Basic to display the address book contents. The following form is defined in the chap07\addrbook project:

Figure 7.3.

The form is named *frmAddressBook*. There is a listbox control named *lbAddresses* and a pushbutton named *pbShow*. The listbox's *Sorted* property is set to true, and the form and pushbutton captions are set as shown in the figure.

The code for this form starts with a declaration of an object to hold the instance of a *NotesSession* OLE object.

```
Option Explicit
Dim session As Object    ' Notes session
```

We initialize the *session* object inside the *Form_Load* method by calling a private function called *openSession*. If this method fails, a message box is displayed and the program ends.

```
Private Sub Form_Load()
     ' initialize the session
     If Not openSession Then
          MsgBox "Could not initialize session"
          End
     End If
End Sub
```

Here is the definition for *openSession*. It sets up a loop to retry the creation of the OLE object three times before failing. This works around some flaky behavior of the OLE objects in version 4.0 of Notes. The ProgId of a Notes session is Notes.NotesSession. In the version of Notes used here (4.1), there is no type library supplied. One may be supplied in later releases, but until then it is necessary to create the object at runtime. There is no type library that can be used to add a reference for early binding of the object.

```
Private Function openSession() As Boolean
     Dim numTries As Integer
     Const notesObject = "Notes.NotesSession"

     ' try to open a Notes session
     On Error Resume Next
     numTries = 0
```

```
    While numTries < 3
        Set session = CreateObject(notesObject)
        If session Is Nothing Then
            numTries = numTries + 1
        Else
            openSession = True
            Exit Function
        End If
    Wend

    openSession = False
End Function
```

When our program ends, we need to delete the session object. *Form_QueryUnload* calls a function called *closeSession* to handle the cleanup.

```
Private Sub Form_QueryUnload(Cancel As Integer,
                              UnloadMode As Integer)
    ' terminate the session
    closeSession
End Sub
```

The *closeSession* method does two things. First, if the session was created, the *Close* method is called and the object variable is set to *Nothing*. Second, the current implementation of the Notes OLE interface automatically starts a minimized client user interface window when a *NotesSession* object is created. Again, a later release may change this, so until then we also terminate the client as part of our cleanup routine. This is done by activating the client window using *AppActivate* and sending it the Alt-F4 key sequence to close it. This is admittedly a kludge, but it works.

```
Private Sub closeSession()
    ' close the session if it is open
    On Error Resume Next
    If Not (session Is Nothing) Then
        session.Close
```

```
        Set session = Nothing
    End If

    ' terminate the Notes UI
    AppActivate "Lotus Notes"
    SendKeys "%{F4}", True
End Sub
```

When the program starts, the Notes session is created and the form is displayed. Clicking the button executes the *pbShow_Click* event, which fills the listbox with entries from the address book. The click event handler code starts by declaring some variables, and setting the Notes server to use, and setting the database name for the address book.

```
Private Sub pbShow_Click()
    ' this function fills the listbox with the
    ' address book entries
    Dim db As Object, curdoc As Object,
    Dim lastdoc As Object
    Dim server As String, dbname As String
    Dim v As Variant, fn As Variant
    Dim ln As Variant, email As Variant

    server = ""
    dbname = "NPGaddr.NSF"
```

For this example, the server name is blank to indicate that the database resides on the local machine. You should copy the database to your \notes\data directory before running this example, or modify the *dbname* to include the appropriate pathname.

The *GetDatabase* method opens the database and returns a *db* object:

```
    ' open the sample database
    On Error Resume Next
    Set db = session.GetDatabase(server, dbname)
    If db Is Nothing Then GoTo Notes_Err
```

If you look at the database design in the Notes client, you will see that one of the views (shown above) for a Notes address book is named "People." We can retrieve a Notes OLE object corresponding to this view by calling the *NotesDatabase* object's *GetView* method.

```
' get the view of the people in the address
' book
Set v = db.GetView("People")
If v Is Nothing Then GoTo Notes_Err
```

To list all of the documents in the view, the first document is retrieved using the method *GetNthDocument.* Then, a loop iterates through each document using the *GetNextDocument* method, which takes the last document object as an argument.

For each document retrieved, we extract the value of three fields, "FirstName", "LastName", and "FullName" obtained from the database design. The values are extracted by calling *GetItem-Value* on the *NotesDocument* object. The first and last names are concatenated, followed by the email address, into a string that is then added to the form's listbox control.

```
' list all names for documents in this view
Set curdoc = v.GetNthDocument(1)

     While Not (curdoc Is Nothing)
     fn = curdoc.GetItemValue("FirstName")
     ln = curdoc.GetItemValue("LastName")
     email = curdoc.GetItemValue("FullName")
     lbAddresses.AddItem ln(0) & ", " & fn(0) & _
     " (" & email(0) & ")"

     Set lastdoc = curdoc
     Set curdoc = Nothing
     Set curdoc = v.GetNextDocument(lastdoc)
     Set lastdoc = Nothing
Wend
Set curdoc = Nothing
```

To clean up, we call the *Close* method on the database, set the object to *Nothing*, and exit the event handler. The *Notes_Err* label is branched to if any errors were encountered in calling the Notes OLE object methods.

```
    ' close the database
    db.Close
    Set db = Nothing
    Exit Sub

Notes_Err:
    MsgBox "A Notes error occurred"
    If Not (db Is Nothing) Then db.Close
    Set db = Nothing

End Sub
```

If you run the program, you should see a window similar to this:

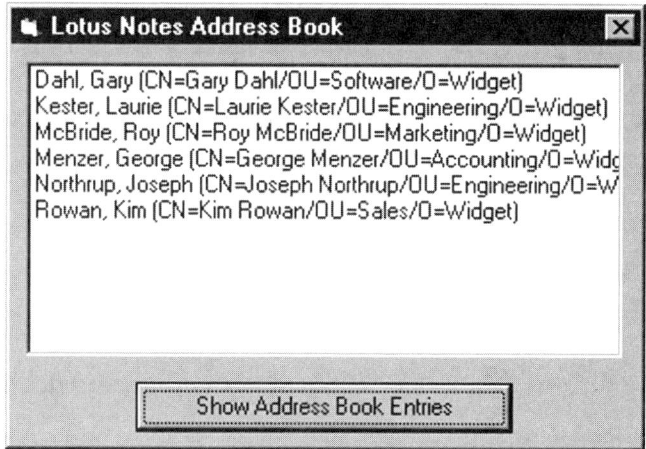

Figure 7.4.

A Notes Discussion Interface

Now that we've seen how to use the Notes OLE objects, we will adapt them to provide an interface to a Notes discussion database.

A sample Notes discussion is included on the CD-ROM in chap07\nsf in the file npg.nsf. The database is a brief, mock discussion of this book, with main topics corresponding to the first three chapters. There are responses to the main topic for the first and third topic entries. A response to a response is included for the third topic.

Notes shows this hierarchy of topics and responses in a view named "($All)." This view is shown in the following screen capture of the Lotus Notes client's view window:

Our goal is to provide a Netscape browser interface to the discussion database. The HTML document should provide a hierarchical view of the topics and responses similar to the one shown above. When a topic or response is selected, the text of the discussion should be shown in another browser window. Finally, we want to add new topics or responses to the database using an HTML form. Let's get started!

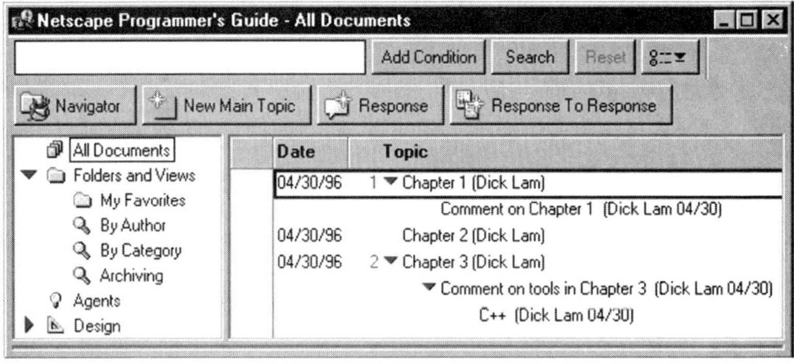

Figure 7.5. Contents of the example Notes discussion database.

clsLotusNotes

Before writing our custom protocol handler for discussions, we need to encapsulate the Notes OLE object interfaces. This encapsulation should provide interfaces specific to our needs for reading and writing topics and responses to a Notes discussion database. In this section, a set of Visual Basic OLE objects are developed to do just that. You can find the code for these objects in the chap07\clsnotes project.

We start by setting up a VB project with the usual empty *Sub Main* function in a modMain.bas module. We then insert three new class modules: *clsLotusNotes*, *clsNotesDiscussion*, and *clsDiscussionDocument*. These classes are all set to public, and their instancing is set to Creatable MultiUse because we want to compile this project as an in-process OLE server.

The *clsLotusNotes* class encapsulates the *NotesSession* interface that will be used by a test program and by the protocol handler. The following private variables are declared in the class declarations section:

```
Option Explicit

Private session As Object      ' NotesSession object
Private created As Boolean     ' True if created ok,
                               ' False if not
```

A function is defined to return true if the Notes session is created with no errors:

```
Public Function createdOK() As Boolean
    createdOK = created          ' returns True if
                                 ' Notes session was
                                 ' created
End Function
```

In the initialization and termination functions, the private *session* variable is handled by calling private *openSession* and *closeSession* methods. These are the same ones we defined earlier, so we will not repeat the code here.

```
Private Sub Class_Initialize()
    ' initialize variables
    Set session = Nothing
    created = openSession()
End Sub
```

```
Private Sub Class_Terminate()
     closeSession
End Sub
```

For our purposes, this class only needs to open a discussion database. A public function called *openDiscussion* does this by accepting a Notes server name and a discussion database filename as arguments. The database is then opened by calling the *NotesSession GetDatabase* method. This method returns a *NotesDatabase* object. An instance of the class *clsNotesDiscussion* is created to encapsulate the *NotesDatabase* instance and to hold the value of the *UserName* property for the current session. The *clsNotesDiscussion* object is then returned.

```
Public Function openDiscussion(serverName As String, _
                               fileName As String) _
                               As clsNotesDiscussion
     Dim db As Object, notesdb As Object
     Dim opened As Boolean
     Dim notesuser As String

     ' make sure session is valid
     On Error Resume Next
     If Not created Then GoTo Open_Err

     ' open the Notes database
     Set notesdb = session.GetDatabase(serverName, _
                                       fileName)
     If notesdb Is Nothing Then GoTo Open_Err

     ' create an encapsulating object for the
     ' discussion
     Set db = CreateObject("NPG.clsNotesDiscussion")
     If db Is Nothing Then GoTo Open_Err

     ' initialize the clsNotesDiscussion object with
     ' the NotesDatabase object and the user name
     ' for this session
```

```
    notesuser = session.UserName
    opened = db.Init(notesdb, notesuser)
    If Not opened Then GoTo Open_Err

    Set openDiscussion = db
    Exit Function

Open_Err:
    Set db = Nothing
    Set notesdb = Nothing
    Set openDiscussion = Nothing

End Function
```

clsNotesDiscussion

The code for *clsNotesDiscussion* begins with a set of private variable declarations, initialized by the *Class_Initialize* method. *Class_Terminate* closes the database.

```
Option Explicit

Private notesdb As Object         ' Notes database
                                  ' object
Private myUserName As String      ' user name for this
                                  ' session
Private opened As Boolean         ' True if database is
                                  ' open, False if not

Dim docs() As Object              ' cache of documents
Private curDimension As Long

Private numDocs As Long           ' number of documents
Private cached As Boolean         ' True if docs are
                                  ' cached, False if
                                  ' not

Private Sub Class_Initialize()
    Set notesdb = Nothing
```

```
    opened = False
    curDimension = 0
    numDocs = 0
    cached = False
End Sub

Private Sub Class_Terminate()
    If opened Then notesdb.Close
    Set notesdb = Nothing
End Sub
```

The *Init* method called from the *openDiscussion* function above is invoked after the object is created. It accepts the instance of the *NotesDatabase* class and the *UserName*, storing them in *notesdb* and *myUserName*, respectively. A Boolean flag is also set to indicate that the database is open.

```
Public Function Init(ndb As Object, notesuser As
                        String) As Boolean
    ' save the Notes database object
    Set notesdb = ndb
    myUserName = notesuser
    opened = False

    ' check that database is open
    If Not (notesdb Is Nothing) Then opened = True
    Init = opened
End Function
```

As this object encapsulates the representation of a Notes discussion, we provide a property to return the database title.

```
Property Get Title() As String
    Title = notesdb.Title
End Property
```

Another property is called by clients of this object to return the number of documents in the discussion database. In our implementation of *clsNotesDiscussion*, we will hold all of the discussion documents in a private array (or cache). Each object in the array is an instance of *clsDiscussionDocument* which we define below. Now you can see the reason for declaring *docs*, *curDimension*, *numDocs*, and *cached* as private variables.

The *DocumentCount* property caches the documents if necessary and then returns the actual number of documents in the array.

```
Property Get DocumentCount() As Long
     If Not cached Then cacheDocs
     DocumentCount = numDocs
End Property
```

The *Document* method again checks that the documents are cached. The value of *index* is checked for validity, and the requested instance of *clsDiscussionDocument* is returned as an object.

```
Public Function Document(index As Long) As Object
     ' cache the documents and verify the index
     If Not cached Then cacheDocs
     If (index < 1) Or (index > numDocs) Then
          Set Document = Nothing
          Exit Function
     End If

     ' return the requested document
     Set Document = docs(index)
End Function
```

As *cacheDocs* is only called by internal methods, it is declared private. The document list is obtained by opening the default view for all of the discussion documents using the *GetView* method.

```
Private Sub cacheDocs()
     Dim curdoc As Object, lastdoc As Object
     Dim curview As Object
     Dim curtype As Integer, lasttype As Integer
```

```
' open the default view
On Error Resume Next
Set curview = notesdb.GetView("($All)")
If curview Is Nothing Then
     numDocs = 0
     cached = False
     Exit Sub
End If
```

The documents are retrieved by iterating through the view using *GetFirstDocument* and *GetNextDocument*. As each document is retrieved, it is stored in the *docs* array by calling another private method, *storeDoc*. The type of the document is set in *curtype* by calling *IsResponse* on the *NotesDocument* object. The type is set to 0 for a main topic, 1 for a response, and 2 for a response to a response.

```
' set up a loop to cache all of the documents
' in the view as clsDiscussionDocument objects
Set curdoc = curview.GetFirstDocument
Set lastdoc = Nothing
curtype = 0
lasttype = 0
numDocs = 0          ' reset the count of cached
                     ' documents

While Not (curdoc Is Nothing)
     ' store the current document
     storeDoc curdoc, curtype

     ' save as the last document and get the
     ' next one
     Set lastdoc = Nothing
     Set lastdoc = curdoc
     lasttype = curtype

     Set curdoc = Nothing
     Set curdoc = curview.GetNextDocument(lastdoc)
```

```
        ' see if the new document is a response
        If Not (curdoc Is Nothing) Then
            curtype = 0
            If curdoc.IsResponse Then
                Select Case lasttype
                    Case 0
                        curtype = 1
                    Case Else
                        curtype = 2
                End Select
            End If
        End If
    Wend

    Set curview = Nothing
    cached = True    ' mark documents as cached
End Sub
```

The *storeDoc* method increments the number of documents in the cache, and increases the size of the array for holding the objects if necessary.

```
Private Sub storeDoc(thisdoc As Object, _
                    doctype As Integer)
    Dim newdoc As Object
    Dim id As String

    ' increment the count and redimension the
    ' cache array if necessary
    numDocs = numDocs + 1
    If numDocs > curDimension Then
        curDimension = curDimension + 100
        ReDim Preserve docs(curDimension) As Object
    End If
```

An instance of *clsDiscussionDocument* is then created. An *Init* method is called to set up the instance of the document with the unique *NoteID* of the document in the database. The new object is also passed a reference to *notesdb* and a value for the type of the document. Finally, the object is added to the *docs* array.

```
    ' create clsDiscussionDocument and initialize it
    Set newdoc = New clsDiscussionDocument
    id = thisdoc.NoteID
    newdoc.Init notesdb, id, doctype

    ' store the document in the cached array (so
    ' it can be returned by the Document method)
    Set docs(numDocs) = newdoc
    Set newdoc = Nothing
End Sub
```

The last function we need in this interface is a way to add appends to the discussion. We need to provide at a minimum the subject and the body, or text, of the append. We also need to provide a parent document reference to indicate if the new append is a main topic or a response to another document. The following method creates a new document in the database using the *Create-Document* method.

```
Public Sub appendNewDocument(subject As String, _
                             body As String, _
                             parentDoc As Object)
    ' creates new document and stores it in the
    ' database
    Dim newdoc As Object, ndoc As Object
    Dim i As Long

    ' create the new document or response
    On Error Resume Next
    Set newdoc = notesdb.CreateDocument
    If newdoc Is Nothing Then Exit Sub
```

Once the new *NotesDocument* object *newdoc* is created, the *ReplaceItemValue* method sets the author, subject, and text fields of the document. This is where the value of the user name from the *clsLotusNotes* object comes in.

```
' set the document properties
newdoc.ReplaceItemValue "From", myUserName
newdoc.ReplaceItemValue "Subject", subject
newdoc.ReplaceItemValue "Body", body
```

Now the input argument is checked to see if this new document is a main topic or a response. If no parent was set, the document is just saved. Otherwise, the *NotesDocument* corresponding to the *clsDiscussionDocument* parent object is retrieved. This is done by calling *GetDocumentByID* using the parent's unique NoteID. The *MakeResponse* method is called with the instance of the parent document to mark the new document as a response. Then the document is saved.

```
' if this is not a response, just save it -
' otherwise make it a response
If parentDoc Is Nothing Then
     newdoc.Save False, False
Else
     ' get NotesDocument object corresponding
     ' to the parent
     ' (which is of type clsDiscussionDocument)
     Set ndoc = notesdb.GetDocumentByID _
                (parentDoc.NoteID)
     While ndoc Is Nothing
          Set ndoc = notesdb.GetDocumentByID _
                     (parentDoc.NoteID)
     Wend

     ' make the new document a response
     newdoc.MakeResponse ndoc
     newdoc.Save False, False

     Set ndoc = Nothing
End If
```

We could manage the cache intelligently, but it is adequate for this example to simply delete the current cache of document objects.

```
    ' remove the current cache of documents
    If cached Then
        For i = 1 To curDimension
            Set docs(i) = Nothing
        Next i
        numDocs = 0
        cached = False
    End If
End Sub
```

clsDiscussionDocument

The *clsDiscussionDocument* class that encapsulates *NotesDocument* starts by defining the constants corresponding to the three document types. The document type, NoteID, and reference to the discussion database are all stored in member variables. The author, subject, and body fields of the document are also stored in strings. A Boolean variable indicates whether the fields have been read from the database yet.

```
Option Explicit

' document types
Const DOCTYPE_TOPIC = 0
Const DOCTYPE_RESPONSE = 1
Const DOCTYPE_SUBRESPONSE = 2

Private myDocType As Integer     ' one of DOCTYPE_
                                 ' constants
Private myNotesID As String      ' NoteID of the
                                 ' document
Private notesdb As Object        ' Notes discussion
                                 ' database
```

```
Private myAuthor As String      ' contents of the
                                ' document
Private mySubject As String
Private myBody As String
Private cached As Boolean       ' True if doc
                                ' contents are cached
```

The class initialization and termination methods take care of the member variable settings:

```
Private Sub Class_Initialize()
     ' initialize variables
     myDocType = DOCTYPE_TOPIC
     myNotesID = ""
     Set notesdb = Nothing
     myAuthor = ""
     mySubject = ""
     myBody = ""
     cached = False
End Sub

Private Sub Class_Terminate()
     ' clean up
     Set notesdb = Nothing
End Sub
```

The *Init* method called after one of these objects has been created sets the reference to the *NotesDatabase* object, the NoteID, and the document type.

```
Public Function Init(ndb As Object, id As String, _
                    doctype As Integer) As Boolean
     ' save the input variables
     Set notesdb = ndb
     myNotesID = id
     myDocType = doctype
```

```
    ' make sure id string is 8 characters
    While Len(myNotesID) < 8
        myNotesID = "0" & myNotesID
    Wend

    ' return True to indicate initialization
    ' succeeded
    Init = True
End Function
```

Clients that need to access the id, document type, or one of the three document fields simply call one of the following properties:

```
Property Get NoteID() As String
    NoteID = myNotesID
End Property

Property Get DocumentType() As Integer
    DocumentType = myDocType
End Property

Property Get Author() As String
    If Not cached Then cacheContents
    Author = myAuthor
End Property

Property Get Subject() As String
    If Not cached Then cacheContents
    subject = mySubject
End Property

Property Get Body() As String
    If Not cached Then cacheContents
    body = myBody
End Property
```

Note that the contents of the document are not read unless they are requested through one of the properties. The private method *cacheContents* actually retrieves the information by first getting a reference to the database document using *GetDocumentByID*. *GetItemValue* then retrieves the named field values.

```
Private Sub cacheContents()
     ' read the document information and store it
     Dim ndoc As Object
     Dim v As Variant

     ' make sure we can open the document
     On Error Resume Next
     If notesdb Is Nothing Then Exit Sub
     Set ndoc = notesdb.GetDocumentByID(myNotesID)
     While ndoc Is Nothing
        Set ndoc = notesdb.GetDocumentByID(myNotesID)
     Wend

     ' get the contents
     v = ndoc.GetItemValue("From")
     myAuthor = v(0)

     v = ndoc.GetItemValue("Subject")
     mySubject = v(0)

     v = ndoc.GetItemValue("Body")
     myBody = CStr(v(0))
     If Len(myBody) = 0 Then myBody = v

     ' clean up and set the flag to indicate the
     ' contents are available
     Set ndoc = Nothing
     cached = True
End Sub
```

Testing the Discussion Interface

Our Notes discussion interface now consists of three classes. A total of ten public methods exposed from these classes are all we need to construct a usable discussion interface. Before moving on to the next section where we will write the Netscape protocol handler, let's test the OLE server (you should have compiled the project and registered the in-process server on your system).

The test program is found in chap07\clsnotes\test. It consists of three forms. The first one, *frmDiscussion*, contains a tree view control named *tvTopics* and two pushbuttons that allow the user to make a new topic or a response to a selected topic:

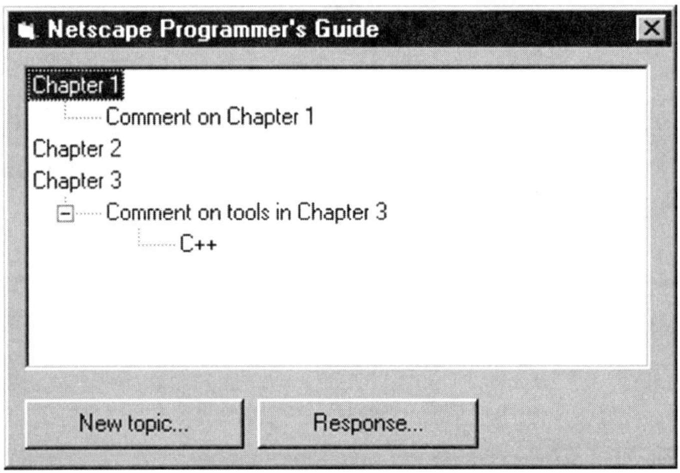

Figure 7.6.

The private declarations section of this form's code holds instances of the *clsLotusNotes* and *clsNotesDiscussion* objects. The *Form_Load* function creates the NPG.clsLotusNotes object and calls *openDiscussion* to obtain an instance of the discussion interface object. It then sets the titlebar of the window to the database title and calls *fillView* to set up the tree view control.

```
Option Explicit

Dim notes As Object        ' clsLotusNotes object
Dim db As Object           ' clsLotusDiscussion object
```

```
Private Sub Form_Load()
     ' create a Lotus Notes session
     On Error Resume Next
     Set notes = CreateObject("NPG.clsLotusNotes")
     If notes Is Nothing Then
          MsgBox "Could not initialize session"
          End
     End If

     ' open the database
     Set db = notes.openDiscussion("", "npg.nsf")
     If db Is Nothing Then
          MsgBox "Could not open discussion"
          End
     End If

     ' set the caption of the form to the database
     ' title and fill the tree view with discussion
     ' topics
     Caption = db.Title
     fillView
End Sub
```

Form_QueryUnload cleans up the private variables:

```
Private Sub Form_QueryUnload(Cancel As Integer, _
                              UnloadMode As Integer)
     ' clean up database and Notes session objects
     Set db = Nothing
     Set notes = Nothing
     End
End Sub
```

The tree view control is initialized by populating it with the main topics and responses from the database. Our *DocumentCount* property and *Document* method allow iteration through the discussion documents to retrieve the document type and subject. Response documents are added to the control as children of their parent document.

```
Private Sub fillView()
    ' gets topics and responses from the database
    ' and puts them into a tree view
    Dim curdoc As Object
    Dim i As Long
    Dim doctype As Integer
    Dim doctopic As String, lastmain As String
    Dim lastresp As String, nextresp As String
    Dim curnode As Node

    On Error Resume Next
    tvTopics.Nodes.Clear        ' clear the tree view
                                ' control

    For i = 1 To db.DocumentCount
        ' get the next document and determine its
        ' type and subject
        Set curdoc = db.Document(i)
        doctype = curdoc.DocumentType
        doctopic = curdoc.subject

        ' add the document to the tree view control
        Select Case doctype
            Case 0          ' main topic
                lastmain = "t" & Trim(Str(i))
                Set curnode = tvTopics.Nodes.Add _
                    (, , lastmain, doctopic)

            Case 1          ' response to main topic
                lastresp = "r" & Trim(Str(i))
                Set curnode = tvTopics.Nodes.Add( _
                    lastmain, tvwChild, _
                    lastresp, doctopic)

            Case Else       ' response to response
              nextresp = "r" & Trim(Str(i))
              Set curnode = tvTopics.Nodes.Add( _
                  lastresp, tvwChild, _
                  nextresp, doctopic)
        End Select
```

```
        curnode.EnsureVisible   ' make all nodes visible
        Set curdoc = Nothing
    Next i
End Sub
```

Double clicking on a tree view selection invokes the following event handler. This handler retrieves the requested document from the *clsNotesDiscussion* instance and loads an instance of *frmView*. The caption of the form is set to the database title, and the author, subject, and body controls on the form are set to their corresponding document values before. Then the form is made visible to the user.

```
Private Sub tvTopics_DblClick()
    ' view the append for the current selection
    Dim i As Long
    Dim curdoc As Object

    ' get the selected item
    On Error Resume Next
    i = tvTopics.SelectedItem.Index
    Set curdoc = db.Document(i)
    If curdoc Is Nothing Then Exit Sub

    ' load the form for viewing the document
    Load frmView
    With frmView
        .Caption = Caption
        .lblSubject.Caption = "Subject: " _
                            & curdoc.subject
        .lblAuthor.Caption = "Author: " _
                           & curdoc.Author
        .txtBody.Text = curdoc.body
    End With

    ' clean up and show the form
    Set curdoc = Nothing
    frmView.Show vbModal
End Sub
```

Here is the sample output for frmView:

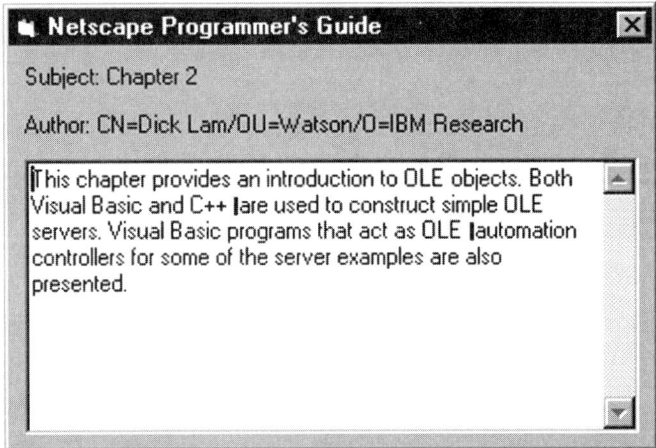

Figure 7.7.

Pressing either of the buttons on the main form brings up a modal dialog box defined as *frmAppend*:

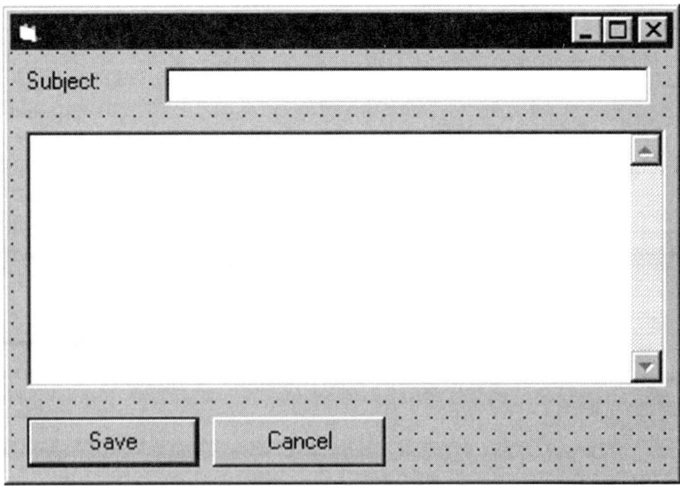

Figure 7.8. The design view for *frmAppend*.

This form allows the user to specify a subject and body for a new append and save the new document in the database. The code for this form is very simple:

```
Option Explicit
Public saveIt As Boolean      ' set to True if data
                              ' should be saved

Private Sub pbCancel_Click()
    saveIt = False
    Hide
End Sub

Private Sub pbSave_Click()
    saveIt = True
    Hide
End Sub
```

All of the work is actually done in the main form's pushbutton event handlers. For example, pressing the button for creating a new main topic loads *frmAppend* and sets the *txtSubject* and *txtAppend* controls to empty strings. Once the form is displayed modally, the public *saveIt* variable is checked. If the value is true, a private method called *saveAppend* is invoked to store the new document in the database.

```
Private Sub pbTopic_Click()
    ' compose a new topic
    Dim body As String

    ' load the form for entering the new append
    On Error Resume Next
    Load frmAppend
    With frmAppend
        .Caption = "New Topic"
        .txtSubject.Text = ""
        .txtAppend.Text = ""
    End With
```

```
    ' show the form and see if new append is to be
    ' saved
    frmAppend.Show vbModal
    If frmAppend.saveIt Then
        ' save the new append
        body = frmAppend.txtAppend.Text
        saveAppend frmAppend.txtSubject.Text, body,
        Nothing
    End If
End Sub
```

The document is added to the database by calling the *append-NewDocument* method of the *clsNotesDiscussion object.* A parent document of *Nothing* indicates that this is a new main topic.

```
Private Sub saveAppend(subject As String, _
                       body As String, _
                       parent As Object)
    ' save the document in the database and update
    ' the view
    On Error Resume Next
    db.appendNewDocument subject, body, parent
    fillView
End Sub
```

The pushbutton for adding a response to a document first checks the tree view control for the currently selected document. This document is then retrieved and used as the parent when calling *appendNewDocument.*

```
Private Sub pbResponse_Click()
    ' compose a response to the selected topic
    Dim i As Long
    Dim curdoc As Object
    Dim body As String

    ' get the selected item
    On Error Resume Next
```

```
    i = tvTopics.SelectedItem.Index
    Set curdoc = db.Document(i)

    ' load the form for entering the new append
    Load frmAppend
    With frmAppend
        .Caption = tvTopics.SelectedItem.Text
        .txtSubject.Text = "Re: " & curdoc.subject
        .txtAppend.Text = ""
    End With

    ' show the form and see if new append is to be
    ' saved
    frmAppend.Show vbModal
    If frmAppend.saveIt Then
        ' save the new append
        body = frmAppend.txtAppend.Text
        saveAppend frmAppend.txtSubject.Text, body,
        curdoc
    End If

    ' clean up
    Set curdoc = Nothing
End Sub
```

You can compile this program as a standalone executable and test it with the clsnotes in-process server created above.

From Notes to Netscape

Now that we know how to interface to a Lotus Notes discussion database, we can write a Netscape protocol handler. This handler will provide an interface similar to the test program we just saw. The difference is that we will be using the browser for an interface rather than Visual Basic forms.

Defining the URLs

Let's start by defining the protocol name "conference." As the *openDiscussion* method requires both a server and filename, our URL should probably start out with those:

```
conference://server/filename
```

If there is no server (i.e., if a local database is being accessed), the URL will be:

```
conference:///filename
```

In the test program, the tree view showed the list of topics. We can define an HTML page that provides a similar view by extending the URL to:

```
conference://server/filename/topic/list
```

We handle documents as either a main topic, or a response to another document. We also either create a new document or show an existing one, so the following URLs will carry out these operations:

```
conference://server/filename/topic/new
conference://server/filename/topic/show
conference://server/filename/response/new
conference://server/filename/response/show
```

To create a new document, any URL that ends with /new should specify the subject and contents. This can be done through form data, as in the following example:

```
Subject=New+Main+Topic&Body=This+is+a+new+topic
```

To retrieve a given document in response to /show, the form data appended to the URL should be the index of the document.

```
id=1
```

Writing the Protocol Handler

At the end of Chapter 6, we created a localexec protocol handler that included form data parsing. We do the same thing now for a new OLE server that implements our conference protocol. The C++ source code for this OLE server is found in chap07\phconf. The mkoleobj program was used to generate the code for NPG.conference.

The standard changes to the code generated by mkoleobj for protocol handlers are necessary for the new *Iconference* interface. *Initialize* and *Open* methods are added to iobject.h, objimpl.h, objimpl.C, and phconf.odl. The STL type declarations for the queue of URL tokens and the form data array are declared at the top of objimpl.h, and the parsing functions we wrote in the last chapter are also added as members of *myImplOfconference.*

The *Initialize* method is identical to the one for localexec (see Chapter 6), except that the protocol is compared to "conference" rather than "localexec." The big change is in the *Open* method. It must create a new instance for one of five classes to handle the five valid URLs we decided to allow. Here are the first few lines of *Open*, which pulls the name of the Lotus Notes server and the filename of the Notes discussion database from the token queue.

```
void STDMETHODCALLTYPE myImplOfconference::
Open(LPCTSTR url)
{

    // get URL from wide char input
    char myURL[256];
    wstrcpy(myURL, url);

    // extract the server and filename
    string serverName = myURLQueue.front();
    myURLQueue.pop();
    string dbFilename = myURLQueue.front();
    myURLQueue.pop();
```

These values will be used to open the discussion database,

using a C++ interface to the Visual Basic OLE server classes *clsLotusNotes* and *clsNotesDiscussion* we developed earlier.

```
// create a session object and open the discussion
// database
string filename("");
{
 clsLotusNotes session;
 clsNotesDiscussion *db = session.openDiscussion(
                              serverName,dbFilename);
  if (!db)
     return;
```

The *filename* variable will be used at the end of the method to load a generated HTML document into the browser. This dynamically generated HTML page is constructed by one of five object types. We can pull off the next two tokens from the queue. These tokens represent the object and the request being made.

```
// extract the object (topic or response)
// and request (new, show, or list) types
string docObject = myURLQueue.front();
myURLQueue.pop();
string request = myURLQueue.front();
myURLQueue.pop();
```

For example, a *docObject* of “topic” and a *request* of “show” should result in the creation of an HTML page that displays a particular main topic from the discussion database. We define a factory object from the class *HTMLDocumentFactory* to create a derived class of *HTMLDocument*. There is one derived class for each of the five URL types.

```
// create an object to handle the object and
// request
HTMLDocumentFactory factory;
HTMLDocument *doc = factory.create(docObject,
                                   request);
```

```
        if (!doc)
            return;
```

Once the correct derived class is created, a *process* method is invoked to generated the correct HTML page. This method returns the name of the new document file.

```
        // call the document object's process method
        // to handle the request
        // and return the filename for the browser
        // to load
        filename = doc->process(*db, myFormData);
        delete doc;
    }
```

Finally, the *Open* method concludes by invoking another OLE server that uses the Netscape DDE interface to load the file in the current browser window.

```
    // load the file in the browser
    clsNetscapeLoader nsloader;
    nsloader.loadFile(filename.c_str(), false);
}
```

The C++ Interface to Notes

We need a C++ interface to the three VB classes we developed to provide a high-level discussion interface to Notes. The three interface class definitions are provided in clsnotes.h.

The first class is *clsDiscussionDocument*, defined by the OLE server NPG.clsDiscussionDocument. This class defines the properties for accessing the document type, author, subject, and contents of the discussion append. The *get_property* template method we developed in Chapter 3 is used to get the property values.

```
class clsDiscussionDocument :
public OLEDispatchInterface {
```

```
public:
    // constructors and destructors
    clsDiscussionDocument(const char *progid =
                        "NPG.clsDiscussionDocument")
        : OLEDispatchInterface(progid) {}
    clsDiscussionDocument(IDispatch *dispatch)
        : OLEDispatchInterface(dispatch) {}

    virtual ~clsDiscussionDocument() {}

    // clsDiscussionDocument interface
    short DocumentType()
    {
        return get_property(this, "DocumentType",
                            (short)0);
    }

    string Author()
    {
        char *p = get_property(this, "Author",
                                (char *)0);
        string s(p);
        delete p;
        return s;
    }

    string Subject()
    {
        char *p = get_property(this, "Subject",
                                (char *)0);
        string s(p);
        delete p;
        return s;
    }

    string Body()
    {
        char *p = get_property(this, "Body",
                                (char *)0);
```

```
        string s(p);
        delete p;
        return s;
    }
};
```

The discussion database class, *clsNotesDiscussion*, provides interface methods to append new discussion topics, access the database title, and iterate through the documents in the database. In addition, two protected members have been added to the C++ interface to access the server name and database filename. These are set by *clsLotusNotes* after an instance of this class is created.

```
class clsNotesDiscussion :
public OLEDispatchInterface {
public:
    // constructors and destructors
    clsNotesDiscussion(const char *progid =
                      "NPG.clsNotesDiscussion")
        : OLEDispatchInterface(progid) {}
    clsNotesDiscussion(IDispatch *dispatch)
        : OLEDispatchInterface(dispatch) {}

    virtual ~clsNotesDiscussion() {}

    // methods to get/set the server and database
    // filename
    void setServer(const string& s) { myServer =
                                      s; }
    string getServer() const { return myServer; }

    void setDatabase(const string& f) { myDatabase =
                                        f; }
    string getDatabase() const { return myDatabase; }

    // clsNotesDiscussion interface
```

```
void appendNewDocument(string& subject,
                       string& body,
                       clsDiscussionDocument
                       *parent)
{
    IDispatch *dispatch = 0;
    if (parent)
        dispatch = parent->getDispatch();

    method_threeargs(this, "appendNewDocument",
                     (int)0,
                     subject.c_str(),
                     body.c_str(),
                     dispatch);
}

string Title()
{
    char *p = get_property(this, "Title",
                           (char *)0);
    string s(p);
    delete p;
    return s;
}

long DocumentCount()
{
    return get_property(this, "DocumentCount",
                        (long)0);
}

clsDiscussionDocument *Document(long index)
{
    IDispatch *dispatch = method_onearg
                          (this, "Document",
                           (IDispatch *)0,
                           index);
    return new clsDiscussionDocument(dispatch);
}
```

```
protected:
    string myServer;        // Notes server and
                            // database
    string myDatabase;
};
```

The Lotus Notes session is created by NPG.clsLotusNotes. The *openDiscussion* method creates an instance of *clsNotesDiscussion* using the *IDispatch* pointer returned by the Visual Basic function (*IDispatch* is equivalent to Visual Basic's *Object* declaration).

```
class clsLotusNotes : public OLEDispatchInterface {
public:
    // constructors and destructors
    clsLotusNotes(const char *progid =
                  "NPG.clsLotusNotes")
        : OLEDispatchInterface(progid) {}
    clsLotusNotes(IDispatch *dispatch)
        : OLEDispatchInterface(dispatch) {}

    virtual ~clsLotusNotes() {}

    // clsLotusNotes interface
    bool createdOK()
    {
        return method_noargs(this, "createdOK",
                             (bool)0);
    }

    clsNotesDiscussion *openDiscussion
                        (string& server,
                         string& filename)
    {
        IDispatch *dispatch = method_twoargs
                              ( this,
                              "openDiscussion",
                              (IDispatch *)0,
                              server.c_str(),
                              filename.c_str() );
```

```
        clsNotesDiscussion *d =
        new clsNotesDiscussion(dispatch);
        if (!d)
            return 0;

        // set the server and database name
        d->setServer(server);
        d->setDatabase(filename);
        return d;
    }
};
```

The HTMLDocument Base Class and Factory

An *HTMLDocumentFactory* object provides a derived class of the abstract class *HTMLDocument*. The derived class object is constructed by calling a factory method named *create*, passing it an object (topic or response) and a request (list, new, or show). The header file for the factory class is:

```
// htmlfact.h
#include "htmldoc.h"

// forward declaration
class HTMLDocument;

// class declaration
class HTMLDocumentFactory {
public:
    // constructor and destructor
    HTMLDocumentFactory() {}
    virtual ~HTMLDocumentFactory() {}

    // object creation method
    HTMLDocument *create(const string& object,
                         const string& request);
```

```
private:
    // helper methods
    HTMLDocument *createTopic(const string& request);
    HTMLDocument *createResponse(const string&
request);
};
```

The factory method uses two helper methods to create the correct derived class object. The implementations for these functions are straightforward. Each object/request pair maps to a specific derived class of *HTMLDocument.*

```
// create - returns a new instance of an
//          HTMLDocument derived class
HTMLDocument *HTMLDocumentFactory::create
                                  (const string&
                                   object,
                                   const string&
                                   request)
{
    // see if the object is a topic or response
    if ( object == string("topic") )
        return createTopic(request);
    else if ( object == string("response") )
        return createResponse(request);
    else
        return 0;
}

// ---------------------------------------------------

// createTopic - creates one of the topic objects
HTMLDocument *HTMLDocumentFactory::createTopic
                                  (const string&
                                   request)
{
    // see if request is new, show, or list
    if ( request == string("new") )
```

```
        return new NewTopic;
    else if ( request == string("show") )
        return new ShowTopic;
    else if ( request == string("list") )
        return new ListTopics;
    else
        return 0;
}

// -----------------------------------------------------

// createResponse - creates one of the response
//                  objects
HTMLDocument *HTMLDocumentFactory::createResponse
                                    (const string&
                                     request)
{
    // see if request is new or show
    if ( request == string("new") )
        return new NewResponse;
    else if ( request == string("show") )
        return new ShowResponse;
    else
        return 0;
}
```

Here is a partial definition of the abstract base class *HTML-Document*. The pure virtual process method must be defined in each of the five derived classes to generate the specific HTML document for each of our five URL types.

```
// htmldoc.h
#include <ospace/stl.h>
#include <ospace/string.h>
#include "clsnotes.h"

// typedef for the form data
typedef map< string, string, less<string> >
formdata_t;
```

```
// class declaration
class HTMLDocument {
public:
    // constructor and destructor
    HTMLDocument() {}
    virtual ~HTMLDocument() {}

    // method to generate HTML document file and
    // return a filename
    // for the generated file
    virtual string process(clsNotesDiscussion& db,
                          const formdata_t& data) =
                          0;

protected:
    // constructs a unique temporary filename
    string tmpFilename();
};
```

A protected method, *tmpFilename*, is provided for the derived classes to create a unique file to contain the new HTML page. The Windows function *GetTempPath* is used to get the current system's temporary path.

```
string HTMLDocument::tmpFilename()
{
    // get a Windows temporary file
    char fpath[MAX_PATH], fname[MAX_PATH];

    GetTempPath(MAX_PATH, fpath);
    GetTempFileName(fpath, "doc", 0, fname);

    return string(fname);
}
```

The ListTopics Class

The derived class *ListTopics* is created by the factory for a topic/list URL. This derived class implements the pure virtual *process* method of *HTMLDocument* by first creating a temporary file.

```
string ListTopics::process(clsNotesDiscussion& db,
                           const formdata_t& data)
{
    // open up a temporary file
    string filename = tmpFilename();
    ofstream fout( filename.c_str() );
    if (!fout)
        return string("");
```

The HTML header for the database is then written to the new temporary file stream.

```
    // write the HTML header
    fout << "<html>" << endl
         << "<head><title>Topic List</title></head>"
         << endl
         << "<body>" << endl;

    // write the topic list header
    fout << "<h1>" << db.Title().c_str() << "</h1>"
    << endl
         << "Topic List<p>" << endl
         << "<ul>" << endl;
```

The Notes server and discussion database names are retrieved from the *clsNotesDiscussion* object:

```
    // get the server and database names
    string server = db.getServer();
    string database = db.getDatabase();
    short curtype = 0, lasttype = 0;
```

Next, a loop is used to iterate through all of the documents in the database. The document type and subject are extracted from each document and used to generate nested lists of unordered topics in HTML format.

```
// loop to write out all discussion topics
for (long i = 1; i <= db.DocumentCount(); i++) {
    // get the next document
    clsDiscussionDocument *doc = db.Document(i);
    if (doc) {
        // determine the document type and
        // subject
        lasttype = curtype;
        curtype = doc->DocumentType();
        string subject = doc->Subject();

        // write the HTML list item
        if (curtype == lasttype)
            fout << "<li>";
        else if (curtype > lasttype)
            fout << "<ul>" << endl
                 << "<li>";
        else if ( (lasttype - curtype) == 1 )
            fout << "</ul>" << endl
                 << "<li>";
        else
            fout << "</ul>" << endl
                 << "</ul>" << endl
                 << "<li>";

        fout    << "<a href=\"conference://"
                << server.c_str() << "/"
                << database.c_str()
                << ( (curtype == 0)?"/topic/show":
                     "/response/show" )
                << "?id=" <<
                setiosflags(ios::left) << i
                << "\">"
                << subject.c_str() << "</a>"
                << endl;
```

```
            delete doc;
        }
    }
    fout << "</ul>" << endl;
```

Each subject is written as a link to a conference URL to show the topic or response. After all of the discussion topics are listed, we also generate HTML form tags to create a form with a single pushbutton. Pressing this button invokes another conference URL that creates a new main topic.

```
    // write the form that allows entering a new
    // main topic
    fout        << "<hr>" << endl
                << "<form method=\"post\" "
                << "action=\ "conference://"
                << server.c_str() << "/" <
                << database.c_str()
                << "/topic/new\">" << endl
                << "<input type=\"submit\" value=\"New"
                << "Topic...\">"
            << "</form>" << endl;
```

The end of the HTML form is then written and the filename is returned to conclude the *ListTopics::process* method.

```
    // write the trailer
    fout << "</body>" << endl
         << "</html>" << endl;

    return filename;
}
```

Here is the HTML document generated for the contents of the enclosed sample database npg.nsf:

```
<html>
<head><title>Topic List</title></head>
<body>
<h1>Netscape Programmer’s Guide</h1>
Topic List<p>
<ul>
<li><ahref=”conference:///npg.nsf/topic/show?id=1”>
Chapter 1</a>
<ul>
<li><a>href=”conference:///npg.nsf/response/show?id=2
”>
Comment on Chapter 1</a>
</ul>
<li><a href=”conference:///npg.nsf/topic/show?id=3”>
Chapter 2</a>
<li><a href=”conference:///npg.nsf/topic/show?id=4”>
Chapter 3</a>
<ul>
<li><a
href=”conference:///npg.nsf/response/show?id=5”>
Comment on tools in Chapter 3</a>
<ul>
<li><a
href=”conference:///npg.nsf/response/show?id=6”>
C++</a>
</ul>
<hr>
<form method=”post”
action=”conference:///npg.nsf/topic/new”>
<input type=”submit” value=”New Topic...”></form>
</body>
</html>
```

The actual browser page is rendered as:

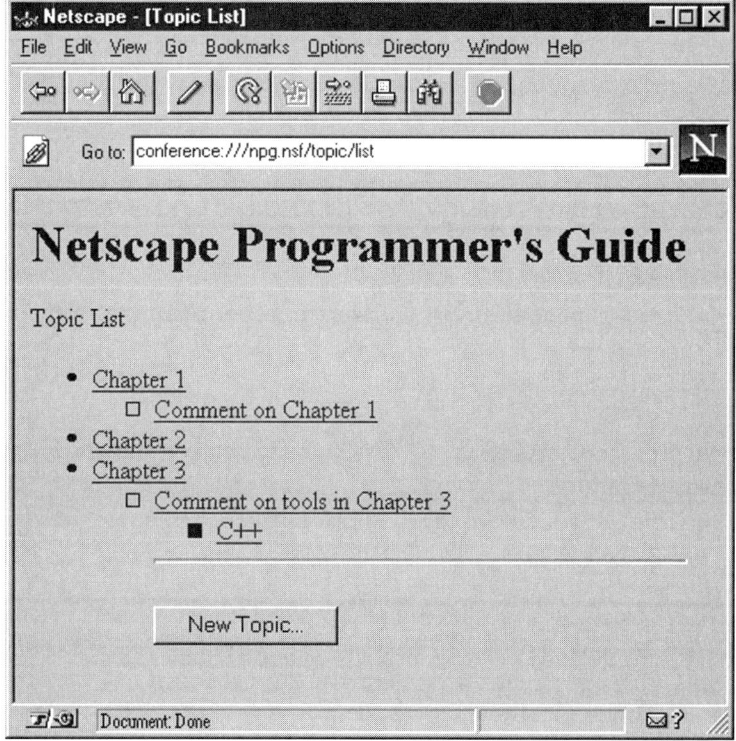

Figure 7.9.

ShowTopic and ShowResponse

Selecting any of the links on thc topic list page generates a URL for showing the corresponding topic or response. In turn, the factory creates a *ShowTopic* or *ShowResponse* object. We will show the code for *ShowTopic::process* here. The code for the *ShowResponse* class is almost identical.

As in the previous implementation of *process*, a new temporary file stream is created. The HTML header is written and the index number of the document to retrieve is obtained from the form data. This index number is appended to the URLs in the HTML page of the last section as an "id" name-value pair.

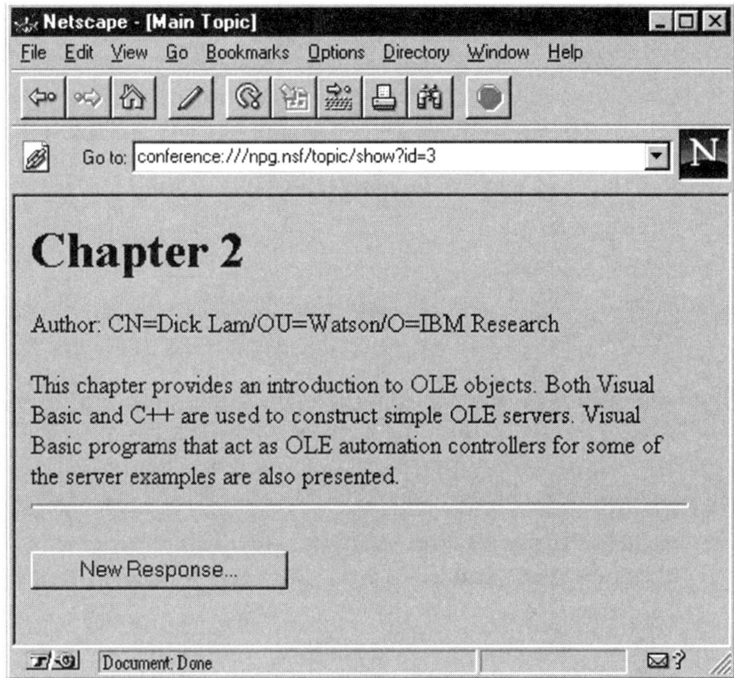

Figure 7.10.

```
string ShowTopic::process(clsNotesDiscussion& db,
                          const formdata_t& data)
{
    // open up a temporary file
    string filename = tmpFilename();
    ofstream fout( filename.c_str() );
    if (!fout)
        return string("");

    // generate HTML to show the topic
    fout   << "<html>" << endl
           << "<head><title>Main Topic</title></head>"
           << endl
           << "<body>" << endl;
```

```
// get the topic number from the form data
long index = 0;

if ( data.find( string("id") ) != data.end() ) {
    // extract the index from the string value
    string strvalue = data[string("id")];
    strstream ss;

    ss << strvalue.c_str() << ends;
    ss >> index;
```

Once the index number is obtained, the document is retrieved and the contents are written to the file in HTML format.

```
    // get the document
    clsDiscussionDocument *doc =
    db.Document(index);
    if (doc) {
        // write the document contents
        fout << "<h1>" << doc->Subject().c_str()
             << "</h1>" << endl
             << "Author: " << doc->Author().c_str()
             << "<p>"
             << endl
             << doc->Body() << endl;
        delete doc;
    }
}
```

The document includes a form that has a single pushbutton for generating a response to the document being viewed:

```
if (index > 0) {
    // get the server and database names
    string server = db.getServer();
    string database = db.getDatabase();
```

```
        // write the form
        fout << "<hr>" << endl
             << "<form method=\"post\" action=\""
             << "conference://"
             << server.c_str() << "/"
             << database.c_str()
             << "/response/new?id="
             << setiosflags(ios::left) << index
             << "\">" << endl
             << "<input type=\"submit\" name=\""
             << "submit\""
             << " value=\"New Response...\">"
             << endl
             << "</form>" << endl;
    }

    // write the trailer
    fout     << "</body>" << endl
             << "</html>" << endl;

    return filename;
}
```

The generated HTML code for the entry on Chapter 2 in the topic list is:

```
<html>
<head><title>Main Topic</title></head>
<body>
<h1>Chapter 2</h1>
Author: CN=Dick Lam/OU=Watson/O=IBM Research<p>
This chapter provides an introduction to OLE
objects. Both Visual Basic and C++ are used to con-
struct simple OLE servers. Visual Basic programs
that act as OLE automation controllers for some of
the server examples are also presented.
<hr>
<form method="post"
```

```
action="conference:///npg.nsf/response/new?id=3">
<input type="submit" name="submit"
value="New Response...">
</form>
</body>
</html>
```

The discussion append as shown by the browser is shown on the opposite page.

The NewTopic and NewResponse Classes

Pressing either the New Topic... or New Response... pushbuttons creates an instance of *NewTopic* or *NewResponse*, respectively. As before, the *NewTopic::process* method creates a temporary file.

```
string NewTopic::process(clsNotesDiscussion& db,
                         const formdata_t& data)
{

   // open up a temporary file
   string filename = tmpFilename();
   ofstream fout( filename.c_str() );
   if (!fout)
      return string("");

   // generate HTML form to create a new main topic
   fout << "<html>" << endl
        << "<head><title>New Topic</title></head>"
        << endl
        << "<body>" << endl;

   // get server and database
   string server = db.getServer();
   string database = db.getDatabase();
```

This time, however, there are two possible HTML documents that this URL can generate. The first document is a blank form that enables the user to enter a subject and body for a new append to the discussion. This is done if no "Body" name-value pair is contained in the form data.

```
// if no Body in form data, output a blank form
// for entering
// a new append - otherwise add new append to
// the discussion
// database and re-display the list of topics
if ( data.find("Body") == data.end() ) {
    // blank form
    fout << "<h1>" << db.Title().c_str()
         << "</h1>" << endl
         << "<form method=\"get\" "
         << "action=\"conference://"
         << server.c_str() << "/"
         << database.c_str()
         << "/topic/new\">" << endl
         << "Subject:" << endl
         << "<input type=\"text\" name=\"Subject\""
         << " value=\"\" size=30><p>"
         << endl
         << "<textarea name=\"Body\" value=\"\" "
         << "rows=8 cols=40>"
         << endl
         << "</textarea><p>" << endl
         << "<input type=\"submit\" name=\"sub "
         << "mit\" value=\""
         << "Append New Main Topic\">" << endl
         << "</form>" << endl;
} else {
```

If there is form data corresponding to a completed form, the subject and body of the new append are extracted. The *append-NewDocument* method is then called to create a new main topic.

```
    // get the subject and body fields for the
    // new append
```

```
        string subject = data["Subject"];
        string body = data["Body"];

        db.appendNewDocument(subject, body, 0);
        fout << "<h1>" << db.Title().c_str()
             << "</h1>" << endl
             << "A new main topic has been appended!<p>"
             << endl
             << "You can view the updated " << endl
             << "<a href=\"conference://"
             << server.c_str() << "/"
             << database.c_str()
             << "/topic/list\">list</a>" << endl
             << " of topics." << endl;
    }

    // write the trailer
    fout << "</body>" << endl
         << "</html>" << endl;

    return filename;
}
```

The code for NewResponse is almost identical. One major difference is that a new response must provide a pointer to its parent document. The index of the parent document is extracted from the "id" name-value pair. The pointer to the retrieved parent document is then used as the last argument to *appendNewDocument*.

```
        // need to specify parent - get it from the
        // id field
        string id = data["id"];
        strstream ss;
        long index;

        ss << id.c_str() << ends;
        ss >> index;
```

```
    // get the parent document
    clsDiscussionDocument *parent =
    db.Document(index);

    // append the document and write a message
    // to the user
    db.appendNewDocument(subject, body, parent);
```

The following HTML is generated by pressing the New Topic . . . button:

```
<html>
<head><title>New Topic</title></head>
<body>
<h1>Netscape Programmer's Guide</h1>
<form method="get"
action="conference:///npg.nsf/topic/new">
Subject:
<input type="text" name="Subject" value=""
size=30><p>
<textarea name="Body" value="" rows=8 cols=40>
</textarea><p>
<input type="submit" name="submit"
value="Append New Main Topic">
</form>
</body>
</html>
```

Note that when the button on this form is pressed, form data for the conference:///npg.nsf/topic/new URL will be automatically appended and submitted for processing. This form data will include Subject and Body name-value pairs, and the *process* method will then create a new append to the discussion database.

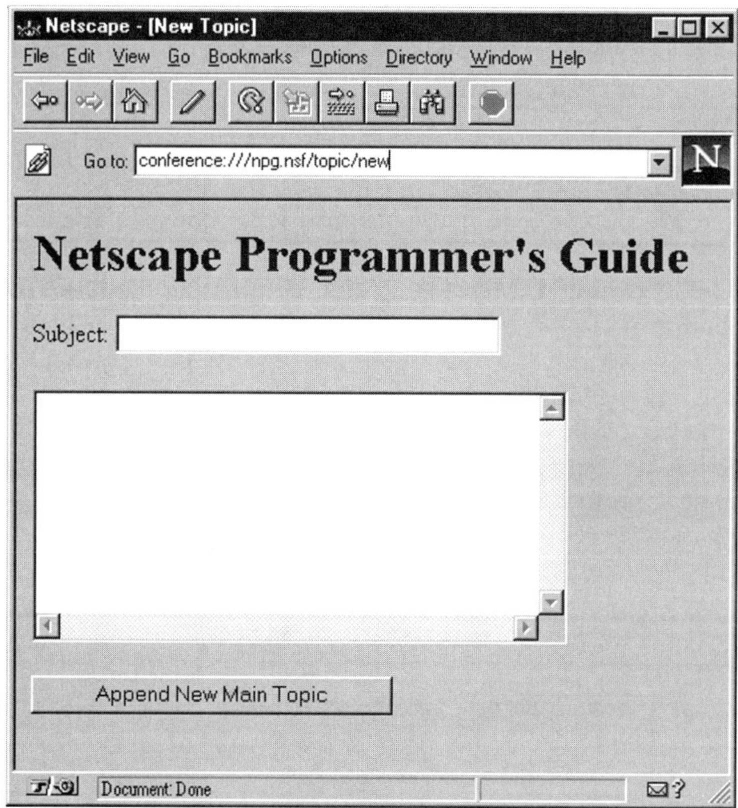

Figure 7.11.

Loading Files Using clsNetscapeLoader

The last part of the code we need to define for our Netscape discussion interface protocol handler is the OLE server for loading a file in the browser window. The code for this project is included in chap07\nsloader. It is based on code we developed in Chapter 4 for communicating with Netscape using DDE.

Recall that in Visual Basic, DDE communications requires a text box control. The following invisible form is defined to provide a control named *txtDDE*.

Figure 7.12.

The form is declared as a private variable in the *clsNetscape-Loader* class module. Instances of the form are loaded and unloaded when instances of the class are created and destroyed.

```
Option Explicit
Private myForm As New frmDDE

Private Sub Class_Initialize()
     myForm.txtDDE = ""
End Sub

Private Sub Class_Terminate()
     Unload myForm
     Set myForm = Nothing
End Sub
```

Two public interface methods are provided. The first one is called to tell Netscape to load a specific URL. You should recognize this code from Chapter 4. A Boolean variable is used to specify whether the URL should be opened in a new instance of a browser window.

```
Public Sub loadURL(url As String, _
newWindow As Boolean)
     ' loads a URL in a browser window
     Dim args As String, retstr As String
     Dim wid As Long

     ' get the URL to load
     args = Trim(url)
     If Len(args) = 0 Then Exit Sub
```

```
    ' see if user wants to open a new window or
    ' use the last active one
    If newWindow Then
        args = args & ",,0,1,,,"
    Else
        args = args & ",,0xFFFFFFFF,1,,,"
    End If

    ' set up the DDE call
    On Error Resume Next
    myForm.txtDDE.Text = ""
    myForm.txtDDE.LinkTopic = "NETSCAPE|WWW_OpenURL"
    myForm.txtDDE.LinkItem = args
    myForm.txtDDE.LinkMode = vbLinkManual
    myForm.txtDDE.LinkRequest
    myForm.txtDDE.LinkMode = vbLinkNone
End Sub
```

The second function explicitly loads a local file in the browser. This is accomplished by translating the filename into a file URL. For example,

```
c:/windows/temp/doc01.tmp
```

is converted to the corresponding local file URL

```
file:///c|/windows/temp/doc01.tmp
```

Once the file URL is constructed, *loadURL* is called to load it in the browser.

```
Public Sub loadFile(fname As String, newWindow As
Boolean)
    ' loads a file in the browser window
    Dim pos As Integer
    Dim transformed As String, url As String

    ' look for a colon and change it to |
```

```
    transformed = Trim(fname)
    pos = InStr(1, transformed, ":", 1)
    If pos <> 0 Then
        Mid(transformed, pos, 1) = "|"
    End If

    ' now prepend the file protocol to the filename
    url = "file:///" & transformed
    loadURL url, newWindow
End Sub
```

The corresponding *OLEDispatchInterface* for the NPG.clsNetscapeLoader OLE server is defined in nsloader.h. This code is used by the *Open* method of the protocol handler to display the file in Netscape that was generated by one of the *HTML-Document* derived classes.

```
class clsNetscapeLoader : public
                          OLEDispatchInterface {
public:
    // constructors and destructors
    clsNetscapeLoader(const char *progid =
                      "NPG.clsNetscapeLoader")
        : OLEDispatchInterface(progid) {}
    clsNetscapeLoader(IDispatch *dispatch)
        : OLEDispatchInterface(dispatch) {}

    virtual ~clsNetscapeLoader() {}

    // clsNetscapeLoader interface
    void loadURL(const char *url, bool newWindow)
    {
        method_twoargs(this, "loadURL", (int)0, url,
                       newWindow);
    }

    void loadFile(const char *url, bool newWindow)
    {
```

```
        method_twoargs(this, "loadFile", (int)0, url,
                       newWindow);
    }
};
```

Compiling the protocol handler and registering it with Netscape will allow you to test it with the sample database. Note that if you were not granted access to the Notes discussion database as a Notes user, and the discussion database was sitting on a Notes server, you would not be able to access the documents. Thus, secure access to the database is achieved while using the Netscape browser as a client-side Notes interface.

Summary

We introduced the OLE interface to Lotus Notes and wrote a sample Visual Basic program to access a Notes address book. A set of Visual Basic OLE objects were then written to provide a simple interface to Notes discussion databases. These client-side Notes interfaces were used inside a custom Netscape protocol handler. This illustrated how protocol handlers can be used to interface to Notes databases or any other database or program that provides a programming interface.

In the next chapter, we see how to extend Netscape to handle specialized MIME datatypes by installing MIME viewers.

Reference

1. Lotus Notes Release 4 Programmer's Guide, Part 1, Lotus Development Corp., Cambridge, MA, 1995.

Chapter 8

Custom MIME Viewers

Protocol handlers are not the only mechanism available for extending Netscape. We can also define custom streaming viewers for specific data formats. Each viewer recognizes and handles a specific MIME type. As with protocol handlers, you can define a custom viewer using either DDE[1] or OLE.[2]

This chapter defines a custom MIME type for a set of X,Y data points. A viewer for the data set is created using either Netscape's *WWW_RegisterViewer* DDE topic or the OLE server registration method *RegisterViewer*. Both viewer types then use Visual Basic's Graph control to display the data set when it is downloaded as part of an HTML document. As you might guess by now, the DDE example will be presented in Visual Basic and the OLE example will use a combination of Visual Basic and C++.

Defining a Data Type

We first need to set up a downloadable data file format to hold a set of X,Y data points. For the purposes of the examples in this chapter, we will define a data set format based on an ASCII file representation. As we will eventually use the Visual Basic Graph control to render the data, we might as well include a graph title, axis labels, and the type of graph to draw.

The following shows the contents of a sample data file, poisson.xy, included on the CD-ROM in chap08\xy:

```
Poisson Distribution
n
f(n)
4
9
0         .135
1         .271
2         .271
3         .180
4         .090
5         .036
6         .012
7         .003
8         .001
```

The first three lines of the data file are text strings. The first one is the title for the graph, and the next two are the X and Y axis labels, respectively. These correspond to the Graph control's *GraphTitle*, *BottomTitle*, and *LeftTitle*, respectively. The next line is a numeric value corresponding to the *GraphType*. Valid graph type values are given in the reference manual for the Graph control.[3] In this case, the value four denotes a 3D bar graph. The next line provides the number of X,Y data points in the data set. Each data point X,Y pair is then written on a separate line in the file.

We also need to provide a name for our custom data file format. This name is referred to as the MIME type of the data. We use this MIME type to register a viewer for this data type with Netscape. MIME type names generally have the form main/subtype. Some examples of common MIME types are text/html, video/mpeg, video/quicktime, and image/gif. You can see other examples by looking at Netscape's helper application list (under the General Preferences option on the menu bar). To avoid conflicts with other formats, we will refer to our data format as text/npgxy.

You can create the new MIME type from the helper application list page by providing the MIME main and subtypes. Then associate the new MIME type with files that have an xy extension.

DDE Viewers

Netscape's DDE interface provides the *WWW_RegisterViewer* topic for associating a MIME type with a custom viewer. The interface is quite similar to the *WWW_RegisterProtocol* topic covered in Chapter 6. Netscape acts as a DDE server for this topic, accepting the name of a DDE server, MIME type, and a flag value. The possible flag values are:

Flag value	Netscape action
1	data is saved in a temporary file and *ShellExecute* is called
2	get filename for data using *WWW_QueryViewer*
4	save data in a temporary file and use *WWW_ViewDocFile* topic
8	not supported

Using a flag value of 1 is not recommended because this leaves your computer unsecured from malicious intent. The only value used in the examples for this book is 4, so that the received data is stored in a temporary file. Netscape then uses the

WWW_ViewDocFile topic to inform the viewer (acting as a DDE server) where the data is stored.

Registering a DDE Viewer

The project chap08\ddeview\regview contains a Visual Basic program for registering a DDE server that acts as a MIME viewer. The form and code for this project are modified from the analogous project we created in Chapter 6 for registering protocol handlers.

The MIME viewer registration form asks for a MIME type and the name of the OLE server that will handle the DDE messages.

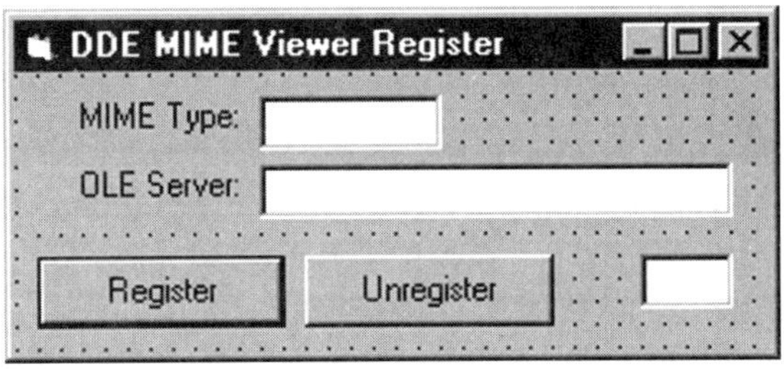

Figure 8.1.

Note that this form contains a *txtDDE* text box to handle the DDE communication with Netscape. The *pbRegister* pushbutton event handler first gets the MIME type and OLE server name from the *txtMIME* and *txtServer* text boxes:

```
Private Sub pbRegister_Click()
     Dim mime As String, oleServer As String
     ' make sure there is a protocol and OLE server
     ' specified
     mime = Trim(txtMIME.Text)
     oleServer = Trim(txtServer.Text)
     If (Len(mime) = 0) Or (Len(oleServer) = 0) _
     Then Exit Sub
```

As in the registration project for protocol handlers in Chapter 6, there is a private variable named *ddeServer* that is set up when the form is loaded. This variable holds an instance of the NPG.DDEServer OLE server we created in Chapter 4. This object is set up to pass Netscape's DDE request topic *WWW_ViewDocFile* to our new viewer object.

```
' set up object with service name and topics
' to handle
ddeServer.setNotifyObject oleServer
ddeServer.addTopic "WWW_ViewDocFile"
ddeServer.registerService "DDEnpgxy"
```

We call the *registerService* method with an argument of "DDEnpgxy" to set up the DDE server that Netscape actually communicates with. The server then passes the topics set by *addTopic* on to the OLE server we specify on the registration form. We will actually write this receiving OLE server object in the next section.

The registration is completed by sending the server name, MIME type, and flag value to Netscape using the *WWW_RegisterViewer* topic. All controls except *pbUnregister* are disabled to indicate a viewer registration is currently active.

```
' set up the DDE call
On Error GoTo Register_Error

txtDDE.Text = ""
txtDDE.LinkTopic = "NETSCAPE|WWW_RegisterViewer"
txtDDE.LinkItem = "DDEnpgxy," & mime & ",4"
txtDDE.LinkMode = vbLinkManual
txtDDE.LinkTimeout = 300      ' set timeout to
                              ' 30 seconds
txtDDE.LinkRequest
txtDDE.LinkMode = vbLinkNone

' enable controls
txtMIME.Enabled = False
txtServer.Enabled = False
pbRegister.Enabled = False
pbUnregister.Enabled = True
Exit Sub
```

```
Register_Error:
     MsgBox "A DDE Error occurred"
     LinkMode = vbLinkNone
End Sub
```

To remove a viewer from the active list, the *WWW_UnRegisterViewer* topic is used.

```
Private Sub pbUnregister_Click()
     ' set up the DDE call
     On Error GoTo Unregister_Error

     txtDDE.Text = ""
     txtDDE.LinkTopic = "NETSCAPE|WWW_UnRegisterViewer"
     txtDDE.LinkItem = "DDEnpgxy," & _
     Trim(txtMIME.Text)
     txtDDE.LinkMode = vbLinkManual
     txtDDE.LinkTimeout = 300      ' set timeout to
                                   ' 30 seconds
     txtDDE.LinkRequest
     txtDDE.LinkMode = vbLinkNone

     ' enable controls
     txtMIME.Enabled = True
     txtServer.Enabled = True
     pbRegister.Enabled = True
     pbUnregister.Enabled = False
     Exit Sub

Unregister_Error:
     MsgBox "A DDE Error occurred"
     LinkMode = vbLinkNone
End Sub
```

Writing the DDE Viewer

When a viewer is registered with the regview.exe program above, an association between a MIME type (text/npgxy) and an OLE server is formed. The server presented in this section is found in chap08\ddeview\dplotter. The server name is NPG.clsPlotter, and it implements the code for actually viewing data of the correct MIME type.

The sequence of events that actually triggers the server to display a view of some data file is as follows:

- A data file of MIME type text/npgxy is delivered to Netscape
- Netscape writes the data to a temporary file and communicates with the NPG.DDEServer object named DDEnpgxy by sending a *WWW_ViewDocFile* topic
- DDEnpgxy receives the XTYP_POKE topic from Netscape and calls the *DDEPoke* method of *clsPlotter*, passing it the temporary filename
- *clsPlotter* creates a new window, reads the data from the file, and graphs it

Thus, we need to create a public *clsPlotter* class module in the dplotter project. This module needs one public method named *DDEPoke*. Note that the *DDERequest* method is not needed because no DDE XTYP_REQUEST messages will be forwarded to this object.

```
Option Explicit

Public Function DDERequest(topic As String, _
                           item As String) _
                           As String
    ' no request topics for this server
    DDERequest = ""
End Function
```

DDEPoke simply checks that the topic being passed in is *WWW_ViewDocFile.*

```
Public Sub DDEPoke(topic As String, item As String, _
                  data As String)
     Dim fname As String
     Dim pos As Integer
     ' make sure this is a topic we are interested in
     If topic <> "WWW_ViewDocFile" Then Exit Sub
```

The *item* argument for this message contains the following comma delimited values:

```
filename, url, mimeType, windowID
```

The temporary filename containing the X,Y data is the value we are interested in, so this is extracted from the *item* string as follows:

```
     ' extract the filename from the item argument
     pos = InStr(1, item, ",", 1)
     fname = Mid$(item, 2, pos - 3)
```

To actually create a window and display a graph of the data in the file, a private method called *setupGraph* is called.

```
     ' and display the graph
     setupGraph fname
End Sub
```

This method is the last one in *clsPlotter*. It creates a new instance of a form named *frmGraph*. It then calls the form method *setDataFile* to pass the temporary filename to the new window.

```
Private Sub setupGraph(fname As String)
     Dim newGraph As frmGraph

     ' create a new graph form
     On Error Resume Next
     Set newGraph = New frmGraph
```

```
    ' hand the filename to the form and delete the
    ' reference
    newGraph.setDataFile fname
    Set newGraph = Nothing
End Sub
```

The *frmGraph* window is shown below. It is a standard form with a fixed dialog border style, and its *Visible* property is set to false. The form contains one Graph control, available as a standard custom control in the Professional Edition of Visual Basic.

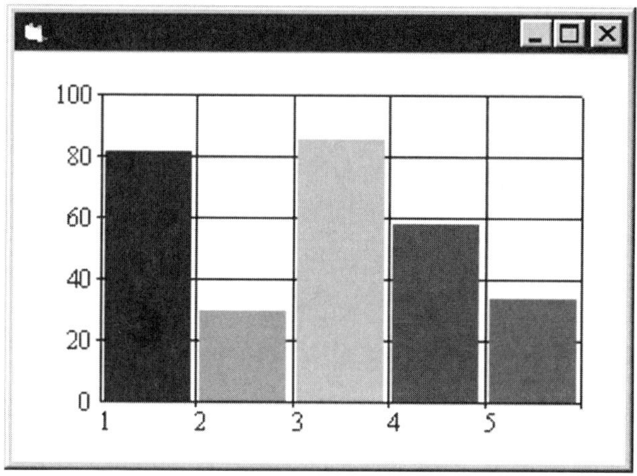

Figure 8.2.

The declarations section of the form contains a private variable that holds a unique file number. The *Form_Load* event also centers the form on the screen.

```
Option Explicit
Private filenum As Integer         ' open file number

Private Sub Form_Load()
    ' center the form
```

```
    Top = (Screen.Height - Height) / 2
    Left = (Screen.Width - Width) / 2
End Sub
```

The only public method required in the form module is *setDataFile*. This passes the filename containing the X,Y data to the window. This method subsequently opens the file using a unique file number. The private method *displayGraph* is called to read in the contents of the file and set up the *gGraph* Graph control. The whole form is then made visible and the file is closed.

```
Public Sub setDataFile(fname As String)
    ' open the file
    filenum = FreeFile
    Open fname For Input As #filenum

    ' show the graph
    displayGraph
    Show

    ' close the file
    Close #filenum
End Sub
```

The actual reading of the file is done is *displayGraph*. The three lines corresponding to the graph title and axis labels are read first. The window titlebar is set to the title text read from the file, and the corresponding *gGraph* properties are also set:

```
Private Sub displayGraph()
    Dim title As String, xlabel As String
    Dim ylabel As String
    Dim gtype As Integer, numpts As Integer,
    Dim i As Integer
    Dim x() As Single, y() As Single

    ' read the title and axis labels
    On Error Resume Next
```

```
With gGraph
     Line Input #filenum, title
     Line Input #filenum, xlabel
     Line Input #filenum, ylabel
     Caption = title      ' set the form caption
                          ' to the graph title
     .GraphTitle = title
     .BottomTitle = xlabel
     .LeftTitle = ylabel
```

Next, the graph type and number of data points are read. The *AutoInc* property is set to off, because the X values will be obtained directly from the file rather than auto-incremented.

```
     ' read the graph type and number of data
     ' points
     Input #filenum, gtype
     Input #filenum, numpts
     .AutoInc = 0
     .GraphType = gtype
     .NumPoints = numpts
```

Once the number of points is determined, the X and Y arrays can be dimensioned to the proper size. It is not necessary to store the X,Y data in arrays for this example, but you may want to modify this code for your own use.

```
     ' dimension the arrays and read in the X,Y
     ' data
     ReDim x(numpts) As Single
     ReDim y(numpts) As Single
```

Finally, each line containing the comma separated X,Y data pair is read and used to set the value of the current graph point.

```
     For i = 1 To numpts
          Input #filenum, x(i), y(i)
```

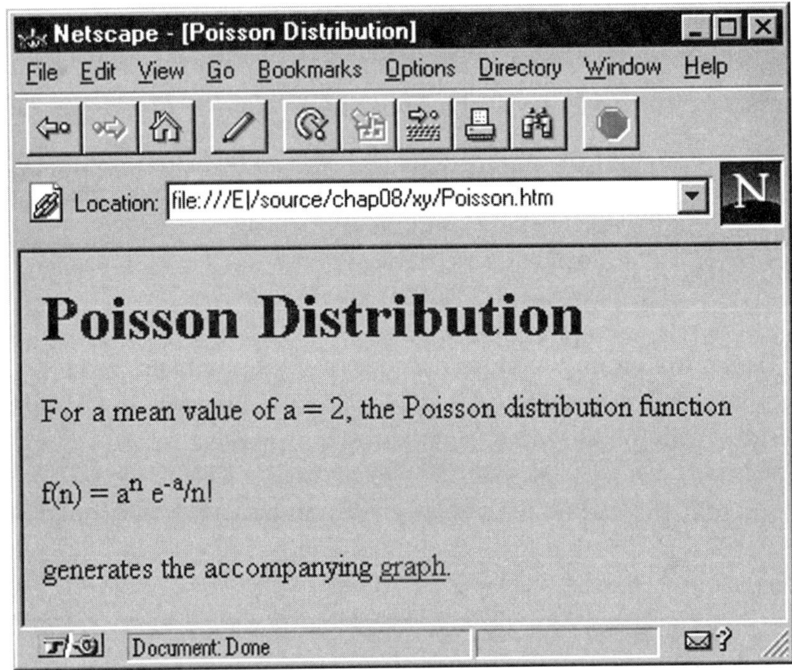

Figure 8.3.

```
                ' set x and y values for the current
                ' point
                .ThisPoint = i
                .XPosData = x(i)
                .GraphData = y(i)
        Next i
    End With
End Sub
```

Testing the X,Y Graph Viewer

To test our new viewer, both NPG.DDEServer (from Chapter 4) and the new NPG.clsPlotter OLE server must be registered with Windows (run each executable with the /r option from the command line). Then run the regview.exe program to associate the plotter with the new MIME type text/npgxy.

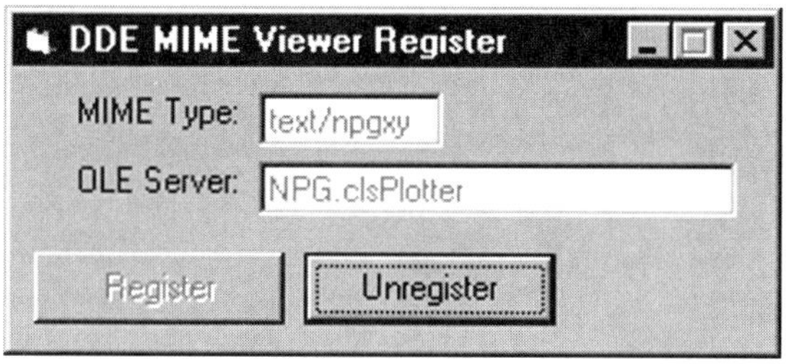

Figure 8.4.

Once the viewer is registered with Netscape, load the HTML file provided in chap08\xy into the Netscape browser. You should see a display similar to the one in Figure 8.5.

If we examine the HTML source for this page, we see an anchor link pointing to the file poisson.xy. Clicking on this link launches our custom viewer for the data in this file. The graph window for the data pops up in a separate window on top of the browser.

```
<html>
<head><title>Poisson Distribution</title></head>
<body>

<h1>Poisson Distribution</h1>
For a mean value of a = 2, the Poisson distribution
function<p>
f(n) = a<sup>n</sup> e<sup>-a</sup>/n!
<p>

generates the accompanying <a
href="poisson.xy">graph</a>.

</body>
</html>
```

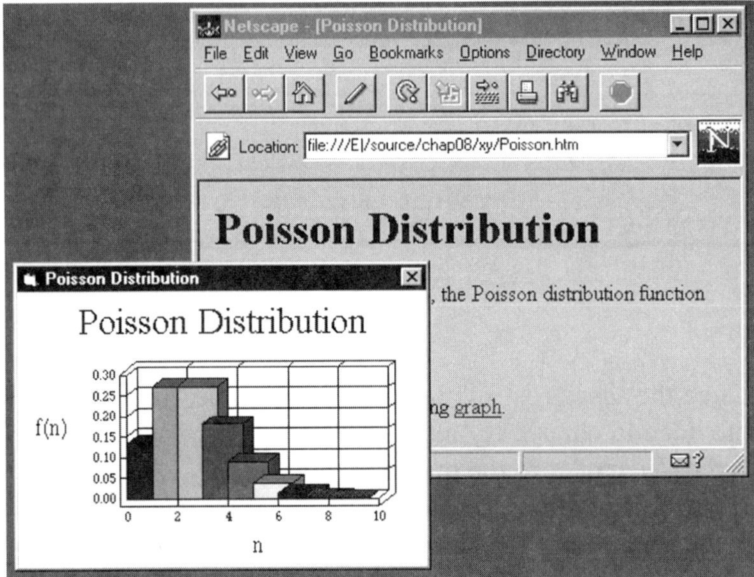

Figure 8.5.

OLE Viewers

Most of the same concerns over protocol handlers registered through DDE also apply to custom MIME viewers. A separate DDE server is required that must register itself with Netscape at runtime. This registration must be repeated if the programs are shut down and restarted.

Netscape once again comes to the rescue by providing an OLE Automation interface for registering a custom viewer implemented as an OLE server. In this section, we show how to register a custom OLE viewer by calling another function in Netscape.Registry.1. We also illustrate the C++ interface that any custom viewer must implement if it is registered through OLE.

An important advantage of a custom viewer implemented by OLE is that the data is streamed to the viewer in chunks. Thus, the viewer can begin processing the data for viewing before the complete data set is received.

Registering an OLE Viewer

An OLE server that acts as a MIME viewer must be registered with Netscape using the *RegisterViewer* API of Netscape.Registry.1. The form and code for this project, which can be found in chap08\oleview\oregview, are quite similar to the corresponding registration form and source code from chap06\oleexec\olereg. The form for the project contains two text boxes for entering the MIME type (*txtMIME*) and the OLE server ProgId (*txtServer*).

Figure 8.6.

The *pbRegister* click event handler first checks for valid entries of the MIME type and OLE server name:

```
Private Sub pbRegister_Click()
    Dim mime As String, oleServer As String
    Dim ns As Object
    Dim rc As Boolean

    ' make sure there is a MIME type and OLE
    ' server specified
    mime = Trim(txtMIME.Text)
    oleServer = Trim(txtServer.Text)
    If (Len(mime) = 0) Or (Len(oleServer) = 0) _
    Then Exit Sub
```

Next, an instance of the Netscape automation interface is created by calling *CreateObject*:

```
    ' create the Netscape.Registry object
    On Error GoTo Register_Error
    Set ns = CreateObject("Netscape.Registry.1")
    If ns Is Nothing Then GoTo Register_Error
```

Finally, the API function is called to install the viewer in Netscape for the corresponding MIME type. A message box is displayed to indicate whether the registration was completed successfully. If the registration was completed, the automation object is deleted and the program ends.

```
    ' register the viewer
    rc = ns.RegisterViewer(mime, oleServer)
    If Not rc Then GoTo Register_Error

    ' display message to user and end program
    MsgBox "The viewer was registered"
    Set ns = Nothing
    End

Register_Error:
    MsgBox "The viewer was not registered", _
    vbOKOnly + vbExclamation
    Set ns = Nothing

End Sub
```

Note that this registration needs to be done once. As in the olereg project of Chapter 6, there is no *pbUnregister* pushbutton because Netscape.Registry provides no function for unregistering an OLE viewer. You remove a viewer by directly editing the system registry key (using regedit.exe):

```
HKEY_CURRENT_USER/Software/Netscape/Netscape
Navigator/Automation Viewers
```

Suggested exercise 8–1 Write a program to unregister OLE viewers by editing the key value in the system registry.

Writing an OLE Viewer

Recall that writing an OLE protocol handler required us to define two functions: *Initialize* and *Open*. OLE MIME viewers require different functions to be exposed for Netscape to call. The prototypes of the four required functions are:

- **void Close(short status)**, used to inform the viewer that downloading of the data stream is complete. If *status* is zero, the stream was transferred successfully. A *status* of -1 indicates that the transfer was interrupted,
- **short Initialize(LPCTSTR mimeType, LPCTSTR url),** initializes the external streaming viewer to receive data of the specified MIME type from a given URL. The function should return one to indicate the viewer is ready, and zero if it fails to initialize.
- **long Ready(),** this method may be called several times by Netscape. It queries the viewer for the number of bytes of data the viewer is prepared to handle. If zero is returned, Netscape will retry the operation.
- **void Write(BSTR *data, long numBytes),** streams data stored in a BSTR to the viewer. The *numBytes* argument holds the number of valid bytes contained in the BSTR.

A sample MIME viewer implemented as an OLE server is included on the CD-ROM in chap08\oleview\oplotter. The source code was generated by mkoleobj, and the ProgId of the OLE server is NPG.Plotter.

The interface declaration in the oplotter.odl file must be modified to reflect the four exposed methods of our viewer. This example follows Netscape's OLE interface description in Reference 2.

```
interface IPlotter : IUnknown
    {
        // methods
        [
            helpstring("download is complete"),
            id(1)
        ]
        void Close([in] short status);

        [
            helpstring("Initializes the viewer"),
            id(2)
        ]
        short Initialize([in] BSTR mimeType, [in]
        BSTR url);

        [
            helpstring("Determines how much data to
                        handle"),
            id(3)
        ]
        long Ready();

        [
            helpstring("Streams data to the viewer"),
            id(4)
        ]
        void Write([in] BSTR *data,
                   [in] long numBytes);
    };
```

Once the ODL file is written, you should compile it with mktyplib to construct the oplotter.tlb type library.

We modify the iobject.h file to include our four viewer functions as pure virtual declarations:

```
// IPlotter methods
// Informs viewer that download is complete
virtual void STDMETHODCALLTYPE Close
   (short status) = 0;

// Initializes the viewer
virtual short STDMETHODCALLTYPE Initialize
   (BSTR mimeType,BSTR url) = 0;

// Query to determine how much data viewer can
// handle
virtual long STDMETHODCALLTYPE Ready() = 0;

// Streams data to the viewer
virtual void STDMETHODCALLTYPE Write
   (BSTR *data, long numBytes) = 0;
```

These declarations are also made in the public section of objimpl.h, with the pure virtual declarations removed. We also add the following two declarations to objimpl.h in the protected section. These variables hold a temporary filename and the file contents that will be written to the temporary file.

```
protected:

   string tempFilename;   // temporary filename
   string fileContents;   // data provided by
                          // Netscape
```

We now cover the implementation of the four required viewer methods. The first one called by Netscape is *Initialize*. Our example implementation creates a temporary filename and stores it in the *tempFilename* member of the object. The *fileContents* are then set to an empty string and a one is returned to indicate the viewer is ready.

```
// Initialize - Initializes the viewer
short STDMETHODCALLTYPE
myImplOfPlotter::Initialize(BSTR, BSTR)
{
    // create a temporary filename
    char fpath[MAX_PATH], fname[MAX_PATH];

    GetTempPath(MAX_PATH, fpath);
    GetTempFileName(fpath, "xy", 0, fname);
    tempFilename = string(fname);

    // set up the contents string
    fileContents = string("");
    return 1;
}
```

Once the viewer is initialized, Netscape begins downloading the data in chunks. Netscape calls the *Ready* method to determine how many bytes of data the viewer can handle in one chunk. This method may be called any number of times, depending on the size of the data. In this example, we simply return an arbitrary number to Netscape because we are not doing any processing of partial streams of data. Rather, the data is just accepted by the Write method and stored in the *fileContents* string.

```
// Ready - Query to determine how much data viewer
//         can handle
long STDMETHODCALLTYPE myImplOfPlotter::Ready()
{
    return 8192L;
}
```

Netscape calls the *Write* method for each chunk of data available. The data is passed in as a BSTR, along with a *numBytes* parameter indicating how many valid bytes of data are contained in the stream. A simple loop adds each data byte to the *fileContents* string.

```
// Write - Streams data to the viewer
void STDMETHODCALLTYPE myImplOfPlotter::Write
     (BSTR *data, long numBytes)
{
    // make sure there is data
    if (numBytes <= 0)
        return;

    // get data from BSTR and append to the contents
    // string
    char *sb = (char *)(*data);
    char c;

    for (long i = 0; i < numBytes; i++) {
        c = *sb++;
        fileContents += c;
    }
}
```

If the data transfer is interrupted for any reason, Netscape calls the viewer's *Close* method with a *status* value of -1. If the *status* is zero, the downloading is complete. Thus, the start of the *Close* method code is:

```
// Close - Informs viewer that download is complete
void STDMETHODCALLTYPE myImplOfPlotter::Close
   (short status)
{
    // check status
    if (status == -1)
        return;  // download was not completed
```

At this point in development, I found that Netscape had appended an extra carriage return to the carriage return/line feed sequences of the downloaded data. Therefore, I simply stripped out the "\r" characters from the string before writing the entire string to the new temporary file.

```
    // remove extra CR from CRCRLF sequence
    size_t pos = 0;

    while ( ( pos = fileContents.find("\r") ) !=
            os_npos )
        fileContents.remove(pos, 1);
```

The *tempFilename* variable is used to create an output file stream, and the *fileContents* are written to the new file.

```
    // write the file
    {
        ofstream fout( tempFilename.c_str() );
        if (!fout)
            return;

        fout << fileContents.c_str() << endl;
    }
```

To complete the current OLE viewer, we will reuse the NPG.clsPlotter object created in the section on DDE viewers. This NPG.clsPlotter OLE object displays a graph of a filename provided through the *DDEPoke* method. Thus, the following code creates an instance of the object and simulates a DDE topic call to pass in the filename of the data to graph.

```
    // create a clsPlotter interface and call DDE
    // Poke to invoke the graph viewer window
    clsPlotter plotter;

    string s = string("\"") + tempFilename +
                                string("\", ");
    plotter.DDEPoke("WWW_ViewDocFile",
                    s.c_str(), "");
}
```

All we need to complete our viewer is the C++ interface to call the clsPlotter OLE object (written in Visual Basic). Of course, this means using the trusty *OLEDispatchInterface* base class:

```
class clsPlotter : public OLEDispatchInterface {
public:
    // constructors and destructors
    clsPlotter(const char *progid = "NPG.clsPlotter")
        : OLEDispatchInterface(progid) {}
    clsPlotter(IDispatch *dispatch)
        : OLEDispatchInterface(dispatch) {}

    virtual ~clsPlotter() {}

    // clsPlotter interface
    void DDEPoke(const char *topic,
                 const char *item, const char *data)
    {
        method_threeargs(this, "DDEPoke", (int)0,
                         topic, item, data);
    }
};
```

Once this code has been compiled as a DLL, you should register the OLE server with Windows using the regsvr32. Then the oregview program can be used to register NPG.Plotter as a text/npgxy viewer with Netscape.

Testing the OLE Viewer

Another HTML file and associated xy data file is provided in chap08\xy. This data is intended to provide a scatter plot example (which has a *GraphType* of 9). Clicking on the link in the HTML file provides the following display of the browser window and associated graph.

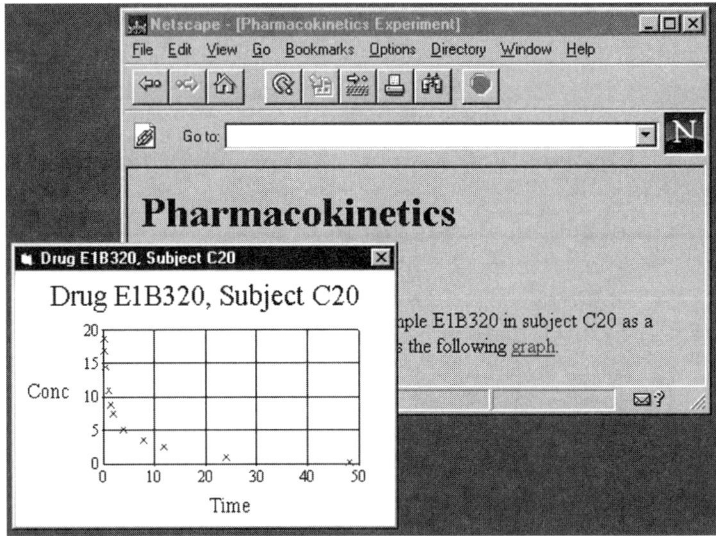

Figure 8.7.

Summary

In this chapter, custom viewers for new MIME types were introduced. Both DDE and OLE were used to register viewers with Netscape. We also wrote general registration programs that tell Netscape to associate a MIME type with a viewer.

We have now extended the Netscape browser using both custom protocol handlers and custom MIME viewers. Combining these techniques with the methods we developed earlier for controlling the browser provides powerful tools for constructing applications. In the next chapter, we look at the new Netscape API for creating plug-ins. The plug-in specification allows us to write a custom viewer for some form of data, but the browser itself provides a window for rendering the data.

References

1. For DDE: Netscape Communications Corporation, http://home.netscape.com/newsref/std/ddeapi.html
2. For OLE: Netscape Communications Corporation, http://home.netscape.com/newsref/std/oleapi.html
3. Custom Control Reference, Microsoft Visual Basic Professional Edition, Microsoft Corporation, Redmond, WA, 1995.

Chapter 9

Netscape Plug-ins

Plug-ins are a very hot extension technology for adding functionality to Netscape Navigator. Plug-ins are used for a variety of purposes: playing multimedia movies, showing slide presentations, loading OLE components, etc. Visit the Netscape home page[1] for a comprehensive list of vendors supplying plug-ins. Many books on using Netscape also describe some of the available plug-ins, and how to install and use them.

Plug-ins can be written for the Windows, UNIX, and Macintosh versions of Netscape, using each platform's native shared library and window APIs. In the Windows environment, plug-ins are simply DLLs that export a specific set of functions that the Netscape browser calls. In addition, Netscape defines a second set of APIs that a plug-in can use in turn to access specific browser functionality.

In this chapter, we explore the plug-in API, and write our own plug-in to load applications written in Visual Basic. This plug-in allows you to write your own Visual Basic forms that can be loaded directly in the browser window. These client side applets are similar to downloaded Java applets that run inside a browser. But, they are written as Visual Basic OLE objects and installed on the local client. These trusted client applets can carry out any operation available in Visual Basic, including reading and writing disk files, accessing databases, and calling functions in other DLLs or OLE servers. Try doing that with a Java applet!

Plug-in Capabilities

The Netscape plug-in API and documentation is available on the network.[2] A summary of the functions is provided in Appendix C. Netscape's current plug-in API for Windows allows you to write a plug-in to do any of the following operations:

- Register a MIME type
- Draw text, graphics, and controls in the Navigator window
- Receive keyboard and mouse events
- Request a URL from the network
- Post data to a URL
- Add a hyperlink or hotspot that links to a URL

The actual plug-in window can either be an embedded child window in the browser, or a full size client window of the Netscape window.

In the rest of this chapter, we will develop our own plug-in in C++. This plug-in will accept a custom MIME data file that contains the ProgId name of an OLE server. If that OLE server is installed on the client machine, an instance of the named server will be instantiated. Most plug-ins provide a single user interface that allows operations on data of a particular type. Our plug-in will load any OLE server we can create. For illustration, we will write several completely different OLE servers using Visual Basic and have them instantiated by the plug-in. Our single plug-in thus provides a way to embed many different kinds of user interface and functionality in the Netscape browser.

Writing a Plug-in

Once you download the plug-in API from Netscape and unpack the files, a new plug-in project can be started. See the example included on the CD-ROM in chap09\npoleobj. Note that the source code of this example has been modified to compile with Borland's C++ compiler. Netscape's examples all use Visual C++.

Defining the MIME Type

The first thing to define for a new plug-in is the MIME type of the data it will support. This is done in the resource file for the project. In the following example, npoleobj.rc contains the resource definitions for a MIME type of npo/ole-plug-in. Files with the extension npo will then be handled by our new plug-in.

```
// npoleobj.rc
VS_VERSION_INFO VERSIONINFO
    FILEVERSION 1,0,0,1
    PRODUCTVERSION 1,0,0,1
    FILEFLAGSMASK 0x3fL
    FILEFLAGS 0x0L
    FILEOS 0x4L
    FILETYPE 0x2L
    FILESUBTYPE 0x0L
    BEGIN
    BLOCK "StringFileInfo"
        BEGIN
        BLOCK "040904e4"
            BEGIN
                VALUE "CompanyName", "NPG\0"
                VALUE "FileDescription", "NPOLEOBJ
Plugin DLL\0"
```

```
            VALUE "FileExtents", "npo\0"
            VALUE "FileOpenName", "Netscape Plugin
                                   OLE server
                                   (*.npo)\0"
            VALUE "FileVersion", "1, 0, 0, 1\0"
            VALUE "InternalName", "NPOLEOBJ\0"
            VALUE "LegalCopyright", "Copyright NPG
                                     \251 1996\0"
            VALUE "MIMEType", "npo/ole-plugin\0"
            VALUE "OriginalFilename",
                   "NPOLEOBJ.DLL\0"
            VALUE "ProductName", "NPOLEOBJ Dynamic
                                  Link Library\0"
            VALUE "ProductVersion", "1, 0, 0, 1\0"
        END
    END
    BLOCK "VarFileInfo"
    BEGIN
        VALUE "Translation", 0x409, 1252
    END
END
```

The "FileExtents" and "MIMEType" values should be modified with the file extension and MIME types handled by the plug-in. The "OriginalFilename" should also be set to the DLL containing the plug-in functions.

The Module Definition File

The plug-in DLL must start with the letters "np" and reside in the Netscape \program\plug-ins directory when Netscape is first started. Netscape loads each DLL at startup to query its MIME type information and the addresses of each plug-in's exported functions. The Navigator calls three standard functions that the module definition file for the DLL must export: *NP_GetEntryPoints*, *NP_Initialize*, and *NP_Shutdown*. Implementations of these three functions are already provided in Netscape's npwin.cpp module.

```
; npoleobj.def
LIBRARY NPOLEOBJ

CODE PRELOAD MOVEABLE DISCARDABLE
DATA PRELOAD SINGLE

EXPORTS
    NP_GetEntryPoints    @1
    NP_Initialize        @2
    NP_Shutdown          @3
```

Setting up the Project

The Borland project file should point to the \include and \lib directories where you installed the plug-in API. The npshell.cpp and npwin.cpp modules from the \sample\shell directory should also be copied to the new project directory. Then you can compile the plug-in module to create npoleobj.dll.

The npwin.C module included on the CD-ROM and used in the plug-in project is a modified version of npwin.cpp. The modified version compiles cleanly with Borland C++. Changes include adding extern "C" declarations to the functions, and fixing a couple of calls to *sizeof* that did not compile correctly. In addition, the following declaration was added at the top of the module:

```
HINSTANCE hinstDLL = (HINSTANCE)0;
```

Inside *DllEntryPoint*, this global variable is set to the instance handle of the DLL module:

```
// DllEntryPoint - handles DLL initialization and
//                 termination
extern "C"
BOOL WINAPI DllEntryPoint(HINSTANCE hinst,
                          DWORD fdwReason, LPVOID)
{
    // save module handle
    hinstDLL = hinst;
```

```
    switch (fdwReason) {
        case DLL_PROCESS_ATTACH:
        case DLL_THREAD_ATTACH:
        case DLL_PROCESS_DETACH:
        case DLL_THREAD_DETACH:
            break;
    }

    return TRUE;
}
```

To finish writing our plug-in, we make modifications to npshell.cpp. For this project, the module is renamed to npoleobj.C. Our modifications will be rather extensive, so the next section shows the complete source code for the module.

The npoleobj Module

A data structure is associated with each plug-in instance, and this structure is declared at the top of npoleobj.C as:

```
// instance state information about the plugin
typedef struct _PluginInstance {
    NPWindow *fWindow;
    HWND hWnd;
    uint16 fMode;
    FARPROC lpfnOldWndProc;
    NPSavedData *pSavedInstanceData;
} PluginInstance;
```

Custom plug-ins typically subclass the plug-in window provided by Netscape in order to intercept and process some standard Windows messages. These messages include WM_PAINT and WM_QUERYPALETTE. But to process these messages, the subclassed window procedure needs access to the *PluginInstance* data structure.

Netscape did not create any extra bytes in defining the plug-in window class. Thus, there is no place in the window class to store information that associates a particular plug-in window to the instance data structure. So the plug-in API added a field to the *Plug-inInstance* structure to allow the structure to be used as part of a linked list. There is also a global variable named *g_pHeadInstanceList* and two additional functions declared in npshell.cpp to manage the linked list. These functions are named *AssociateInstance* and *GetInstance.*

We will use another technique to associate the plug-in instance data with its corresponding plug-in window. Thus, our data structure does not need the extra field, nor do we need to include the linked list manager functions or global variable. The technique we will use in our plug-in is covered a bit later.

For our plug-in to create instances of OLE servers, it must call *CoInitialize.* This can be done once when the DLL is loaded in the *NPP_New* function that Netscape calls. A global flag named *oleInitialized* is set if the initialization succeeds.

```
#include <ole2.h>

// global variable indicating whether OLE was
// initialized
int oleInitialized = 0;

// NPP_Initialize - one time initialization of the
//                  plugin
extern "C" NPError NPP_Initialize()
{
    // initialize COM
    if ( FAILED( CoInitialize(0) ) )
        return NPERR_MODULE_LOAD_FAILED_ERROR;

    oleInitialized = 1;
    return NPERR_NO_ERROR;
}
```

Netscape calls the termination routine *NPP_Shutdown* when there are no more instances of the plug-in loaded by the browser.

This is a good place to call *CoUninitialize.*

```
// NPP_Shutdown - termination function called after
//                all instances of the plugin are
//                deleted
extern "C" void NPP_Shutdown()
{
    // terminate COM
    if (oleInitialized) {
        CoUninitialize();
        oleInitialized = 0;
    }
}
```

Netscape's new LiveConnect specification describes how to communicate among plug-ins, Java, and JavaScript programs. We will not use this feature for the npoleobj plug-in, but npwin.C calls a function named *NPP_GetJavaClass* to facilitate this communication, so we define it here.

```
// NPP_GetJavaClass - gets the Java class associated
//                    with the plugin
extern "C" jref NPP_GetJavaClass()
{
    return 0;
}
```

When Netscape encounters data with a MIME type of npo/ole-plug-in, it loads and initializes npoleobj.dll. After the DLL is initialized, Netscape calls the plug-in's *NPP_New* function to create a new instance of the plug-in for the current browser window. This function is passed the MIME type, so a plug-in can support more than one MIME type if desired. It also passes in an NPP instance pointer that uniquely identifies the new instance.

To store our *Plug-inInstance* data structure, Netscape's *NPN_MemAlloc* API function is called to allocate memory for the structure. The *instance->pdata* field holds the data structure so other plug-in functions can access it. The mode denotes whether the plug-in is:

- Drawn in a child window of the current page (NP_EMBED)
- Drawn using the entire Netscape window client area (NP_FULL)
- Invisible (NP_BACKGROUND)

```
// NPP_New - creates a new plugin instance
extern "C" NPError NP_LOADDS NPP_New
           (NPMIMEType pluginType, NPP instance,
            uint16 mode, int16 argc, char *argn[],
            char *argv[], NPSavedData *saved)
{
    if (!instance)
        return NPERR_INVALID_INSTANCE_ERROR;

    instance->pdata = NPN_MemAlloc(
                          sizeof(PluginInstance) );
    PluginInstance* This =
          (PluginInstance *)instance->pdata;
    if (!This)
        return NPERR_OUT_OF_MEMORY_ERROR;

    // *Developers*: Initialize fields of your plugin
    // instance data here.  If the NPSavedData is
    // Nnon-ULL, you can use that data (returned by
    // you from NPP_Destroy) to set up the new
    // plugin instance.
    This->fWindow = 0;

    // mode is NP_EMBED, NP_FULL, or NP_BACKGROUND
    // (see npapi.h)
    This->fMode = mode;
    This->hWnd = 0;
    This->pSavedInstanceData = saved;
```

```
    return NPERR_NO_ERROR;
}
```

Any name-value pair tags included in an HTML <EMBED> tag are also passed to this function for handling. If a previous instance of the plug-in stored data that can be used by the current instance, the data is made available through the *saved* parameter.

The *NPP_Destroy* function is called to destroy an instance of the plug-in created by Netscape and initialized by calling *NPP_New*. However, we defer looking at the code for *NPP_Destroy* until we examine the next function, *NPP_SetWindow*.

NPP_SetWindow is called to provide the plug-in DLL with the window handle of a child window that Netscape creates inside the browser. This function is also called when the child window is moved or resized, to give the plug-in a chance to update itself in response to browser window operations. Inside *NPP_SetWindow*, the *PluginInstance* data structure associated with a particular plug-in *instance* is retrieved into the variable *This*.

```
// NPP_SetWindow - handles a new or resized plugin
//                 window
extern "C" NPError NP_LOADDS NPP_SetWindow
                   (NPP instance, NPWindow *window)
{
    if (!instance)
        return NPERR_INVALID_INSTANCE_ERROR;

    PluginInstance *This = (PluginInstance *)
                           instance->pdata;

    // *Developers*: Before setting fWindow to point
    // to the
    // new window, you may wish to compare the new
    // window
    // info to the previous window (if any) to note
    // window
    // size changes, etc.
```

An *NPWindow* pointer is passed as a parameter to this function, and it is examined to determine how to process the window. If no window handle is currently saved for this plug-in instance and the *NPWindow* structure contains one, this is a new child window. The handle of the child is saved in *This->hWnd*, and the child window is subclassed by calling *SetWindowLong*. We pass in the address of a window function (*SubClassFunc*) defined later in the npoleobj.C module. Subclassing allows our window function to process window messages first, before passing them on to the child window.

```
if ( (window->window) && (!This->hWnd) ) {
    This->fWindow = window;
    This->hWnd = (HWND)(DWORD)
                 This->fWindow->window;

    // subclass the window
    This->lpfnOldWndProc = (WNDPROC)
        SetWindowLong(This->hWnd,
        GWL_WNDPROC, (DWORD)SubClassFunc);
    SetProp(This->hWnd, "npoleobj.instancedata",
            (HANDLE)This);
}
```

Note the call to *SetProp* after the window has been subclassed. This associates a user-defined property named "npoleobj.instancedata" with the plug-in window. The value of the property is set to be the pointer to the *PluginInstance* structure. Thus, we avoid using the linked list functions originally defined in the plug-in API and still do not use any extra bytes defined for window-specific data (which may not be available).

To be fair, this property technique only works with 32 bit Windows applications. So Netscape's linked list solution is probably more general, but arguably not as elegant.

The other case arises if the currently saved window handle does not match the new one specified in *window->window*. In this case, the new window is saved and the user-defined property is removed from the old window by calling *RemoveProp*. The window subclass is removed by calling *SetWindowLong*, passing in the address of the original window procedure saved in *lpfnOld-WndProc*.

```
    else {
        // if window handle changed
        if (This->hWnd != (HWND)(DWORD)
                        window->window) {
            // remember the new window
            This->fWindow = window;

            // remove the subclass for the old client
            // window
            RemoveProp(This->hWnd,
                    "npoleobj.instancedata");
            SetWindowLong(This->hWnd, GWL_WNDPROC,
                        (DWORD)This->lpfnOldWndProc);
```

The new window must be subclassed, so its handle is saved and it is subclassed as above using *SetWindowLong* and *SetProp*.

```
            // remember the new window handle
            This->hWnd = (HWND)(DWORD)
                        This->fWindow->window;

            if (This->hWnd) {
                // subclass the new one
                This->lpfnOldWndProc =
                (WNDPROC)SetWindowLong(This->hWnd,
                    GWL_WNDPROC, (DWORD)SubClassFunc);
                SetProp(This->hWnd,
                        "npoleobj.instancedata",
                        (HANDLE)This);
            }
        }
    }

    return NPERR_NO_ERROR;
}
```

Now that we see how the window property associates a window handle with a corresponding *PluginInstance* structure, we can write *NPP_Destroy*. This function examines the structure for a valid window handle. If there is a window handle, the property and the subclass of the window are removed.

```
// NPP_Destroy - destroys a plugin instance
extern "C" NPError NP_LOADDS NPP_Destroy
                    (NPP instance,
                     NPSavedData **save)
{
    if (!instance)
        return NPERR_INVALID_INSTANCE_ERROR;

    PluginInstance *This = (PluginInstance *)
    instance->pdata;

    // *Developers*: If desired, call NP_MemAlloc to
    // create a
    // NPSavedData structure containing any state
    // information
    // that you want restored if this plugin
    // instance is later
    // recreated.
    if (This) {
        // remove the subclass for the client window
        if (This->hWnd) {
            RemoveProp(This->hWnd,
            "npoleobj.instancedata");
            SetWindowLong(This->hWnd, GWL_WNDPROC,
                          (DWORD)This->lpfnOldWndProc);
        }
```

The rest of the function is the same as in the plug-in API example. If you want to save data associated with this instance, it is done by allocating memory with *NPN_MemAlloc* and copying the data to an *NPSavedData* structure.

```
        // make some saved instance data if
        // necessary
        if (!This->pSavedInstanceData) {
            // make a struct header for the data
            This->pSavedInstanceData = (NPSavedData *)
                                        NPN_MemAlloc(
                sizeof(NPSavedData) );

            // fill in the struct
            if (This->pSavedInstanceData) {
                This->pSavedInstanceData->len = 0;
                This->pSavedInstanceData->buf = 0;

                // replace the def below and
                // references to it with your data
                #define SIDATA "aSavedInstanceDataBlock"

                // the data
                This->pSavedInstanceData->buf =
                NPN_MemAlloc(sizeof SIDATA);

                if (This->pSavedInstanceData->buf) {
                    strcpy( (char *)
                    This->pSavedInstanceData->buf,
                    SIDATA );
                    This->pSavedInstanceData->len =
                        sizeof(SIDATA);
                }
            }
        }

        // save some instance data
        *save = This->pSavedInstanceData;

        NPN_MemFree(instance->pdata);
        instance->pdata = 0;
    }
```

```
    return NPERR_NO_ERROR;
}
```

The next function, *NPP_NewStream*, is called by the browser to inform the plug-in that there is a new data stream. In our case, we want the whole data file at once rather than receiving the file a piece at a time. Therefore, we set the return value of *stype* to NP_ASFILE. Netscape will stream the data to a local data file and call another function to let the plug-in know in what file the new data resides.

```
// NPP_NewStream - informs plugin of a new stream
//                 of data
extern "C" NPError NP_LOADDS NPP_NewStream
                   (NPP instance, NPMIMEType type,
                    NPStream *stream,
                    NPBool seekable, uint16 *stype)
{
    if (!instance)
        return NPERR_INVALID_INSTANCE_ERROR;

    pluginInstance *This = (pluginInstance *)
                           instance->pdata;
    *stype = NP_ASFILE;

    return NPERR_NO_ERROR;
}
```

The next few functions are copied more or less verbatim from the plug-in API. There are some minor formatting changes, and extern "C" declarations have been added so the functions will compile with Borland C++. These functions are not used in our npoleobj.C plug-in, so we do not cover them in detail here. Look at the descriptions of the functions in Appendix C for more details.

```
// *Developers*:
// These next 2 functions are directly relevant in
// a plugin
```

```
// which handles the data in a streaming manner.
// If you want
// zero bytes because no buffer space is YET
// available,
// return 0.  As long as the stream has not been
// written to
// the plugin, Navigator will continue trying to
// send bytes.
// If the plugin doesn't want them, just return
// some large
// number from NPP_WriteReady(), and ignore them in
// NPP_Write().  For a NP_ASFILE stream, they are
// still called
// but can safely be ignored using this strategy.
int32 STREAMBUFSIZE = 0x0fffffff;   // If we are
                                    // reading from
                                    // a file in
                                    // NP_ASFILE
                                    // mode, we can
                                    // take any
                                    // size stream
                                    // in our
                                    // write call
                                    // (since we
                                    // ignore it)

// ---------------------------------------------

// NPP_WriteReady -  queries the plugin for the
//                   number of  bytes of data it is
//                   ready to handle
extern "C" int32 NP_LOADDS NPP_WriteReady(
NPP instance, NPStream *stream)
{
    if (instance)
        PluginInstance *This = (PluginInstance *)
                                 instance->pdata;
    return STREAMBUFSIZE;
}
```

```
// ------------------------------------------------

// NPP_Write - data is written to the plugin
extern "C" int32 NP_LOADDS NPP_Write(NPP instance,
NPStream *stream, int32 offset, int32 len,
void *buffer)
{
    if (instance)
        PluginInstance *This = (PluginInstance *)
                                 instance->pdata;
    return len;    // The number of bytes accepted.
                   // Return a
                   // negative number here if, e.g.,
                   // there was
                   // an error during plugin
                   // operation and you
                   // want to abort thestream
}

// ------------------------------------------------

// NPP_DestroyStream - informs plugin that a stream
//                     is being destroyed
extern "C" NPError NP_LOADDS NPP_DestroyStream
                   (NPP instance, NPStream *stream,
                    NPError reason)
{
    if (!instance)
        return NPERR_INVALID_INSTANCE_ERROR;

    PluginInstance *This = (PluginInstance *)
    instance->pdata;
    return NPERR_NO_ERROR;
}

// ------------------------------------------------

// NPP_Print - requests that the plugin print
//             itself
```

```
extern "C" void NP_LOADDS NPP_Print(NPP instance,
NPPrint *printInfo)
{
    if (!printInfo)    // trap invalid parm
        return;

    if (instance) {
        PluginInstance* This = (PluginInstance*)
                                 instance->pdata;

        if (printInfo->mode == NP_FULL) {
            // *Developers*: If your plugin would
            // like to take
            // over printing completely when it is in
            // full-
            // screen mode, set printInfo->plugin-
            // Printed to
            // TRUE and print your plugin as you see
            // fit.  If
            // your plugin wants Netscape to handle
            // printing in
            // this case, set printInfo->pluginPrint-
            // ed to FALSE
            // (the default) and do nothing.  If you
            // do want
            // to handle printing yourself, printOne
            // is true if
            // the print button (as opposed to the
            // print menu)
            // was clicked. On the Macintosh,
            // platformPrint
            // is a THPrint; on Windows,
            // platformPrint is a
            // structure (defined in npapi.h)
            // containing the
            // printer name, port, etc.
            void *platformPrint =
            printInfo->print.fullPrint.platformPrint;
```

```
        NPBool printOne =
        printInfo->print.fullPrint.printOne;
        printInfo->print.fullPrint.pluginPrinted =
        FALSE;
    } else {      // if not fullscreen, we must
                  // be embedded
        // *Developers*: If your plugin is
        // embedded, or is
        // full-screen but you returned false in
        // plugin
        // Printed above, NPP_Print will be
        // called with
        // mode == NP_EMBED.  The NPWindow in the
        // printInfo
        // gives the location and dimensions of
        // the
        // embedded plugin on the printed page.
        // On the
        // Macintosh, platformPrint is the
        // printer port; on
        // Windows, platformPrint is the handle to
        // the
        // printing device context.
        NPWindow *printWindow =
           &(printInfo->print.embedPrint.window);
        void *platformPrint =
            printInfo->print.embedPrint.platform-
            Print;

        // initialize the pen's "brush"
        LOGBRUSH lb;

        lb.lbStyle = BS_SOLID;
        lb.lbColor = RGB(128, 128, 128);
        lb.lbHatch = 0;
```

```
            HPEN hPen = ExtCreatePen(PS_COSMETIC |
                                     PS_SOLID, 1,
                                     &lb, 0, 0);
            HDC hDC = (HDC)(DWORD)platformPrint;
            HPEN hPenOld = (HPEN)SelectObject(hDC,
            hPen);
            BOOL result = Rectangle( hDC,
                               (int)(printWindow->x),
                (int)(printWindow->y),
                (int)(printWindow->x + printWindow-
                     >width),
                (int)(printWindow->y + printWindow-
                     >height) );
            SelectObject(hDC, hPenOld);
            DeleteObject(hPen);
        }
    }
}
```

The final function that Netscape calls in the plug-in DLL is *NPP_StreamAsFile*. This is called to let the plug-in know the filename of the data received from the given stream. This function is called for npoleobj because we returned an *stype* of NP_ASFILE in the *NPP_NewStream* function above.

```
// NPP_StreamAsFile - provides the filename for data
//                    coming from a stream
extern "C" void NP_LOADDS NPP_StreamAsFile
                (NPP instance, NPStream *stream,
                 const char *fname)
{
    if (!instance)
        return;

    PluginInstance *This = (PluginInstance *)
instance->pdata;
}
```

The last thing to define for our general plug-in is the window function that we used above to subclass the child window provided by the browser. This is a simply a standard window function. To access the *Plug-inInstance* data structure, the *GetProp* function is called to get the property associated with the window.

```
#define BACKGROUND_COLOR RGB(0, 0, 255)

// SubClassFunc - subclass window function
extern "C" DWORD NP_LOADDS WINAPI SubClassFunc
                 (HWND hWnd, WORD Message,
                  WORD wParam, DWORD lParam)
{
    // get the instance data associated with this
    // window
    PluginInstance *This = (PluginInstance *)
    GetProp(hWnd, "npoleobj.instancedata");
```

Two messages are intercepted: WM_PALETTECHANGED and WM_PAINT. For now, these functions just update the child window, painting a blue rectangle where the browser places the embedded child window:

```
    switch (Message) {
        case WM_PALETTECHANGED:
            InvalidateRect(hWnd, 0, TRUE);
            UpdateWindow(hWnd);
            return 0;

        case WM_PAINT:
            {
                PAINTSTRUCT paint;

                HDC hDC = BeginPaint(hWnd, &paint);
                HBRUSH hBrush = CreateSolidBrush
                                (BACKGROUND_COLOR);
                HBRUSH hBrushOld = (HBRUSH)
                                   SelectObject
                                   (hDC, hBrush);
```

```
                FillRect(hDC, &paint.rcPaint, hBrush);
                SelectObject(hDC, hBrushOld);
                DeleteObject(hBrush);
                EndPaint(hWnd, &paint);
            }
            return 0;

        default:
            if (!This && !This->lpfnOldWndProc)
                return DefWindowProc(hWnd, Message,
                                     wParam, lParam);
            else
                return CallWindowProc(This->
                                      lpfnOldWndProc,
                                      hWnd, Message,
                                      wParam, lParam);
    }
}
```

If you compile this code and copy the resulting npoleobj.dll to the Netscape \program\plug-ins directory, the plug-in will be initialized the next time the browser is started. To test the plug-in functionality so far, try loading the test.html file included in chap09\html. This file contains the following <EMBED> tag.

```
<embed src="test.npo" width=300 height=150>
```

The resulting browser display is shown in Figure 9.1.

The Plug-in–OLE Connection

We now add the functionality to this base plug-in code so OLE objects can be loaded according to their ProgId. This ProgId will be read from the npo file, and used to create an instance of the requested OLE server object. Once we have an instance of the OLE object, we will query for its window handle, and reparent the window. The new parent will be the Netscape plug-in child win-

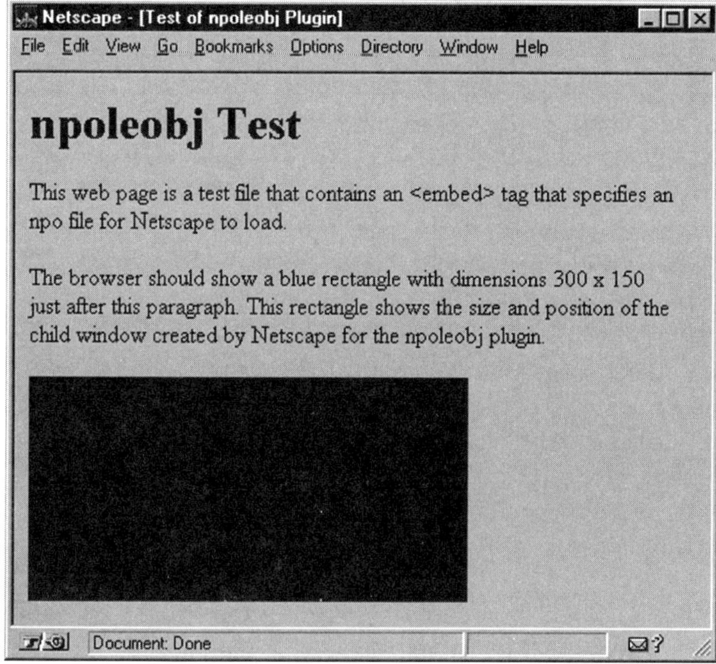

Figure 9.1.

dow—thus, the OLE object will appear embedded in the browser window!

We start by adding two fields to the instance-specific data structure. The new structure is:

```
#include "oleplug.h"

typedef struct _PluginInstance {
    NPWindow *fWindow;
    HWND hWnd;
    uint16 fMode;
    WNDPROC lpfnOldWndProc;
    NPSavedData *pSavedInstanceData;
    OLEPluginObject *oleObject;
    HWND hole;
} PluginInstance;
```

The oleplug.h file that defines the class *OLEPlug-inObject* is covered later. *oleObject* is a pointer to the new object to be created, and *hole* is a handle for the object's window. These fields should be initialized by adding the following two statements to *NPP_New*:

```
// initialize OLE fields
This->oleObject = 0;
This->hole = (HWND)0;
```

The object should be deleted in *NPP_Destroy*:

```
// delete the OLE object
delete This->oleObject;
This->oleObject = 0;
This->hole = (HWND)0;
```

The OLE object is created by reading the ProgId of the OLE server from the MIME data file. This filename is passed to *NPP_StreamAsFile*, so the following function call is added to that function:

```
// initialize the object
initObject(This, fname);
```

initObject opens a input file stream on the file written by Netscape, and the ProgId of the OLE server is read from the first line of the file.

```
// initObject - initializes the object based on the
//              stream input
void initObject(PluginInstance
*This, const char *filename)
{
    // open the file stream to see which OLE object
    // to load
    ifstream fin(filename);
```

```
if (!fin)
    return;

char oleObjectName[256];
fin >> oleObjectName;
```

A new instance of the server is created by instantiating an *OLEPluginObject* using the provided object name.

```
// load the appropriate object
This->oleObject = new OLEPluginObject
                    (oleObjectName);
if (!This->oleObject)
    return;
```

Once the object is created, its window handle property must be retrieved and stored in the *hole* field of the *Plug-inInstance* structure.

```
// get the object's window handle and save it
OLEPluginObject& object = *(This->oleObject);
This->hole = object.windowHandle();
if (!This->hole)
    return;
```

Finally, the OLE instance window's parent is changed to be the child window created by the browser. Thus, all movement and drawing of the OLE object window will be controlled by the browser. Once the parent has been modified, another property of the OLE object is used to provide the MIME data filename. Thus, the object can read any other information that may be included in the file in order to initialize the object's state.

```
// re-parent the OLE object's window so its
// parent is the plugin
// window - then give the filename to the OLE
// object
```

```
    SetParent(This->hole, This->hWnd);
    object.MIMEFile(filename);
}
```

We need to change one last thing in the DLL before moving on to define the oleplug.h interface. This is a modification to the WM_PAINT message processing in *SubClassFunc* to be sure the OLE object window gets updated.

```
    case WM_PAINT:
        if (!This || (This && !This->hole)) {
            // no OLE object window, so just paint a
            // rectangle
            PAINTSTRUCT paint;

            HDC hDC = BeginPaint(hWnd, &paint);
            HBRUSH hBrush = CreateSolidBrush
            (BACKGROUND_COLOR);
            HBRUSH hBrushOld = (HBRUSH)SelectObject
                                (hDC, hBrush);

            FillRect(hDC, &paint.rcPaint, hBrush);
            SelectObject(hDC, hBrushOld);
            DeleteObject(hBrush);
            EndPaint(hWnd, &paint);
        } else {
            // update the OLE object window
            InvalidateRect(This->hole, 0, TRUE);
            UpdateWindow(This->hole);

            PAINTSTRUCT paint;
            HDC hDC = BeginPaint(hWnd, &paint);
            EndPaint(hWnd, &paint);
        }
        return 0;
```

The Plug-in-VB Interface

We now define oleplug.h, which is based on our trustworthy *OLEDispatchInterface* class. This header file defines *OLEPluginObject* and includes the two methods called by the plug-in's *initObject* method.

```
#include "oledisp.h"

// class declaration
class OLEPluginObject : public OLEDispatchInterface
{
public:
    // constructors and destructor
    OLEPluginObject(const char *progid)
        : OLEDispatchInterface(progid) {}
    OLEPluginObject(IDispatch *dispatch)
        : OLEDispatchInterface(dispatch) {}

    virtual ~OLEPluginObject() {}

    // OLE automation methods
    // retrieves the window handle
    HWND windowHandle()
    {
        long h = get_property(this, "windowHandle",
                              (long)0);
        return (HWND)h;
    }

    // sets the MIME filename
    void MIMEFile(const char *fname)
    {
        set_property(this, "MIMEFile", fname);
    }
};
```

The *windowHandle* property must be implemented by any OLE server that the plug-in loads. This property simply returns the

HWND of the OLE object's main window. The plug-in also uses the *MIMEFile* property to hand off the filename downloaded by Netscape to the OLE object.

The corresponding implementation of this class in Visual Basic begins with a declaration of a form and the filename in a clsOLEPluginObject.cls module:

```
Option Explicit

Private myform As frmMain
Private myfile As String
```

When the object is created, a new instance of a form (named frmMain.frm) is created and stored in *myform*. The form is unloaded when the OLE object is subsequently destroyed. These operations are carried out in the initialization and termination methods of *clsOLEPluginObject*.

```
Private Sub Class_Initialize()
     Dim f As New frmMain
     Load f
     Set myform = f
End Sub

Private Sub Class_Terminate()
     If myform Is Nothing Then Exit Sub
     Unload myform
     Set myform = Nothing
End Sub
```

Each OLE object loaded by the plug-in must supply a window handle. For our Visual Basic examples, we will use a PictureBox control as the window shown inside the Netscape browser. This control will have the name *picFrame*, and the *windowHandle* property simply returns the *hWnd* property of the PictureBox.

```
Property Get windowHandle() As Long
     Dim h As Long

     If myform Is Nothing Then
          windowHandle = 0
     Else
          h = myform.picFrame.hWnd
          windowHandle = h
     End If
End Property
```

The *MIMEFile* property required for the object stores the file-name passed in from the plug-in DLL in the private string *myfile.* The *picFrame* window is then made visible, so the OLE object will appear in the browser window.

```
Property Let MIMEFile(fname As String)
     myfile = fname
     myform.picFrame.Visible = True
End Property
```

Embedded VB Program Examples

We now show several examples of VB plug-in windows that can be loaded by the npoleobj.dll plug-in module. The clsOLEPlug-inObject.cls module and an empty main function inside mod-Main.bas are included in each example project. Thus, each project needs to define a frmMain.frm module that includes a PictureBox control named *picFrame.* This ensures that each OLE server will be compatible with the plug-in.

Playing Videos

The first example is a video player that plays AVI movie files. The VB project files for this example are found in chap09\vidplay. The frmMain form (shown in Figure 9.2) contains a PictureBox control named *picFrame*, and both the form and the control are marked

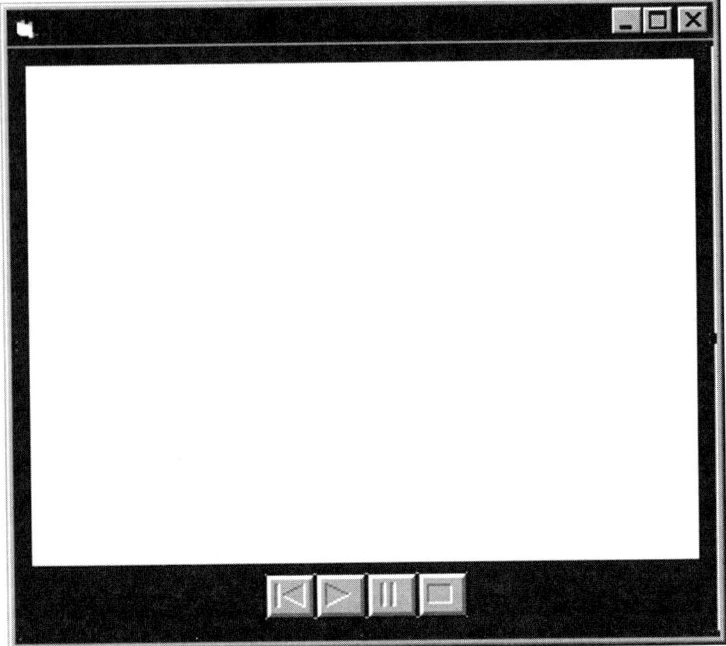

Figure 9.2.

invisible. Two child controls are added to *picFrame*. The first one is *picVideo*, another PictureBox control slightly smaller than its parent PictureBox. The second control is a VB Multimedia control named *MMControl1*.

The multimedia control's *DeviceType* property is set to *AVIVideo*, and the *FileName* property contains the pathname to some video file on the system.

The code for the form module sets up the window for display of the video as *picVideo.hWnd*. The multimedia file is opened and closed when the form is loaded and unloaded, respectively. Setting the *MMControl1.Command* value to "Play" starts playing the video file.

```
Option Explicit

Private Sub Form_Load()
     MMControl1.hWndDisplay = picVideo.hWnd
```

```
    MMControl1.Command = "Open"
End Sub

Private Sub Form_Unload(Cancel As Integer)
    MMControl1.Command = "Close"
End Sub

Private Sub MMControl1_PlayClick(Cancel As Integer)
    MMControl1.Command = "Play"
End Sub
```

Once this example OLE server is compiled, you can load the video player in Netscape using an HTML file such as:

```
<html>
<head><title>Video Player Example</title></head>
<body>

<h1>Video Player Example</h1>

This web page contains an embedded npo file that
contains the name of an OLE server. The OLE server
plays video files, with the video window created as
a plugin window of the browser.<p>

<embed src="vidplay.npo" width=360 height=300>

</body>
</html>
```

The vidplay.npo file contains only one line, which is the ProgId of our video player object, namely NPGVideoExample.clsOLEPluginObject. The resulting Netscape browser display in Figure 9.3 shows the embedded VB window, which plays the loaded video when the play button is pressed.

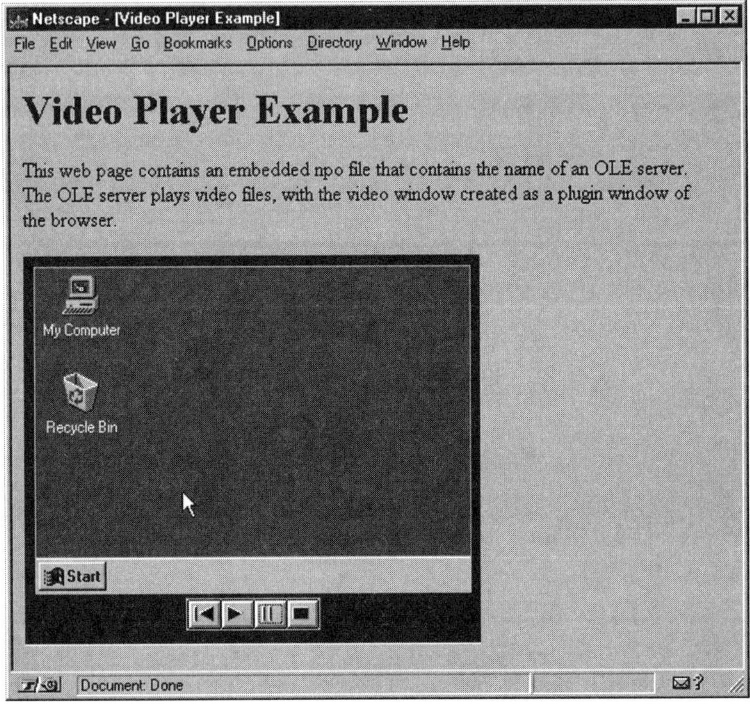

Figure 9.3.

An Embedded RTF Editor

The second example OLE object loaded by the plug-in is an RTF editor, based on the VB RichTextBox control. The Visual Basic form for this project (in chap09\rtfedit) is set up as in the previous example, with a main form containing a *picFrame* PictureBox control. The form design is shown in Figure 9.4. There are three controls placed on the PictureBox as child controls. These are a RichTextBox control named *rtfEditor*, a pushbutton named *pbBrowse*, and a common dialog control named *dlgFile*.

The dialog control properties are set to select RTF files, and the editor is set to display both horizontal and vertical scrollbars. The only code is for the pushbutton, which uses the dialog control to pop up a file dialog box. An RTF file is then selected and loaded into the editor control.

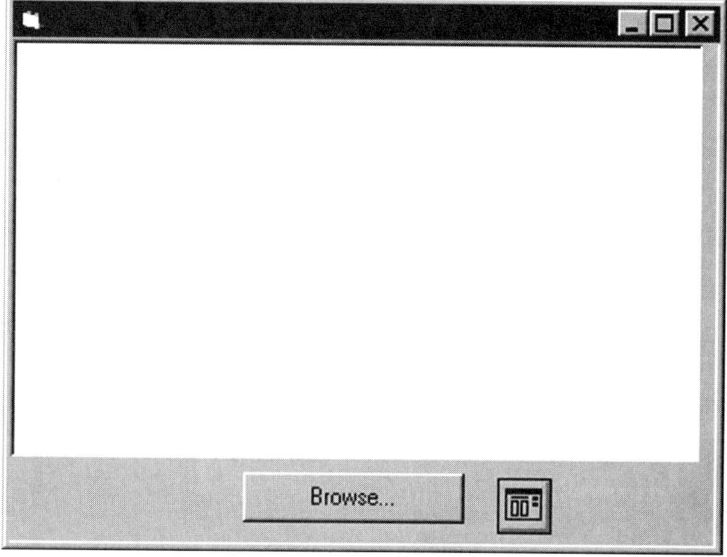

Figure 9.4.

```
Private Sub pbBrowse_Click()
     dlgFile.ShowOpen
     rtfEditor.filename = dlgFile.filename
End Sub
```

A sample HTML file (rtfedit.html) containing an <EMBED> tag for rtfedit.npo displays an NPGEditorExample.clsOLEPlug-inObject instance in the browser window. Clicking the browse button then brings up the file dialog box on top of the browser window, as shown in Figure 9.5.

When an RTF file is selected, it is loaded in the editor control and the browser appears as in Figure 9.6.

Summary

This chapter covered the Netscape plug-in API. The complete source code for a new plug-in was presented. This plug-in allows custom, client-side Visual Basic OLE objects to be loaded inside

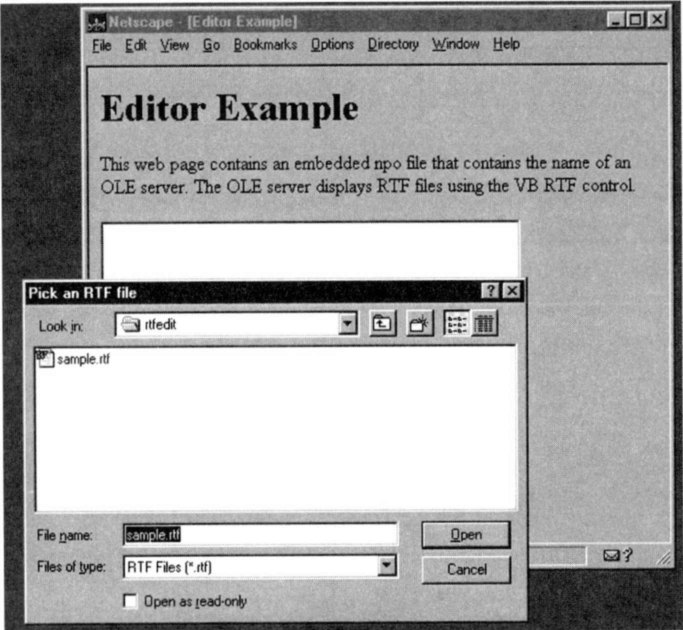

Figure 9.5.

the browser window using standard HTML syntax. Several OLE object examples are created for use with the plug-in, and they are shown embedded in the Netscape browser window.

In the next chapter, we write another plug-in that has a more limited function. This plug-in will graph an equation that the user supplies through an HTML form. JavaScript code is used to evaluate the user's expression and pass the data directly to a plug-in for plotting.

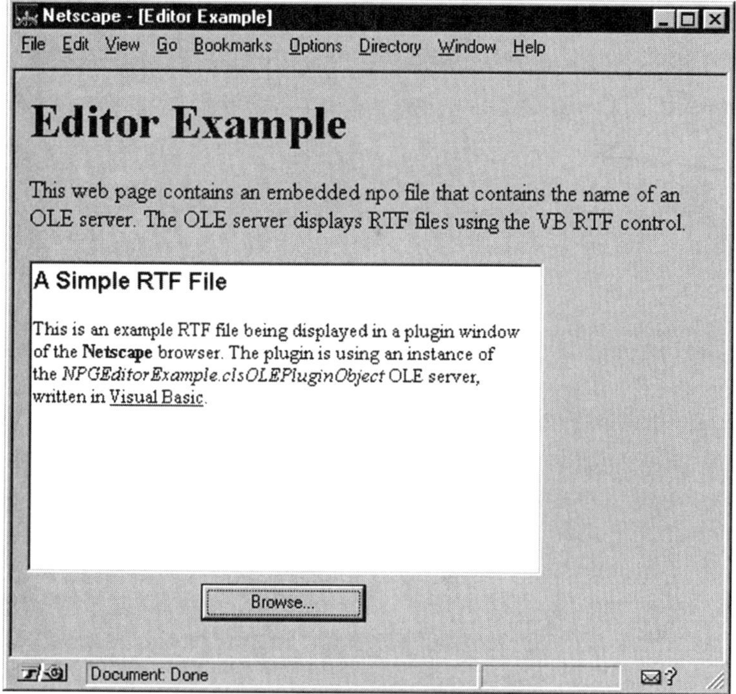

Figure 9.6.

References

1. Netscape Communications Corporation, http://home.netscape.com/comprod/products/navigator/version_2.0/plug-ins/plug-in_developers.html
2. Netscape Communications Corporation, http://home.netscape.com/comprod/development_partners/plug-in_api/index.html

Chapter 10

Graphing with JavaScript and Plug-ins

In this final chapter, we write another plug-in. This time, the plug-in will be designed to have a specific function, as opposed to the much more general plug-in we saw in the last chapter. Our new plug-in will handle X,Y data similar to the custom MIME data viewers we wrote in Chapter 8. However, this time we will use JavaScript to create the data that gets passed to the plug-in.

The example we create allows the direct typing of an equation into an HTML form on a web page. JavaScript is used to evaluate the equation over some range of the independent variable to create an array of X,Y data. The JavaScript program then opens a new browser window and writes the data directly to the window. Our new plug-in DLL is called to read the data and graph it directly in the new browser window. Let's see how to accomplish this task by integrating together all of the necessary components.

JavaScript

JavaScript is an embedded scripting language that is interpreted and executed in an HTML page. The language is loosely typed, with certain standard objects defined with corresponding methods and properties. We will not cover very much of JavaScript here—refer to the references for more information on the language.[2] The only objects we are concerned with for this example are the *document*, *window*, *Math*, and *form* objects. References to these objects and other declared variables are made within <script></script> tags in the HTML source.

Some JavaScript Objects

The *document* object enables the dynamic creation of HTML text directly inside the web page that the object represents. This is done through either the *write* or *writeln* methods, which write out strings (followed by a carriage return in the case of *writeln*) to the page:

```
<script language="JavaScript">
document.open();
document.write("<title>This is the document
title</title>");
document.close();
</script>
```

If a document contains one or more HTML forms, they can be referenced through a *forms* array. In the following statement, a variable named *firstForm* is declared and initialized to point to the first form defined in the current document.

```
var firstForm = document.forms[0];
```

Any HTML form contains a set of named controls with corresponding values. The values of these controls are accessed using a name.value syntax. For example, here is a partial HTML form definition containing an input entryfield named *userinput*:

```
<form>
Enter a value:<br>
<input type="text" name="userinput" value=""
size=50><p>
<input type="button" name="showinput"
value="Show the input" onClick="showIt()">
</form>
```

When the *showinput* button of this form is clicked, the JavaScript *onClick* handler function named *showIt* is invoked. This function, which should be defined in the <head> portion of the HTML document, can access the value of the text field as follows:

```
<script language="JavaScript">
function showIt()
{
   // get the value typed in by the user
   var text = document.forms[0].userinput.value;

   // pop up an alert dialog with the contents of
   // the text field
   alert(text)
}
</script>
```

It is also possible to open a browser window through JavaScript. Simply call the *window* object's *open* function, passing in the URL that the new browser window should load, a name to use to refer to the window, and the desired window properties.

```
var aNewWindow = window.open
                 ("http://home.netscape.com",
                  "nswin", "width=500,height=400");
```

Generating X,Y Data

For our plug-in example, we want to define an HTML form that plots an equation of the form y = f(x) over some range of the independent variable x. The form should ask for the minimum and maximum values of x, generate the array of X,Y values in a particular MIME format, and write the data to the plug-in.

The plotter.html web page is on the enclosed CD-ROM in the chap10\js directory. The head of the document contains a JavaScript function named plotIt. When this function is called, it accesses the first (and only form) defined in plotter.html, and retrieves the equation to be plotted, the range of the independent variable, and the number of points to use in approximating the continuous function over that range.

```
<html>
<head>
<script language="JavaScript">
// plotIt - plots an equation
function plotIt()
{
    // get the input values from the form
    var eqn = document.forms[0].equation.value;
    var xMin = document.forms[0].xlo.value;
    var xMax = document.forms[0].xhi.value;
    var numPoints = document.forms[0].npts.value;
```

The variable *deltaX* defines the incremental x value to use in setting up the range of X,Y data for the graph:

```
    // compute the delta value between each point
    var deltaX = (xMax - xMin)/(numPoints - 1)
```

Next, a new browser window is opened with no URL specified. The name of the window is *plotWindow*, and the document object of the new window is opened to receive MIME type data of the form xydata/plug-in. This MIME type is similar to the data format we used in Chapter 8. Our plug-in that we develop later in this chapter will handle this data type.

```
    // create a window to do the plotting
```

```
var plotWindow = window.open("", "plotWindow",
                                "width=300,height=20
                                0");
plotWindow.document.open("xydata/plugin");
```

The title and axis labels for the graph are written to the new document using *writeln*. The type of graph to plot and the number of points are also written on separate lines.

```
// write the title, axis labels, graph type, and
// number of points
plotWindow.document.writeln(eqn);
plotWindow.document.writeln("X\nY");
plotWindow.document.writeln("6\n" + numPoints);
```

The actual array of X,Y data must now be computed and sent, one line at a time, to the new document. A loop is used to increment over the range of the independent variable, whose current value is stored in *X*. We can use JavaScript's *Math* object to evaluate the equation typed in by the user for the current x. The value returned by *Math.eval* is saved in *Y*. The X,Y pair is then written as a comma-separated value string to the graph window.

```
// generate the array of points
var X = xMin - deltaX;
var Y;

for (var i = 1; i <= numPoints; i++) {
    // get next value of X
    X += deltaX;

    // evaluate the equation at the current X
    // value
    with (Math) {
        Y = eval(eqn);
    }
    plotWindow.document.writeln(X + ", " + Y);
}
```

To complete the header for plotter.html, the graph window's *document* object is closed and the function returns.

```
    // close the document
    plotWindow.document.close();
}
</script>
<title>General Equation Plotter</title>
</head>
<body>
```

The body of the HTML document simply defines the form that accepts the user's input:

```
<h1>General Equation Plotter</h1>

<form>
Enter the equation to plot (the equation must be a
valid JavaScript expression, with X used as the
independent variable):<br>
<input type="text" name="equation" value="X"
size=50><p>

Enter the range of X values:<br>
Low: <input type="text" name="xlo" value="0"
size=5><br>
High: <input type="text" name="xhi" value="1"
size=5><p>

Enter the number of points to use in the plot:
<input type="text" name="npts" value="100"
size=5><p>

<input type="button" name="plot"
value="Plot the equation" onClick="plotIt()">
</form>
</body>
</html>
```

Note that the <input> tags have names that correspond to the control names used in the JavaScript function implementation (*equation*, *xlo*, *xhi*, and *npts*). The form's button defines our JavaScript function as its *onClick* handler. The browser renders plotter.html as shown on the next page.

Of course, before using this form, we must define the plug-in that handles MIME data of xydata/plug-in format.

An X,Y Graphing Object

As we did in Chapter 8, a Visual Basic OLE object is constructed to handle the X,Y plotting. The chap10\xyplot directory contains a VB project that defines an OLE server named NPG.clsXYData. The modMain.bas module contains the usual blank *Sub Main* start-up code, and the frmGraph.frm module defines the *frmGraph* form:

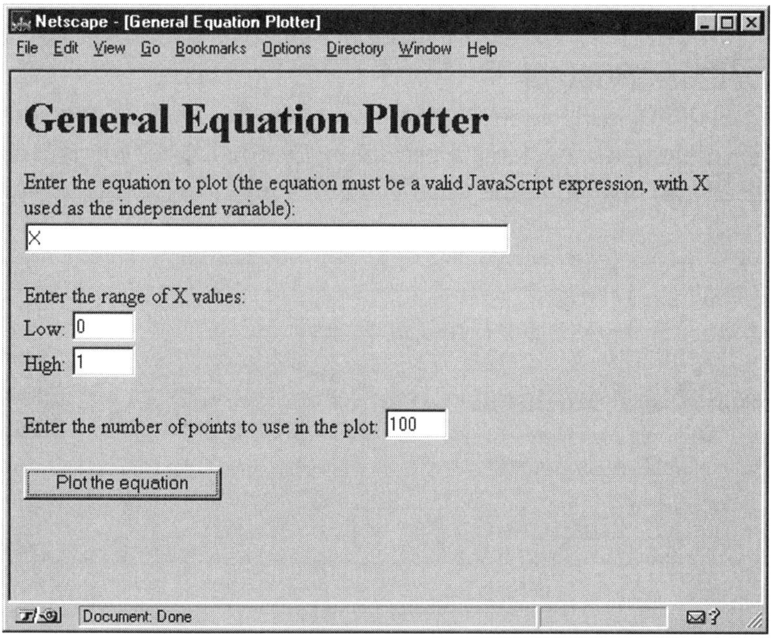

Figure 10.1.

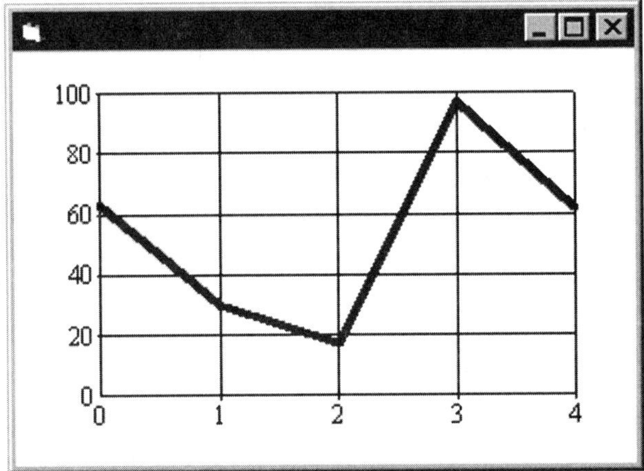

Figure 10.2.

The form contains a PictureBox control named *picFrame*—this control also has a single child Graph control named *gGraph.*

The Class Module

The clsXYData.cls module contains code for loading the form. This module first declares a private *myform* instance, which is initialized and deleted in the *Class_Initialize* and *Class_Terminate* functions.

```
Option Explicit
Private myform As frmGraph

Private Sub Class_Initialize()
     Dim f As New frmGraph

     Load f
     Set myform = f
End Sub

Private Sub Class_Terminate()
     If myform Is Nothing Then Exit Sub
```

```
    Unload myform
    Set myform = Nothing
End Sub
```

To use this OLE server in our plug-in, the window handle of the PictureBox control needs to be accessible. The *windowHandle* property returns the handle of *picFrame* to the plug-in:

```
Property Get windowHandle() As Long
    Dim h As Long

    If myform Is Nothing Then
        windowHandle = 0
    Else
        h = myform.picFrame.hWnd
        windowHandle = h
    End If
End Property
```

Note that the browser window size is set from the JavaScript code we defined in the last section. We want to adjust the graph window size to match the plug-in window created by Netscape. Thus, we provide a method for the plug-in DLL to call for changing the graph window size. The *ScaleMode* property of *picFrame* should be set to three at design time, as the window width and height are specified in pixels.

```
Public Sub setWindowSize(w As Integer, h As Integer)
    With myform
        .picFrame.ScaleWidth = w
        .picFrame.ScaleHeight = h
        .gGraph.Width = .picFrame.ScaleWidth
        .gGraph.Height = .picFrame.ScaleHeight
    End With
End Sub
```

The final method in the clsXYData.cls module passes in a string containing the MIME data to plot. This function makes the current graph invisible, calls a function defined in the form module to pass the data to the form for plotting, and then shows the form.

```
Public Sub setData(data As String)
     myform.picFrame.Visible = False
     myform.setData data
     myform.picFrame.Visible = True
End Sub
```

The Form Module

The form maintains a copy of the MIME data to be plotted, along with a pointer to the current position within the data. These variables are declared in the private declarations section.

```
Option Explicit
Private mydata As String     ' private copy of data
                             ' to graph
Private pos As Integer       ' current position in
                             ' the string
```

The *setData* method of the form is called from the *setData* method of the class we implemented in the last section. This method makes a private copy of the data and calls the private *displayGraph* method to actually plot the data.

```
Public Sub setData(data As String)
     ' show the graph
     mydata = data
     displayGraph
End Sub
```

The plotting of the data starts by declaring all of the variables needed for reading the MIME type, and setting the current position within the data to the beginning of the data stream.

```
Private Sub displayGraph()
     Dim title As String, xlabel As String
```

```
Dim ylabel As String
Dim pair As String, xstr As String
Dim ystr As String
Dim gtype As Integer, numpts As Integer
Dim i As Integer
Dim commaPos As Integer
Dim x() As Single, y() As Single

' read the title and axis labels
On Error Resume Next
With gGraph
    pos = 1
```

The graph title and axis labels are read from the first three lines, and used to set the Graph control's corresponding properties:

```
title = nextLine
xlabel = nextLine
ylabel = nextLine
Caption = title          ' set the form
                         ' caption to the
                         ' graph title
.GraphTitle = title
.BottomTitle = xlabel
.LeftTitle = ylabel
```

Next, the graph type and number of X,Y data pairs to read are obtained from two separate lines. These values are used to set those properties of the Graph control, and two arrays are also initialized to hold the data as it is read from the stream.

```
' read the graph type and number of data
' points
gtype = Val(nextLine)
numpts = Val(nextLine)
.AutoInc = 0
.GraphType = gtype
.NumPoints = numpts
```

```
        ' dimension the arrays and read in the X,Y
        ' data
        ReDim x(numpts) As Single
        ReDim y(numpts) As Single
```

Each pair of points is extracted from the remaining lines, read by a loop over the total number of points to plot. The *gGraph.XPosData* and *gGraph.GraphData* properties are then set to the X,Y value for each pair to complete the graph.

```
        For i = 1 To numpts
            ' extract the next line and separate
            ' the x and y strings
            pair = nextLine
            commaPos = InStr(1, pair, ",", 1)
            xstr = Mid(pair, 1, commaPos - 1)
            ystr = Mid(pair, commaPos + 1)

            ' get the x,y data values
            x(i) = Val(xstr)
            y(i) = Val(ystr)

             ' set x and y values for the current
             ' point
            .ThisPoint = i
            .XPosData = x(i)
            .GraphData = y(i)
        Next i
    End With
End Sub
```

The last function in this OLE server is *nextLine*. It simply breaks the input data stream into separate lines by searching for a newline character starting from the current stream position.

```
Private Function nextLine() As String
    Dim s As String
    Dim nextPos As Integer
```

```
    nextPos = InStr(pos, mydata, Chr$(10), 1)
    s = Mid(mydata, pos, nextPos - pos)
    pos = nextPos + 1

    nextLine = s
End Function
```

This project should be compiled as an OLE server and registered in order to be accessed from the Netscape plug-in DLL, which we will write in the next section.

The X,Y Plug-in

The plug-in module is written in a manner similar to the one we wrote in the last chapter—the source code is available on the CD-ROM in chap10\npxydata. We have already defined the MIME type xydata/plug-in that this plug-in should recognize (see the JavaScript code at the beginning of the chapter). Therefore, we start writing the DLL by putting the plug-in name (NPXYDATA) and the MIME type in the npxydata.rc resource file:

```
VS_VERSION_INFO VERSIONINFO
   FILEVERSION 1,0,0,1
   PRODUCTVERSION 1,0,0,1
   FILEFLAGSMASK 0x3fL
   FILEFLAGS 0x0L
   FILEOS 0x4L
   FILETYPE 0x2L
   FILESUBTYPE 0x0L
   BEGIN
   BLOCK "StringFileInfo"
      BEGIN
      BLOCK "040904e4"
         BEGIN
            VALUE "CompanyName", "NPG\0"
            VALUE "FileDescription", "NPXYDATA
            Plugin DLL\0"
            VALUE "FileExtents", "npo\0"
```

```
                VALUE "FileOpenName", "X,Y data plot-
                ting (*.xydata)\0"
                VALUE "FileVersion", "1, 0, 0, 1\0"
                VALUE "InternalName", "NPXYDATA\0"
                VALUE "LegalCopyright", "Copyright NPG
                \251 1996\0"
                VALUE "MIMEType", "xydata/plugin\0"
                VALUE "OriginalFilename",
                "NPXYDATA.DLL\0"
                VALUE "ProductName", "NPXYDATA Dynamic
                Link Library\0"
                VALUE "ProductVersion", "1, 0, 0, 1\0"
            END
        END
        BLOCK "VarFileInfo"
        BEGIN
            VALUE "Translation", 0x409, 1252
        END
    END
```

In the npxydata.C module, we change the definition of *PluginInstance* to hold an instance of the NPG.clsXYData OLE server written in the last section. There is also an instance of an *strstream* declared, which will hold the data streamed to the plug-in from the JavaScript code.

```
#include "xydata.h"

typedef struct _PluginInstance {
    NPWindow *fWindow;
    HWND hWnd;
    uint16 fMode;
    WNDPROC lpfnOldWndProc;
    NPSavedData *pSavedInstanceData;

    // *** for npxydata functionality ***
    clsXYData *oleObject;
    strstream *dataStream;
```

```
    HWND hole;
    // *** end for npxydata functionality ***
} PluginInstance;
```

Inside *NPP_New*, these new pointers are initialized. One difference from the previous plug-in we developed is the creation of the OLE object here rather than when a new data stream is available. The object can be created here because the plug-in handles only one type of data, and the OLE server is the same in each case.

```
// NPP_New - creates a new plugin instance
extern "C" NPError NP_LOADDS NPP_New
                    (NPMIMEType pluginType,
                     NPP instance,
                     uint16 mode, int16 argc,
                     char *argn[], char *argv[],
                     NPSavedData *saved)
{
    // ...

    // *** for npxydata functionality ***
    // initialize OLE fields
    This->oleObject = new clsXYData();
    This->dataStream = 0;
    This->hole = (HWND)0;
    // *** end for npxydata functionality ***

    return NPERR_NO_ERROR;
}
```

The pointers are cleaned up in *NPP_Destroy*:

```
// NPP_Destroy - destroys a plugin instance
extern "C" NPError NP_LOADDS NPP_Destroy
                    (NPP instance,
                     NPSavedData **save)
```

```
{
    // ...
        // *** for npxydata functionality ***
        // delete the OLE object
        delete This->dataStream;
        This->dataStream = 0;
        delete This->oleObject;
        This->oleObject = 0;
        This->hole = (HWND)0;
        // *** end for npxydata functionality ***
    // ...
    return NPERR_NO_ERROR;
}
```

Another difference in this plug-in is the initialization of *dataStream* inside *NPP_NewStream*. This function is called by Netscape whenever a new data stream is being sent to the plug-in. The *dataStream* is initialized with a new instance of *strstream*, and a stream type of NP_NORMAL is returned to Netscape.

```
// NPP_NewStream - informs plugin of a new stream
//                  of data
extern "C" NPError NP_LOADDS NPP_NewStream
            (NPP instance, NPMIMEType type,
             NPStream *stream, NPBool seekable,
             uint16 *stype)
{
    if (!instance)
        return NPERR_INVALID_INSTANCE_ERROR;

    PluginInstance *This = (PluginInstance *)
    instance->pdata;
    if (This->dataStream) {
        delete This->dataStream;
        This->dataStream = 0;
    }
    This->dataStream = new strstream();
```

```
    // if your plugin must operate file based, you
    // may wish to do this:
    //     *stype = NP_ASFILE;
    // remember, though, that use of NP_ASFILE is
    // strongly
    // discouraged; your plugin should attempt to
    // work with
    // data as it comes in on the stream if at all
    // possible
    *stype = NP_NORMAL;
    return NPERR_NO_ERROR;
}
```

After Netscape calls this function, it proceeds to call *NPP_WriteReady* to determine how many characters the plug-in is prepared to handle, and *NPP_Write* to pass up to that number of characters to the DLL. When this plug-in receives a chunk of data, it writes it to the *dataStream* instance.

```
// NPP_WriteReady - queries the plugin for the
//                  number of bytes of data
//                  it is ready to handle
extern "C" int32 NP_LOADDS NPP_WriteReady
                 (NPP instance, NPStream *stream)
{
    if (instance)
        PluginInstance *This = (PluginInstance *)
                               instance->pdata;

    return 80;
}

// ------------------------------------------------

// NPP_Write - data is written to the plugin
```

```
extern "C" int32 NP_LOADDS NPP_Write
                  (NPP instance, NPStream *stream,
                   int32 offset, int32 len,
                   void *buffer)
{
   if (instance) {
      PluginInstance *This = (PluginInstance *)
                             instance->pdata;
      strstream& ss = *(This->dataStream);
      ss.write( (char *)buffer, len );
   }

   return len;     // The number of bytes accepted.
                   // Return a
                   // negative number here if, e.g.,
                   // there was
                   // an error during plugin
                   // operation and you want to
                   // abort the stream
}
```

Once Netscape writes all of the data to the plug-in, it calls *NPP_DestroyStream* to let the plug-in know that the streaming is complete. At this point, our plug-in should pass the data stream to the OLE object for subsequent plotting. This is done by first terminating the data stream with a '\0' character, and then calling *initObject*, passing it the data as a string.

```
// NPP_DestroyStream - informs the plugin that a
//                     stream is being destroyed
extern "C" NPError NP_LOADDS NPP_DestroyStream
           (NPP instance, NPStream *stream,
            NPError reason)
{
   if (!instance)
      return NPERR_INVALID_INSTANCE_ERROR;
```

```
    PluginInstance *This = (PluginInstance *)
    instance->pdata;
    strstream& ss = *(This->dataStream);
    ss << ends;

    // initialize the object with the new data
    // stream
    initObject( This, ss.str() );

    // delete the stream
    delete ss.str();
    delete This->dataStream;
    This->dataStream = 0;

    return NPERR_NO_ERROR;
}
```

The *initObject* function obtains the window handle of the OLE server's form by accessing the *windowHandle* property. This is used to re-parent the *picFrame* of the form so that the Netscape plug-in window is the new parent. Thus, the graph will be embedded in the browser window as in the npoleobj plug-in examples.

The size of the client rectangle for the parent is then obtained by calling *GetClientRect*. This information is used to set the size of the graph window by calling the OLE server method *setWindowSize*. Finally, *setData* is called to pass in the data captured from the stream delivered by Netscape.

```
// initObject - initializes the object based on the
//               stream input
void initObject(PluginInstance *This,
const char *data)
{
    // get the object's window handle and save it
    clsXYData& object = *(This->oleObject);
    This->hole = object.windowHandle();
    if (!This->hole)
        return;
```

```
    // re-parent the OLE object's window so its
    // parent is the
    // plugin window - then set the plugin window size
    // parameters and data for the OLE object
    SetParent(This->hole, This->hWnd);

    RECT rect;
    GetClientRect(This->hWnd, &rect);

    object.setWindowSize( (short)rect.right,
                          (short)rect.bottom);
    object.setData(data);
}
```

The last thing to define is the C++ interface to the VB OLE server NPG.clsXYData. This interface is provided in the xydata.h header file, using the *OLEDispatchInterface* base class and companion template functions as usual.

```
#include "oledisp.h"

class clsXYData : public OLEDispatchInterface {
public:
    // constructors and destructor
    clsXYData(const char *progid = "NPG.clsXYData")
        : OLEDispatchInterface(progid) {}
    clsXYData(IDispatch *dispatch)
        : OLEDispatchInterface(dispatch) {}

    virtual ~clsXYData() {}

    // OLE automation methods

    // retrieves the window handle
    HWND windowHandle()
    {
```

```
        long h = get_property(this, "windowHandle",
        (long)0);
        return (HWND)h;
    }

    // sets the MIME data and the window size
    void setWindowSize(short width, short height)
    {
        method_twoargs(this, "setWindowSize",
                        (short)0, width, height);
    }

    void setData(const char *data)
    {
        method_onearg(this, "setData", (short)0,
        data);
    }
};
```

This file implements the three public methods of clsXYData.cls: *windowHandle, setWindowSize,* and *setData.*

Once you compile the files for this project, copy the resulting npxydata.dll file to the program\plug-ins directory where Netscape is installed. Then restart the browser to activate the plug-in.

Tying It All Together

The following screen shows user input for a plot of the function $f(x) = 1/(1 + e^{-4x})$ over the range -1 to 1. Note that in the text field for entering the equation, the independent variable is defined as capital *X*. This must be the same as the name of the variable in the JavaScript function that uses this equation in the *Math.eval* call to evaluate the function.

Netscape - [General Equation Plotter]

File Edit View Go Bookmarks Options Directory Window Help

General Equation Plotter

Enter the equation to plot (the equation must be a valid JavaScript expression, with X used as the independent variable):

1/(1 + exp(-4*X))

Enter the range of X values:

Low: -1

High: 1

Enter the number of points to use in the plot: 100

Plot the equation

Document: Done

Figure 10.3.

When the button is pressed, the JavaScript function is called. This opens a new browser window and writes MIME data for the equation directly to the window. The resulting graph is displayed directly in the browser window:

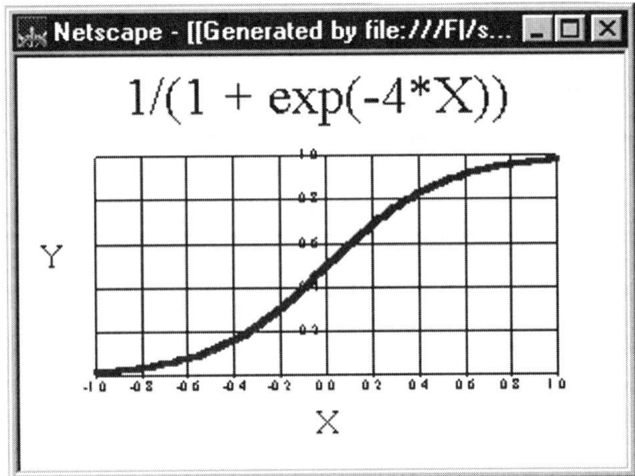

Figure 10.4.

Another example is a plot of the equation f(x) = x sin x/e^{-x}, over the range 0 to 2. The equation is input to the HTML form as X * sin(X)/exp(-X), and the resulting plot is:

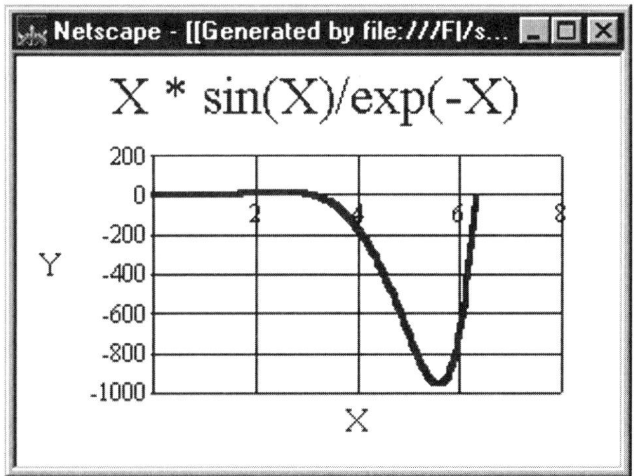

Figure 10.5.

Summary

In this, the last chapter, we wrote another Netscape plug-in to graph a set of X,Y data as a continuous function. Data is provided to the plug-in by asking the user to type in an equation from a standard HTML form. JavaScript is then used to evaluate the equation over a selected range for the independent variable, and the X,Y data is written directly to a new browser window. This application illustrates many of the componentware aspects I have tried to stress in this book. C++, Visual Basic, OLE, a plug-in DLL, JavaScript code, and the Netscape browser all work together to accomplish some useful task.

References

1. Netscape Communications Corporation, http://home.netscape.com/eng/mozilla/Gold/handbook/javascript/index.html
2. Tim Ritchey, "Programming JavaScript for Netscape 2.0", New Riders Publishing, Indianapolis, IN, 1996.

Epilogue

I hope that, in reading this book and studying the example code, you have gained an appreciation of the power inherent in Netscape's browser. One of my aims has been to show the various extension options available for harnessing Netscape's power to access intranets and the Internet. You should now be able to intelligently choose among a myriad of options to address specific programming problems.

In addition, I have tried to illustrate the value of Microsoft's OLE component technology. The facile communication techniques that OLE makes possible between Visual Basic and C++ are a powerful addition to your Windows programming skills. The resulting control over integration among existing applications and custom OLE servers provides the opportunity to create unique and powerful solutions.

Of course, the web environment is dynamic—new languages, APIs, and emerging component standards are all competing for your attention. With the background and extensive examples provided here, I believe you (and I!) will be better prepared for the continued rapid explosion of web programming technologies. Happy computing!

DDE Topics Reference

This appendix lists the DDE topics currently supported by Netscape. Each topic contains a brief description and its arguments (the DDE item), along with any return type(s).

WWW_Activate (XTYP_REQUEST)

Activates a browser window

Arguments: window id (use 0xFFFFFFFF to activate the last active window)

flags (reserved, use 0)

Returns: window id of activated window (0 if error)

WWW_Alert (XTYP_REQUEST)

Sent to a DDE server to request that an alert box be displayed

Arguments: message

type (0 for an error, 1 for a warning, 2 for a question, 3 for a status dialog) buttons (0 for OK, 1 for OK/Cancel, 2 for Yes/No, 3 for Yes/No/Cancel)

Returns: answer (0 indicates the dialog could not be displayed, 1 if OK was pressed, 2 if Cancel was pressed, 3 if No was pressed, 4 if Yes was pressed)

WWW_BeginProgress (XTYP_REQUEST)

Sent to a DDE server that is to receive progress reports (the server is specified in the *WWW_OpenURL* topic item)

Arguments: window id
message to display

Returns: transaction id (will be sent in other progress topics, return 0 if you do not want to receive other progress messages)

WWW_CancelProgress (XTYP_POKE)

Cancels the operation specified by a transaction id

Arguments: transaction id

WWW_EndProgress (XTYP_POKE)

Sent to a DDE server when an operation has completed

Arguments: transaction id

WWW_Exit (XTYP_POKE)

Closes the Netscape application

Arguments: (none)

WWW_GetWindowInfo (XTYP_REQUEST)

Retrieves the current URL and title loaded in the specified browser window.

Arguments: window id (use 0xFFFFFFFF to specify the last active window)

Returns: url,title (as a comma-separated pair)

WWW_ListWindows (XTYP_REQUEST)

Returns an array of window ids (as an array of 4 byte values) representing all open browser windows

Arguments: (none)

Returns: array

WWW_MakingProgress (XTYP_REQUEST)

Sent to a DDE server to indicate the current status of an operation.

Arguments: transaction id
message (may be empty)
progress (ranges from 0 to the maximum value set by
WWW_SetProgressRange)

Returns: 0 to continue, 1 to stop the current operation

WWW_OpenURL (XTYP_REQUEST)

If Netscape is acting as a DDE server, it loads the requested URL. If the browser is acting as a DDE client, this message directs a DDE server to handle a particular URL request (the DDE server is registered through *WWW_RegisterProtocol*)

Arguments: url

filename (optional, saves data into file instead of displaying it) window id (use 0xFFFFFFFF to load in the last active window, 0 to create a new window) flags (1 to ignore document cache, 2 to ignore image cache, 4 to operate in the background—always 0 for DDE servers)

form data (optional, data that will be posted to URL)

MIME type (optional, specifies MIME type of data to be posted)

server name (optional, specifies server to receive progress topics)

Returns: window id (0 if the operation failed)

WWW_ParseAnchor (XTYP_REQUEST)

Resolves relative into absolute URLs

Arguments: absolute url

relative url

Returns: fully qualified url

WWW_QueryURLFile (XTYP_REQUEST)

Returns the URL from which a file was loaded

Arguments: filename

Returns: url

WWW_QueryViewer (XTYP_REQUEST)

Sent to a DDE server acting as a viewer (registered through *WWW_RegisterViewer*) to request a filename

Arguments: url being loaded by Netscape

MIME type of the document being loaded

Returns: filename

WWW_RegisterProtocol (XTYP_REQUEST)

Registers a DDE server to handle new protocol (or service) types (the server will receive *WWW_OpenURL* topics).

Arguments: server name

protocol (e.g., http, ftp, mailto, etc.)

Returns: 1 if success, 0 if failed

WWW_RegisterURLEcho (XTYP_POKE)

Registers a DDE server that is notified (through *WWW_URLEcho* topics) whenever a new URL is loaded.

Arguments: server name

WWW_RegisterViewer (XTYP_REQUEST)

Registers a DDE server that will handle data of a particular MIME type (it is recommended that the flags argument be set to 6, so your viewer can supply a filename and handle how the data is viewed after loading).

Arguments: server name

MIME type

flags (1 to save the data in a temporary file and call *ShellExecute*, 2 to get a filename through *WWW_QueryViewer*, 4 to save the data in a temporary file and use the *WWW_ViewDocFile* topic)

Returns: 1 if success, 0 if failed

WWW_RegisterWindowChange (XTYP_REQUEST)

Registers a DDE server that will receive *WWW_WindowChange* topics for a particular browser window.

Arguments: server name

window id

Returns: window id if success, 0 if failed

WWW_SetProgressRange (XTYP_POKE)

Sent to a DDE server to indicate the current progress status of an operation. This topic is sent after a *WWW_BeginProgress* message has been handled by the DDE server.

Arguments: transaction id

maximum value

WWW_ShowFile (XTYP_REQUEST)

Loads a file into a browser window.

Arguments: filename

MIME type of data in the file

window id (use 0xFFFFFFFF to use the last active window, 0 to create a new window) url (used to reload the document if necessary)

Returns: window id (0 if failed)

WWW_UnRegisterProtocol (XTYP_REQUEST)

Unregisters a protocol handler.

Arguments: server name

protocol

Returns: 1 if success, 0 if failed

WWW_UnRegisterURLEcho (XTYP_POKE)

Unregisters a server receiving *WWW_URLEcho* topics.

Arguments: server name

WWW_UnRegisterViewer (XTYP_REQUEST)

Unregisters a viewer for a particular MIME type.

Arguments: server name

MIME type

Returns: 1 if success, 0 if failed

WWW_ UnRegisterWindowChange (XTYP_REQUEST)

Unregisters a server that is monitoring window changes for a particular browser window.

Arguments: server name

window id

Returns: 1 if success, 0 if failed

WWW_URLEcho (XTYP_POKE)

Sent to a DDE server registered to receive URLs that are being loaded by the browser.

Arguments: url being loaded

MIME type

window id (0xFFFFFFFF if the data was not loaded into a browser window)

referrer (the URL that contained an anchor which lead to this URL)

WWW_ViewDocFile (XTYP_POKE)

Sent to a DDE server acting as a viewer for a particular MIME type.

Arguments: filename containing the data for the viewer to display url corresponding to the filename

MIME type of the data in the file

window id of the browser window that loaded the URL

WWW_WindowChange (XTYP_POKE)

If Netscape is acting as a DDE client, this topic is sent to a DDE server registered to monitor browser window change events. If the browser is acting as a server, this topic allows direct manipulation of the browser window size and position.

Arguments: window id

flags (1 indicates change in size and/or position, 2 if maximized, 4 if restored, 8 if minimized, 0x10 if window was closed, 0x10000 if Netscape is attempting to exit)

x (horizontal position of browser window)

y (vertical position of browser window)

cx (width of browser window)

cy (height of browser window)

Appendix B

Netscape OLE Automation Reference

This appendix lists the current Netscape OLE Automation functions. The Netscape.Network and Netscape.Registry automation object functions are described.

Netscape.Network Functions

short BytesReady()

Returns the number of bytes ready to be read by calling the *Read* function

void Close()

Disconnects an active connection and resets the object. This must be called after a call to *Open* has been made, even if the open fails. If a download is in progress, calling *Close* will interrupt the transfer.

CString GetContentEncoding()

Returns the MIME encoding of the current document

long GetContentLength()

Returns the total number of bytes in the current document. This is used after a call to *Open* succeeds. The accuracy of the return type depends on the server being contacted

CString GetContentType()

Returns the MIME type of the current document

CString GetErrorMessage()

Returns an error message provided by Netscape. This is used after a call to *GetStatus* indicates that an error message is available.

CString GetExpires()

Returns a string containing the date and time when the current document is no longer valid

BOOL GetFlagFancyFTP()

Returns TRUE if FTP output will contain directory information about the file size, file type, etc.

BOOL GetFlagFancyNews()

Returns TRUE if newsgroups will be listed only when they contain a description. FALSE is returned if the browser will list all newsgroups, even those without a description.

BOOL GetFlagShowAllNews()

Returns TRUE if all newsgroup articles are shown. FALSE is returned if only those articles that are unread will be shown.

CString GetLastModified()

Returns a string containing the date and time when the current document was last modified.

CString GetPassword()

Returns the current password property set by a call to *SetPassword*

short GetServerStatus()

Determines the server's error status

long GetStatus()

Returns one or more mask values that determine the status of the current load. The mask values are:

Mask	Description
0x0000	Normal
0x0001	User name was requested
0x0002	User password was requested
0x0100	Netscape is busy, retry the operation
0x0200	The server reported an error
0x0400	The server was not contacted
0x0800	Netscape has a suggested error message (use *GetErrorMessage*)

CString GetUserName()

Returns the current user name, set previously by a call to *SetUserName.*

BOOL IsFinished()

Returns TRUE if all data has been read for the current load. FALSE is returned if the load is not complete.

BOOL Open(LPCTSTR url, short method, LPCTSTR postdata, long postsize, LPCTSTR posthdrs)

Starts the retrieval of the requested URL given in the first argument. Use a *method* value of 0 to GET the URL, 1 for POST, and 2 for HEAD. If *method* is 1, *postdata* contains the data to post to the server. *postsize* is the number of bytes of data, and *posthdrs* is a string that contains any additional headers you want to post to the URL. The default header is "Content-type: application/x-www-form-urlencoded".

Returns TRUE if the load was started successfully. The return value is FALSE if the request fails. As Netscape may be busy, you should call the *GetStatus* method to see if you should retry the operation.

short Read(BSTR *buffer, short amount)

Reads data that Netscape has retrieved after a successful call to *Open*. The data is stored in *buffer*, up to a maximum number of bytes specified in *amount*.

Returns the number of bytes actually stored in the buffer. If the return value is -1, there is no more data left to read. If the return value is 0, there was no current data to read.

CString Resolve(LPCTSTR base, LPCTSTR relative)

Resolves a relative to an absolute URL. The *relative* argument is an incompletely specified URL relative to *base*.

void SetFlagFancyFTP(BOOL fancy)

Sets the FTP listing property to show (if *fancy* is TRUE) or not show (if *fancy* if FALSE) directory information such as file size, file type, etc.

void SetFlagFancyNews(BOOL fancy)
Sets the newsgroup listings to only show newsgroups with descriptions if *fancy* is TRUE. Otherwise, all newsgroups are shown.

void SetFlagShowAllNews(BOOL all)
If *all* is TRUE, all newsgroup articles will be shown. Otherwise, only unread articles will be displayed.

void SetPassword(LPCTSTR password)
Sets the current password property for any document load that needs access control

void SetUserName(LPCTSTR user)
Sets the current user name property for any document load that needs access control

Netscape.Registry Functions

Netscape allows the definition of external protocol handlers and viewers. These are implemented as separate OLE objects, which are registered by the following two functions. See Chapters 6 and 8 for the methods each registry type must support.

BOOL RegisterProtocol(LPCTSTR protocol,
LPCTSTR registryname)
Registers an OLE Automation server that handles your own protocol types (e.g., http, ftp, mailto, etc.). The protocol (or service) type is given by the *protocol* argument, and *registryname* is the ProgId of the OLE server.

BOOL RegisterViewer(LPCTSTR mimetype,
LPCTSTR registryname)
Registers an OLE Automation server that acts as an external viewer for data of a particular MIME type, given by the *mimetype* argument. The *registryname* is the ProgId of the OLE server.

Appendix C

Netscape Plug-ins Reference

This appendix lists the current Netscape plug-in API functions. These are divided into two groups. The first group contains the plug-in methods that a new plug-in must implement. Netscape calls these functions to initialize and communicate information to the plug-in. The second group contains Netscape functions that can be called directly by the plug-in methods. These functions allow a plug-in to allocate memory, retrieve and post data from and to URLs, and communicate with Java applications.

The npapi.h header file of the plug-in API contains declarations for all of the function prototypes, data types, and structures.

Plug-in Functions

NPP_Destroy

```
NPError NPP_Destroy(NPP instance,
                    NPSavedData **save);
```

NPP_Destroy is called when a plug-in instance is deleted. This is a result of leaving the page that contains the plug-in instance, closing the browser window, or exiting Netscape. In response to this call, any instance data stored in *instance->pdata* should be deleted.

The *save* parameter allows you to save information that is used by other instances of the plug-in with the same URL. The data is passed to new instances using a parameter in *NPP_New*.

NPP_DestroyStream

```
NPError NPP_DestroyStream(NPP instance, NPStream
                          *stream, NPError reason);
```

NPP_DestroyStream is called when the *stream* for a plug-in instance is being destroyed. Any data allocated in *stream->pdata* should be deleted when this function is called.

The *reason* argument indicates why the stream is being destroyed. The normal reason code NPRES_DONE indicates that all data was provided to the plug-in. NPRES_USER_BREAK indicates that the user interrupted the data transfer.

NPP_GetJavaClass

```
jref NPP_GetJavaClass();
```

GetJavaClass returns the Java class associated with the plug-in.

NPP_Initialize

```
NPError NPP_Initialize()
```

This function is called once when a plug-in is first loaded. This allows you to allocate any memory or resources that will be shared by all instances of the plug-in.

NPP_New

```
NPError NPP_New(NPMIMEType *pluginType, NPP
                instance, uint16 mode, int16 argc,
                char *argn[], char *argv[],
                NPSavedData *saved);
```

NPP_New creates a new plug-in instance, using the MIME type specified by *pluginType*. The *mode* parameter equals NP_EMBED if the plug-in instance was created by an HTML <EMBED> tag. If the instance was created by loading a separate file of the specified MIME type, *mode* equals NP_FULL. Any data that is required for this specific instance of the plug-in should be allocated in this function and stored in *instance->pdata*.

The *argc*, *argn*, and *argv* parameters contain a list of name-value pairs passed to the plug-in through the <EMBED> tag. For example, the following tag contains private attributes for the width and height of a plug-in that plays a digital video file. This tag would cause the plug-in's *NPP_New* method to receive an *argc* value of three. The names of the attributes would be passed in through *argn*, and the attribute values would be passed in through *argv*.

```
<embed src="movie.avi" height=128 width=256>
```

Any data saved from invoking *NPP_Destroy* on a previous plug-in instance is received in *saved*. The plug-in is then responsible for deleting the memory associated with this data.

NPP_NewStream

```
NPError NPP_NewStream(NPP instance, NPMIMEType type,
                      NPStream *stream,
                      NPBool seekable,
                      uint16 *stype);
```

NPP_NewStream notifies a plug-in instance that a new *NPStream* has been created. The stream's MIME type is passed in as *type*. The argument *stype* defines the stream mode, which can take on any of the following values:

stype	Description
NP_NORMAL	Stream data is delivered to the instance by *NPP_WriteReady* and *NPP_Write*. The plug-in can process the data as it arrives from the stream.
NP_ASFILEONLY	Netscape saves the stream data in a file. The *NPP_StreamAsFile* function is then called to give the pathname of the new file to the plug-in instance.
NP_ASFILE	This mode is retained for compatibility. Use NP_ASFILEONLY instead.
NP_SEEK	The stream data is randomly accessed as needed using the function *NPN_RequestRead*. The *seekable* argument is TRUE if the stream supports random access.

NPP_Print

```
void NPP_Print(NPP instance,
               NPPrint *platformPrint);
```

NPP_Print is called to request that the plug-in instance print itself.

NPP_SetWindow

```
NPError NPP_SetWindow(NPP instance,
                      NPWindow *window);
```

This function informs the plug-in instance about an *NPWindow* the instance can use for output. This function is also called when the window has been resized. If either the *window* parameter or *window->window* is null, no drawing should be done in the window, and any resources associated with the window should be freed.

NPP_Shutdown

```
void NPP_Shutdown();
```

This function is called once after the last instance of a plug-in is destroyed. Any memory or resources shared among all instances of the plug-in should be freed.

NPP_StreamAsFile

```
void NPP_StreamAsFile(NPP instance,
                      NPStream *stream,
                      const char *fname);
```

NPP_StreamAsFile provides the full pathname (*fname*) to a file for a particular data *stream*.

NPP_URLNotify

```
void NPP_URLNotify(NPP instance, const char *url,
                   NPReason reason,
                   void *notifyData);
```

NPP_URLNotify is called after Netscape completes a URL retrieval or post operation made by a previous call to *NPN_GetURLNotify* or *NPN_PostURLNotify*. The *reason* for the notification is usually NPRES_DONE, which indicates normal completion. NPPRES_USER_BREAK indicates that the request was halted by the user.

The *notifyData* argument is provided as is from the parameter passed to *NPN_GetURLNotify* or *NPN_PostURLNotify* call. You can use it to identify the particular request.

NPP_Write

```
int32 NPP_Write(NPP instance, NPStream *stream,
                int32 offset, int32 len, void *buf);
```

NPP_Write is called to write *len* bytes of *buf* data from a stream buffer to the plug-in. The logical position of the data from the beginning of the stream is given by *offset*. The plug-in should return the number of bytes consumed by the plug-in instance. Returning a negative number will cause the stream to be destroyed.

NPP_WriteReady

```
int32 NPP_WriteReady(NPP instance,
                     NPStream *stream);
```

NPP_WriteReady is called to determine the number of bytes of data that the plug-in instance is ready to consume from the given *stream*. The *NPP_Write* function will subsequently be called to deliver the data to the plug-in.

Netscape Functions

NPN_DestroyStream

```
NPError NPN_DestroyStream(NPP instance,
                          NPStream *stream,
                          NPError reason);
```

A plug-in instance can close and destroy a stream using *NPN_DestroyStream*. The stream can either be one created by Netscape (and passed to the instance using *NPP_NewStream*), or one created by the plug-in using *NPN_NewStream*. Use one of the NPRES constants defined in npapi.h for the *reason* code.

NPN_GetJavaEnv

```
JavaEnv *NPN_GetJavaEnv();
```

NPN_GetJavaEnv returns the Java execution environment. The *JavaEnv* pointer is required for making calls to Java methods from the plug-in.

NPN_GetJavaPeer

```
jref NPN_GetJavaPeer(NPP instance);
```

NPN_GetJavaPeer gets the Java object associated with the plug-in instance.

NPN_GetURL

```
NPError NPN_GetURL(NPP instance, const char *url,
                   const char *window);
```

NPN_GetURL requests that a new stream be created with the contents of the specified URL. If the *window* parameter is not null, the stream is sent to the Netscape browser. The data will be displayed in the browser's named window or frame. If *window* is null, the contents of the URL are delivered to the plug-in instance through a call to *NPP_NewStream*.

NPN_GetURLNotify

```
NPError NP_GetURLNotify(NPP instance,
                        const char *url,
                        const char *target,
                        void *notifyData);
```

This function is identical to *NPN_GetURL*, except that *NPP_URLNotify* is called after the request is completed. To allow the notification method to identify the request, pass in a unique identifier using *notifyData*.

NPN_MemAlloc

```
void *NPN_MemAlloc(uint32 size);
```

NPN_MemAlloc allocates *size* bytes from the Navigator's memory space. This function should be used to allocate any saved instance data in *NPP_Destroy*.

NPN_MemFree

```
void NPN_MemFree(void *ptr);
```

This function frees the block of memory previously allocated with *NPN_MemAlloc*.

NPN_NewStream

```
NPError NPN_NewStream(NPP instance, NPMIMEType type,
                      const char *target,
                      NPStream **stream);
```

NPN_NewStream creates a new stream for the plug-in instance. The MIME *type* of the new stream and the *target* window or frame of the browser is specified in the request. Netscape returns the new *NPStream* in the *stream* variable. *NPN_Write* can then be used by the plug-in to write data to the stream. The plug-in should call *NPN_DestroyStream* after all of the data has been written to the stream.

NPN_PostURL

```
NPError NPN_PostURL(NPP instance, const char *url,
                    const char *window, uint32 len,
                    const char *buf, NPBool file);
```

NPN_GetURL retrieves data from a specified URL. *NPN_PostURL* writes data to the URL. The response from the server is then either displayed in the specified target *window*, or delivered to the plug-in instance.

The data to post resides either in a buffer or a file. To post a particular file to the server, the *file* variable is set to TRUE and *buf* contains the pathname of the file. If *flag* is set to FALSE, *buf* contains the actual data to post, and *len* is set to the length of the buffer.

NPN_PostURLNotify

```
NPError NPN_PostURLNotify(NPP instance,
                          const char *url,
                          const char *window,
                          uint32 len,
                          const char *buf,
                          NPBool file,
                          void *notifyData);
```

This function is identical to *NPN_PostURL*, except that *NPP_URLNotify* is called after the request is completed. To allow the notification method to identify the request, pass in a unique identifier using *notifyData*.

NPN_RequestRead

```
NPError NPN_RequestRead(NPStream *stream,
                        NPByteRange *rangeList);
```

NPN_RequestRead requests that a range of bytes be read from the *stream*. The *rangeList* is a linked list of *NPByteRange* objects. Each object specifies an offset and length into the stream. The data are written to the plug-in through calls to *NPP_WriteReady* and *NPP_Write*.

NPN_Status

```
void NPN_Status(NPP instance, const char *message);
```

NPN_Status requests the browser to display a status message. The message appears in the status bar of the browser client window. You can use this function to simulate the browser's behavior of displaying the URL of a standard HTML link in the browser's status bar.

NPN_UserAgent

```
const char *NPN_Status(NPP instance);
```

This function returns a string containing the Navigator's "user agent" field. This field is a part of the HTTP header that identifies the browser during data transfers.

NPN_Version

```
void NPN_Version(int *plugin_major,
                 int *plugin_minor,
                 int *netscape_major,
                 int *netscape_minor);
```

NPN_Version returns the major and minor version numbers for the plug-in and the Netscape Navigator.

NPN_Write

```
int32 NPN_Write(NPP instance, NPStream *stream,
                int32 offset, int32 len, void *buf);
```

A plug-in instance calls *NPN_Write* after creating a stream with *NPN_NewStream*. This call writes a buffer (*buf*) containing *len* bytes of data from the stream to Netscape. The *offset* is the logical position of the buffer from the start of the stream data.

Netscape returns the number of bytes consumed. A negative return value denotes an error, and the plug-in should call *NPN_DestroyStream*.

Index